MR. MOTHERCOUNTRY

MR. MOTHERCOUNTRY

THE MAN WHO MADE THE RULE OF LAW

KEALLY MCBRIDE

OXFORD
UNIVERSITY PRESS

OXFORD
UNIVERSITY PRESS

Oxford University Press is a department of the University of Oxford. It furthers the University's objective of excellence in research, scholarship, and education by publishing worldwide. Oxford is a registered trade mark of Oxford University Press in the UK and certain other countries.

Published in the United States of America by Oxford University Press
198 Madison Avenue, New York, NY 10016, United States of America.

Library of Congress Cataloging-in-Publication Data
Names: McBride, Keally D., author.
Title: Mr. Mothercountry : the man who made the rule of law / Keally McBride.
Description: New York, NY : Oxford University Press, 2016. |
Includes bibliographical references and index.
Identifiers: LCCN 2016005121 (print) | LCCN 2016005532 (ebook) |
ISBN 9780190252977 (hardcover : alk. paper) | ISBN 9780190252984 (Updf) |
ISBN 9780190252991 (Epub)
Subjects: LCSH: Law—Great Britain—Colonies. | Rule of law—
Great Britain—Colonies. | Law—Great Britain—Colonies—English influences.
Classification: LCC KD5020 .M38 2016 (print) | LCC KD5020 (ebook) |
DDC 349/.171241—dc23
LC record available at http://lccn.loc.gov/2016005121

1 3 5 7 9 8 6 4 2

Printed by Sheridan Books, Inc., United States of America

Dedicated with love and gratitude to my parents,
Richard and Betsy McBride

CONTENTS

ACKNOWLEDGMENTS

MY FIRST THANKS MUST GO to the Faculty Development Fund at the University of San Francisco, as it has allowed me to participate in the wonders of archival research and to receive feedback on the chapters of this book at many different conferences over six years. The university and the Faculty Union provide an invaluable resource without which this book would not have been possible.

An invitation from Bernard Harcourt to present at the Criminal Justice Roundtable at the University of Chicago Law School provided the starting point of this research, and his sage advice to avoid thinking of the rule of law "as a blunt instrument" was key in helping the book find its direction. Jesse Goldhammer pointed out that it was a "Roginesque" project and also helped to fundamentally shape my approach. Sylvia Brownrigg and Ellen Bernard helped shelter me in London as I slowly learned how to use the India Office Records and National Archives and uncovered the personal stories beneath the larger history. My thanks also to Marianne Constable for inviting me to be a visiting scholar in the rhetoric department at University of California at Berkeley so I could access the library's fantastic nineteenth-century holdings.

Audiences at the University of Oregon, University of Chicago, University of Alberta, and the University of San Francisco Law School provided excellent feedback and consistent writing deadlines. Fellow presenters at repeated meetings of the Association of Law, Culture and the Humanities; the Western Political Science Association; and the American Political Science Association also have provided criticism and questions that have made different components of the book much stronger. I promise that I will consider turning the story into a Hollywood screenplay some day!

Colleagues who have read and commented upon pieces of the manuscript include Karl Shoemaker, George Pavlich, Jennifer Culbert, Linda Ross Meyer, Megan Thomas, Samera Esmeir, Austin Sarat, Mark Antaki, Brian Weiner, Renisa Mawani, Jeanne Morefield, Peggy Kohn, David Gutterman, Mary Katzenstein, Bernard Harcourt, Susan Silbey, Uday Mehta, and Mathew Unger. My all-time favorite counsel, Kevin Bundy, has also read pieces in various stages of completion. Jinee Lokaneeta has helped me to understand the police and India far more than I would have without her assistance. James Martel and Sarah Burgess have read multiple drafts of most of these chapters, and I am forever grateful for their generous readings and perceptive comments. Conversations with Patchen Markell, Jeanne Morefield, Samuel Moyn, and Chip Turner about the relationship between history and political theory helped me understand (invent?) my methodology.

Tracy Seeley, Marjolein Oele, and Rachel Brahinsky helped support my writing of the manuscript during key moments. A number of students provided research assistance, including Paola Vu, Zachary Scalzo, Cassandra Sutherland, Keith Calara, Maribel Mercado, Sonja Anderson, and Benjamin Schaub. My editor at Oxford, Angela Chnapko, was intrigued by the romance of my unwieldy project and has been wonderfully supportive and enthusiastic as I have corralled it to completion. Reader evaluations provided excellent advice about the style of my argument and the scope of the content. Carol Specter and Debbie Benrubi at the University of San Francisco did their usual magic and found the map included here.

John Zarobell helped me discover the bizarre mirror provided by colonial history, and has encouraged my archival habit and travels. His brilliant mind helped me sharpen my arguments over many glasses of wine after dinner when the children had fled yet another discussion of "Mom's guy." He has read multiple drafts of much of the manuscript at its various stages of development with (mostly) good cheer. He also procured the fantastic image on the cover of this book with the gracious permission of the artist, Andrew Gilbert.

While I was writing this book, my daughter morphed into a serious scholar and even took time from writing college application essays to help me with the bibliography. Thank you, Celeste.

Image of James Stephen at twenty years of age.
Courtesy of the Cambridge University Library.

MR. MOTHERCOUNTRY

Introduction

> A. A violent order is disorder, and
> B. A Great disorder is an order. These two things are one.
>
> —Wallace Stevens

WHEN POLITICS GO AWRY, PEOPLE instinctively turn to law for resolution. In fact, Alexis de Tocqueville noted the personal tendency to embrace *either* law or politics: "Men who have made a special study of the laws and have derived therefrom habits of order, something of a taste for formalities, and an instinctive love for a regular concatenation of ideas are naturally strongly opposed to the revolutionary spirit and to the ill-considered passions of democracy."[1] The greatest appeal of law is that it stands above the fray, and can resolve intractable differences that could otherwise lead to violence.

The same observation holds true in international politics today. Laws are created and invoked in order to curb tyrants and terrorists—admittedly to uneven effect. International human rights law was created to provide recourse when domestic politics go horribly wrong and populations are not protected by their own regimes. The United Nations provision against genocide implies what has been coined a "Responsibility to Protect," whereby in cases of genocide, external forces have the responsibility to intervene and prevent further loss of life. The United Nations claims, "Sovereignty no longer exclusively protects States from foreign interference; it is a charge of responsibility where States are accountable for the welfare of their people."[2] In other words, international law overrides domestic sovereignty. The United Nations Security Council invoked the Responsibility to Protect doctrine to justify intervention in Libya in 2011.

On July 23, 2009, General Assembly president Miguel d'Escoto Brockmann staged a debate in the United Nations concerning the adoption of Responsibility to Protect as formal policy. Brockmann invited Ngugi wa Thiong'o, Noam Chomsky, and Jean Bricmont to participate in the debate, which mainstream media barely noted. These figures pointed out the realities of international power dynamics. On paper, the principle looks universal. However, in practice, more powerful countries would invade countries with less power in order to enforce "the rule of law." Even idealistic proponents admitted that places like China and the United States would never be subjected to external enforcement. Brockmann closed the debate by encapsulating his resistance to what seemed to be a relatively magnanimous desire to protect vulnerable populations: "Recent and painful memories related to the legacy of colonialism give developing countries strong reasons to fear that laudable motives can end up being misused once more to justify arbitrary and selective interventions against the weakest states."[3] This story caught my attention; it is not every day that someone calls into question the principle of human rights or the rule of law, particularly in the United Nations. Here was an example of politics roaring back and questioning the presumptive impartiality and ordering function of the law.

After all, it seems that what the world needs is a very large dose of the rule of law. Every day I read stories about police graft, judicial coverups, missing lawyers, and state violence against vulnerable populations. These stories are common in countries as diverse as Nigeria, Russia, Mexico, and the United States. There is one overriding principle that is frequently offered up as the answer to such corruption near and far: the rule of law. But the rule of law is a difficult concept to pin down, and is far less self-evident than the policymakers, analysts, and commentators who turn to it as a source of salvation acknowledge.

I began researching the US Agency for International Development's (USAID) rule-of-law initiatives and became increasingly uncomfortable with what I discovered. Frequently, USAID awarded large contracts to different law firms to help build "legal capacity" in countries around the world. This could mean anything from visiting law schools to providing lectures on property rights, to helping map out proper procedures between different courts. The project of providing law for others seemed problematic at best, particularly given Brockmann's comments about a continuation of colonial relationships through the law. How to understand the intermingling of colonial violence, legal order, and political disorder when one term—the rule of law—portends to stand outside and above the other two?

I turned to the history of colonial powers and their dissemination of law in their colonies. What I found was that the common contemporary narrative that postcolonial countries have not been "exposed" to the rule of law was not accurate. In fact, colonial regimes delivered a rule of law to all of their colonies. The rule of law was and is an inextricable element within the inegalitarian global institutions and power dynamics that we had in the nineteenth century and today. Yet it was—and is—offered as the corrective to these same dysfunctions.

This book explores the rule of law and its evolution within nineteenth-century British colonial relationships and institutions. This may sound like an arcane topic, but I pursue it here with contemporary political goals. In some sense, this investigation follows Walter Benjamin's observation that history is filled "with the presence of the now."[4] This book is not a comprehensive historical record of British colonial laws or the Empire's bureaucratic mechanisms; instead I recount particular historical episodes and developments that help explain how we got to where we are today.

Early to mid-nineteenth-century British colonial developments forced a turning point in the administration of the rule of law in British territories, protectorates, and colonies. Skeptics would assume that the rule of law within British colonies was nothing but a flimsy scrim, and I started this project counting myself among them. However, there is a far more complex story to be told from looking at this historical period in some detail.

This era of colonial administrative history reflects international as well as domestic developments. The start of the Victorian era was characterized by fear and anxiety in response to the changes in the British economy and rapid urbanization.[5] International developments only added to the fear of potential revolution; France's continuing revolutionary proclivities might ignite an increasingly restless British working class, and the North American settlements were indeed a disappointment to colonial officials in this regard. Would extending the franchise restore order or only encourage more demands? The ruling classes were driven to assert order and their place in it, and the rule of law was an ideal vehicle for this project. Insisting upon the rule of law was, as Tocqueville observed, a way of discouraging disorderly politics and simultaneously promising that the rights of men would be secure under the British Crown. The impulse to substitute orderly administration for messy politics is common in the contemporary world, and it is no accident that the rule of law continues to be a central aspect of this technocratic vision.

The period I examine was preceded by the dramatic seven-year (1788–1795) impeachment trial of Warren Hastings for abuses of the prerogatives awarded to him in his position in the East India Company. This trial spawned a debate about whether it was appropriate for the Crown of England to delegate the exercise of sovereignty to the British East India Company: Was colonialism an occupation of the state or private corporations? Did acting as a colonial power make the entity a sovereign power? There were many aspects of colonialism that exposed the inadequacies of the basic framework of nation-states and forced new innovations, as Antony Anghie has explored in his work, *Imperialism, Sovereignty, and the Making of International Law* (2005). At the start of the nineteenth century, Britain affirmed that colonial ventures *should* be closely regulated and controlled by the state, even if the state's ability to do so was improbable because of distance or lack of resources.

There was a sense that the uprightness of the colonial order needed to be asserted in order to effectively maintain British honor and its interests. Better technologies meant travel times between London and colonial outposts were decreasing, and reports of colonial atrocities could make their way to the newspapers. However, what has been coined "the Second British Empire" was also under increased economic strain.[6] There was a need to improve profitability generally, and the state wanted a larger share of the returns to help defray the increasing costs of global ambitions. Hence, the colonial administration was centralized and routinized to improve oversight, and economic imperatives started to gain even greater prominence in colonial decision-making.

There was an emphatic embrace of order and morality in British colonial administration, vividly represented in this book by Sir James Stephen. James Stephen was colonial undersecretary and legal counsel who worked in the Colonial Office in various capacities from 1813 until 1847. He was charged with protecting the rule of law in the Empire, and he took this task very seriously, exercising his powers of discretion and earning himself the nickname, "Mr. Mothercountry." He was instrumental in developing a new bureaucracy of colonial administration during his time in the Colonial Office, but even more important, he was driven by a personal mission to use law to create opportunities for the dispossessed persons under British rule.

The rule of law was envisioned by James Stephen as a bulwark against vice and an instrument for promoting freedom during his career. At the end of his period of service, the rule of law as he envisioned it had fallen prey to the very changes he resisted. It became a handmaiden for economic expansion, an instrument of social control and propaganda that accompanied the violence of British rule. This book tells the story of this evolution. I have taken his nickname as the title of the book, and the subtitle indicates that paradoxically, it was one man who tried to achieve the rule of law, contra Aristotle's typology. But the full story shows how his vision failed and the realities of colonial domination resisted the incursion of grand idealism.

Unrest in the colonies was linked with unrest at home. In 1866 there was a high-profile case against Governor Edward John Eyre for the slaughter of Jamaican protesters, and the graphic account of the murders ended up causing riots and political disruption in several locations around Great Britain. Of course, citizens of Great Britain then, just like citizens today, were only so interested in the actions of their countrymen in faraway places. It was not only public pressure that pushed adherence to something called "the rule of law" in the distant reaches of the British Empire. Adherence to the rule of law was the party line in Great Britain in the nineteenth century.

High-profile trials about the behavior and responsibility of colonial officials provided the stage for a public reconciliation of often-violent colonial practices with Great Britain's emphatic embrace of the rule of law. Less spectacular incidents of British settlers engaging in criminal activity throughout the world also caused a crisis of sorts as the proclamation of the white man's burden to civilize the rest of the world was pointedly belied by British behavior.

The British responded in two ways. First, they tried to centralize colonial administration and "clean up the Empire." In debates that might strike the contemporary reader as familiar, the British explored the possibility that more oversight would create more accountability, and the need to recruit more virtuous men into service abroad. Next, given the impossibility of controlling what happened in faraway places, the British changed the way they understood the rule of law. The first response was deliberate and noisily advertised. James Stephen was part of this vaguely realized plan to create more oversight in London. The second response was quiet and evolved in practice; the shifts are not registered in ideological claims about the rule of law, but through examination of historical episodes.

The fact that the British Empire was struggling to reassert and reform itself during this period is relatively well known, as is James Stephen. Scholarly voices speaking from within the paradigm (note the "we" in this passage) observed,

> Criticism of our colonial system came from all sides—religious, humanitarian, political and economic—and after 1830 was reinforced by the Colonial Reformers with their ideas of systematic colonization and the ideal of reviving the ancient glory of British expansion. While Colonial Secretaries, following one another in rapid succession, sought to solve colonial problems in relation to Parliamentary exigencies, one steadfast and penetrating mind was interpreting imperial policy in ethical terms. The intellect and purpose of James Stephen raised colonial government to a higher political plane and contributed greatly to the attempts to solve its new problems.[7]

These "new problems" resulted from the successes of the British Empire as much as from the soul searching following the loss of the North American settlements. As the aspirations of Empire became more developed and widespread, the need for a unified strategy became evident. In London, the Colonial Office was generally, and James Stephen was specifically, charged with being the central clearinghouse for all the colonies with the exception of India, which had its own apparatus, the India Office.

One of my colleagues commented that I was probably expecting to find "an Eichmann" in the Colonial Office. For precisely this reason, I was shocked instead to discover someone with an intense conscience and spiritual belief who was a critic of British colonialism. Stephen was trained as a lawyer and determined that implementing the rule of law in the colonies meant faithful adherence to the tradition of common law. Stephen understood that all too frequently, the colonists abused their powers. He devoted himself to curbing this abuse, whenever possible, through the law. In practice what this meant was sorting through different sources of sovereignty, local practices and arrangements, and distinct legal provisions that had been established particular to each colony in order to excavate the principle that would apply. During Stephen's tenure as colonial undersecretary, a clear system of legal accountability emerges in the books of the Colonial Office. He sorted and recorded the particularities of each colony's political and legal administration in order to create records for present and future administrators. He created paper trails of legal precedent and started to hold colonial officials, who changed very frequently, accountable to the practices established earlier. The maze of specific practices associated with each colony would baffle anyone, and Stephen became irreplaceable given his specific knowledge of the particularities of each colony.

It was a completely unsustainable system. The complexities of common law within one country are enough to defeat the most resolute legal scholar. Trying to follow common-law practice in a mixture of legal systems, shifting boundaries, distinct languages, vastly different populations, and unclear sovereignty is an impossible undertaking. Colonial realities precipitated crisis and change in pursuing the rule of law at an international level. British colonial administration provides an excellent site to trace this evolution because of the centrality of law in its national culture before and during this time frame, as well as its increasing political and military dominance. The increased circulation of British economic interests, citizens, and rapidly accelerating international competition over resources and territories combined to create pressure on the traditional understanding of the rule of law.

After exploring this particular moment of colonial legal administration, the book dwells upon two particular innovations that resulted. These developments paved the way for the current understanding of the rule of law as a universal value, combined with the realities of a deeply unequal international system. Somehow, the rule of law came to be embraced by virtually all powers, great and small, and yet it is consistently trampled. This is not just a matter of inconsistency. Instead, the rule of law came to be subtly redefined so it would facilitate resource extraction and sanctify the ability of some countries to assert sovereignty over others. The rule of law would also be defined to focus upon procedure above all else, thereby dulling its potential for critique and control of powers that be.

The problem of how to control agents of state power in a globalized world is not solved. For the past 140 years, one solution has been to focus upon procedures and stated principles as an indication of allegiance to "the rule of law." Yet, I would argue, this formalism is less and less convincing. People want to live in just polities; they want officials whose powers are bounded; and they want those who abuse their powers to be held accountable. This is ideally what the rule of law means. But what does the rule of law mean in a country that was introduced to its legal system through colonialism? Does it become a tainted instrument that can no longer have power?

The rule of law is supposed to be an eternal and universal principle, yet it has a very particular international history. This history matters for understanding the contemporary potential of the rule of law to create justice, curb the abuse of power, and serve as the foundation for a more peaceful world. I did not set out to write a biography, but James Stephen was a riveting figure for me. As I poured through his notes contained in the archives of the Colonial Office, it became clear that he was a sharp critic of colonialism and no idealist when it came to the law. Why did he go to work every day? It was not uncritical patriotism or blind faith in legal procedure. I came to see my struggle reflected in his; if the rule of law has failed so often to curb power and assert right why do I still venerate it as an ideal worth fighting over? The rule of law is grinding, slow, and impossible work; this book provides a cautionary tale for those who toss it off as a principle that can easily solve issues of power and inequality. Instead, we should look behind its invocation to see what powers and privileges it actually protects.

Above all, I hope to reveal that invoking the rule of law is not a neutral claim. Thomas Carothers observed, "Despite the close ties of the rule of law to democracy and capitalism, it stands apart as a nonideological, even technical solution. In many countries, people still argue over the appropriateness of various models of democracy or capitalism. But hardly anyone these days will admit to being against the idea of law."[8]

Many of the regions that are subject to foreign intervention in this regard have been exposed to colonial versions of the rule of law. What initially appears as complete disorder is the result of a historical economic, political, and legal order. There is a postcolonial perspective on the international circulation of the rule of law; seeing this perspective requires knowing the colonial history.

I

Colonialism and the Rule of Law

ONE OF THE MOST VIGOROUSLY advertised aspects of the British Empire was the claim that the British brought the rule of law with them, planting the principles of the Magna Carta in foreign soils around the globe. Anticolonial and postcolonial critique has assiduously belied this narrative, pointing out how frequently laws were ignored or haphazardly enforced. And this is to put aside the question of whether British notions of the rule of law were appropriate to transfer in the first place. Furthermore, critics point out that the British Empire was more Hobbesian (might makes right) than it was Lockean. In fact, some argue that Locke's work provided the legal justification for colonial appropriation; more recently, his reputation has been tarnished through the colonial link rather than British colonialism being sanitized through its affiliation with Lockean liberalism.[1]

While the focus of this book's inquiry is theoretical and historical, its eye is also aimed at present international ideologies and practices around the rule of law. Though there are particular resonances between past and present, this approach is not designed primarily to provide a distant mirror to our own time. It is an excavation of the present, for many of the laws that are in place around the globe are a direct result of British colonial administration. British administrators did write legal codes and, in often shocking ways, distributed them to British possessions around the globe. While the laws of the Empire had a relationship to English law, codes from different colonies were more likely the immediate source. H. F. Morris noted in his study of criminal laws in British colonies in Africa that "these Codes may be divided, as far as their ancestry is concerned, into three categories: those which ultimately derive from the Indian Penal Code, the St. Lucia Criminal Code of 1889 and the Queensland Criminal Code of 1899 respectively."[2] Sometimes colonists would swap the Indian Code for the Queensland one, or even the reverse.[3] The Indian Penal Code written particularly for India by Thomas Babington (T. B.) Macaulay was deposited in Cyprus, the Seychelles, northern Nigeria, northern Somalia, and the Sudan. In India and many African countries it remains the existing code of law. The past is not so distant after all.

Today, every continent retains elements of the legal code distributed by the British Empire. I am not making normative claims based upon the persistence of British colonial jurisprudence. After all, such claims would amount to either rejecting the laws outright based upon origins, or arguing that their survival indicates either utility or inherent justice. Rather, I make a historical argument. The fact is that the British Empire did create a legal footprint along with political, economic, cultural, and racial ones. It is also a historical fact that violence was a part of British colonialism. What does it mean to say the British Empire introduced ideologies of the rule of law in the context of violence?

There is one primary fact that needs to be acknowledged at the outset. Upon examining the theory behind colonial legal administration in conjunction with colonial practice, one finds it immediately evident that there is a large gap between the two. The British Empire failed miserably to live up to its own rhetoric. It is not a surprise that scholars, practitioners, colonial subjects, and even some British colonial administrators viewed the proclamations about the rule of law within practices of British colonization with cynicism. As Peter Fitzpatrick has commented, "the violence of imperialism was legitimated in its being exercised through law."[4] I assumed that any attention to the rule of law would be perfunctory at best, and most generally driven by a strategic deployment of legality to cover brutal domination. Nasser Hussain's brilliant exploration in *The Jurisprudence of Emergency: Colonialism and the Rule of Law* displayed how the colonies functioned as the actual limits, and the Schmittian exception, of the rule of law.[5] The British might be forced into some adherence to principles of just rule at home; abroad, anything was possible.

There is such a strong justification for this position, it is reasonable to assume that colonial legal history proves that the rule of law is an irretrievably tainted instrument in global politics. And while I hold a great deal of sympathy for this argument, it is difficult to embrace a world absent of the ideal that power can be bound effectively by stated principles and institutional checks. This doesn't mean that I want to salvage the idealization of the rule of law in its current or even past guises, but I do want to complicate the story so we might have a more nuanced view of the way the ideal of the rule of law is *deployed.* I don't want to use history in order to illustrate the failures of empires and individuals to enact the ideal in order to discard the ideal altogether. To call it ideological is to admit that the concept hides, reshapes, and suppresses some activities that happen under its aegis. But to quickly conclude that it needs to be unmasked and discarded would still leave obfuscated how the ideal has nonetheless shaped and continues to inflect the world. Of course the rule of law is ideological. Every idea, when deployed in the world, becomes ideological. To be bitterly disappointed by this fact is to give too much credence to the claims of impartiality that have been attached to the rule of law.

Why look at the rule of law in the context of colonialism? Putting the two inquiries together should mean that we understand both colonialism and the rule of law better by doing so. In theory, colonialism and the rule of law do not seem to go together, as the first term insinuates external control and the second implies bound power. In practice, both in the past and present, the rule of law is a yardstick that is used to measure, reform, control, bribe, and administer governments, elites, and people. In theory, the rule of law portends to "solve" the problem of power, defanging those who are given governmental authority. In practice, the administration of the rule of law is hopelessly erratic. At times, idealists hoist it as a flag and take principled positions in its name; at other times, it serves as a scrim for extortion. Studying its presence within practices of British colonialism reveals this volatility in particularly stark terms. The rule of law was the standard that the British were presumably, yet inconsistently, holding themselves against.

The practices and politics of colonialism and the rule of law virtually disintegrate as coherent categories under close scrutiny. Both terms presume a sense of unity where, in fact, none exists. While colonialism as a historical phenomenon is unquestionable, its methods, impact, and agents are far less unified and coherent once one starts to examine them closely. As already observed, British colonialism failed to live up to its "civilizational" claims, but it also failed to live up to its claims of rule and administration. As Ged Martin asked,

> Was there any real and effective measure of central control over the units which could justify the rhetoric of imperialism? Were there features common to the member territories which make it reasonable to generalize about an Empire? If the answers to both these questions prove to be negative, then it will be necessary to remember that when we talk about the British Empire we are really referring to a loose and often accidental association of units, embodying in their disorganization the worst features of the feudal and federal systems. Such a view would account for the large element in imperial history of the plainly irrational, which was designed to clothe with illusion that which lacked reality.[6]

And in fact, my first response to starting this research was simply shock at the randomness of British administration. To point out how erratic colonial administration was is not to say that it was unintentional or happened in a "fit of absence of mind." Jeanne Morefield's recent work, *Empires without Imperialism: Anglo-American Decline and the Politics of Deflection*, is a reminder that the British and American empires, despite protestations and stated reluctance to take on the imperial role, were and are conscious and deliberate attempts to exercise control over large parts of the globe.[7] Colonialism does not happen by accident.

C. A. Bayly has argued that there was a form of order in what looks like colonial mayhem. Granted, British colonies differed in their patterns, in large part because of the class formation and state-building histories in Asia and Africa that greeted British imperialists. But within the colonial camp there were divergent interests as well; farmers, creoles, settlers, administrators, soldiers, and traders often had distinct and opposing interests in the territories they inhabited. Bayly points out that despite these differences, the British colonial enterprise had a coherence based upon three factors: the fact that colonists needed the British arms to defend them from other colonizing powers, the fear of indigenous groups resisting their presence, and the fact that colonists needed a working relationship with colonial administrators in London to maintain favorable trade relationships. Without these Navigation Acts, the colonial endeavor would cease to be profitable.[8] Colonial politics were ultimately about economics.

My training as a political theorist leads me to read texts, but power relations are articulated largely outside of texts. The rule of law is invoked as an ideal and principle, but in fact, enacting the rule of law is not a matter of idealism but a matter of practice, actions, and small decisions, made by particular individuals in given circumstances. Any investigation of the rule of law needs to focus on the concrete application of the principle, not just invocations of the principle itself.

I am investigating one aspect of Britain's colonial bureaucracy, the legal arm. Modern governments that are based upon the rule of law invariably need bureaucracies to administer it. And bureaucracies, as Weber articulated, are mechanical forms of decision-making and policy implementation that are intended to achieve perfect rationalization and distribution of power. Ideally, bureaucratic implementation of the rule of law would mean that no one figure or group of figures would be able to shape outcomes. As Hannah Arendt observed, bureaucracies are "rule by Nobody," which is not the same as anarchism. Rather, "in a fully developed bureaucracy there is nobody left with whom one can argue, to whom one can present grievances, on whom the pressures of power can be exerted."[9] Modern governance according to the rule of law should function irrespective of the figures that inhabit the bureaucracy and who pays them, who their friends are, and what their personal beliefs are.

On this count, the British Empire was also a spectacular failure. Rather than rule of "Nobody," the rule of law was very much a project of a particular set of personalities. This is not to say that these figures were omnipotent or tyrants. Their directives were not infrequently ignored, and the distance from the Colonial Office to the outposts it was presumably overseeing was indeed vast. But perhaps that gap was really no farther than the distance between the deliberations held in the US Supreme Court and the police officer making a traffic stop in Detroit, the Bronx, or East Oakland today. The rule of law frequently *does* have a particular face, mission, or personality behind it, and bureaucracies cannot easily govern faraway places. Stated differently, the rule of law works differently than it portends and does not achieve its stated goals.

So what does it do? The rule of law organizes institutions, creates patterns of behavior, and broadcasts the presumed values of a regime. The patterns of behavior it creates are not necessarily law-abiding. For instance, prohibition of logging may make it a more lucrative and hence increasingly attractive occupation. Institutions which are intended to disperse the law, such as the police, may also develop in unexpected ways, as Chapter Five explores. The entire book considers the problems that arise when a regime is unable to live up to its professed values. Does the rule of law remain a goal to attain one day, or does it become a cover that works to perpetuate the abuse of power? These two outcomes are too stark in their opposition; the reality of the rule of law is ambiguity without end. This is why it is helpful to rub the theoretical construct up against historical examples.

The British Empire and the Rule of Law

The rule of law played a particularly essential role in the development of the British Empire during the era (1813–1870) I examine in the following chapters. This was an era of consolidation, a period when commercial interests were initially relegated to secondary import behind political strategy. "Economic interests were an important, but not critical, incentive to the creation of this new imperial system. More important was the sharp perception of danger among the ruling class, threatened as they felt themselves to be by the dissolution of social order at home and a fearsome military and ideological challenge abroad."[10] The Reform Act of 1832 that enlarged suffrage in Great Britain led to fears of French-like political chaos. To stave off what they feared would be disastrous shifts in political order, British elites elevated the rule of law to be a central characteristic of the British nation. Systems of policing were traded back and forth between India and Great Britain in case the rule of law needed bolstering through a force other than the pen. The assertion of the right to rule others because their power was bound by law (and hence sanitized of self-interest) was a central justification of British elites home and abroad. Since the time of Edmund Burke, the rule of law was also considered the best weapon for preventing social and political disruptions. The investment in keeping the rule of law and bound power in the colonies cannot be considered insincere because it was so self-interested!

The prosecution, led by Edmund Burke himself, of Warren Hastings for irregularities in his administration of India riveted the elites of the country at the end of the 18th century. Chapter Four recounts the public response to the Morant Bay Rebellion of 1865—another moment of political controversy over the actions of the British in their colonies. Sir James Fitzjames Stephen served as a barrister for the Jamaica Committee, led by John Stuart (J. S.) Mill, for the purposes of investigating the actions of Governor Eyre in suppressing rebellion in Jamaica. Stephen proposed that Eyre be convicted of murder for his role in the bloody suppression of the rebellion. In both instances the defendant was exonerated from the most serious crimes (Eyre was censored, Hastings recalled), which some would argue is an indication that the invocation of the rule of law was less than sincere. Regardless, both cases provided the opportunity for the rule of law in the Empire to be debated. At the very least, we could conclude that at least some segment of the British elite believed that it was important to have colonial administration be bound by the principle.

Though British elites generally embraced the rule of law, there were nonetheless a select few who carried the heaviest burden in achieving and administering it. There were figures such as T. B. Macaulay, who single-handedly wrote the entire penal code that has governed millions of people, up to and including today. Laws in colonies were upheld or struck down on the basis of the colonial undersecretary's opinion. Though there was a colonial apparatus, it was not systematic, nor was it in existence long enough—nor was its importance deemed great enough—that generations and competing parties were able to shape it. This meant that the administration of the rule of law was deeply personal. The political and historical outlooks of these individuals mattered in the circulation of the law. And beyond personal, it was also familial. The British story of civilizational advance was based upon impartial rule that maximizes individual freedom of thinking, reason, and economic production. Yet the rule of law in the 19th-century British Empire was a project of an incestuously intertwined, religiously devout collection of families known as the Clapham Sect. This paradigmatic tool of rationality was wielded by zealots and their offspring, driven to prove themselves worthy to their brothers, fathers, sisters, and friends. What does it mean that a tiny section of the English elite driven by otherworldly fervor took it upon themselves to defend the bureaucratic and mundane principle of legal proceduralism in the British Empire?

This book builds upon the important and nuanced political theoretical work about British colonialism by Jennifer Pitts, Sankar Muthu, Karuna Mantena, and Jeanne Morefield. They demonstrate that British colonial ideologies were not as monolithic as we sometimes make them out to be. Muthu's book, *Enlightenment against Empire* traces critiques of colonial assumptions in Diderot, Herder, and Kant, but admits that such resistance to imperialism waned in Europe by the middle of the 19th century. Jennifer Pitts's *A Turn to Empire* is a close account of this period of transition from critique to myopic narratives of European civilizational superiority and its mission of furthering the rest of the world. "The confidence-even self-righteousness—of imperial liberalism requires a kind of presumption incompatible with the sharply ironic, self-critical stance so characteristic of the eighteenth-century thinkers considered here. We encounter an earnestness in J. S. Mill or a grand high-mindedness in Tocqueville that is quite foreign to the style of Bentham or Burke."[11] Pitts traces a tendency to block out or even consciously refuse local knowledge in the name of high-minded liberal principles of colonial administration.

Karuna Mantena's *Alibis of Empire: Henry Maine and the Ends of Liberal Imperialism* picks up historically where Pitts leaves off in the mid-19th century and explains the subsequent embrace of local knowledge after a series of anticolonial movements and violence rattle the resolve of British liberal colonialists. Mantena's brilliant study investigates what could be termed the entrance of British colonialism into an era of bad faith through the figure of Henry Maine. The British were not going to abandon the project of empire, but they were going to adjust their expectations and storylines to match the very evident fact that the rest of the world was not mutely falling in line and becoming British. She argues that British colonial ideologies moved from being driven by "civilizing justifications" to "culturalist alibis." "In the late nineteenth century, new imperial alibis redefined the terms of debate about empire; foundational questions about the legitimacy of British rule in India were displaced by a presumption of the necessity of foreign rule given by the 'nature' of native societies."[12] Anthropological approaches were embraced, and the indissoluble difference between the British and their colonial subjects, as opposed to the narrative of progress through imperialism, came to structure ideologies of colonial rule.

Emphasizing this difference does not indicate any retreat from colonial ambitions, however; Mantena argues it was just a reformulation of the structure of ruling the Empire. One of the greatest advantages of the embrace of native difference was that it allowed for more flexibility in response to events in the colonies. "On the one hand, as opposed to grand schemes of societal improvement, imperial rule was to accommodate itself to the allegedly unchanging and unchangeable character of native peoples. On the other, impending crises within native society, linked to endemic forms of internecine conflict, or, more often, to traumatic contact with the West, were put forward as retroactive validations for the prolongation of imperial rule."[13] My research shows this same shift in emphases according to the specific situation. If the rule of law failed because of abuses by local officials or policemen, it demonstrated the need for the British oversight to continue. If the rule of law failed to prevent criminality by the native population, it demonstrated the lawlessness inherent in the indigenous culture, once again underscoring the need for outsiders to import the principle.

This book examines the ideas about and implementation of the rule of law in the British colonies during the 19th century, and hence moves across all three of the eras detailed in Muthu's, Pitts's, and Mantena's studies. The juxtaposition of past and present practices and ideas about Empire mirrors Jeanne Morefield's work on the deflection of imperial responsibility. However, my scope is in many ways smaller as I focus upon the legal aspect of colonialism as implemented by a small group of influential persons rather than the ideological logic of colonialism itself.

In addition to the backdrop of colonial economics, colonial ideas, and anticolonial struggles, changing ideas about the rule of law form the backdrop to this investigation. The actions and attitudes I investigate in this book reflect the convergence of two different discussions that often overlapped but are nevertheless distinct. Colonial justifications and alibis intertwined with evolving ideas about the rule of law within

Great Britain as revealed by codification debates that were started with the ideas and advocacy of Jeremy Bentham and his pupil, John Austin.

I have affinity with the critical legal studies tradition and see that colonial laws served British colonial elites and their interests. However, the continued persistence of the legal codes around the world demands that I also make space for a more descriptive approach to these laws. How did these claims operate? How did British administrators formulate and implement law in the colonies?

India was always the exception in terms of colonial administration, and it fell outside of the purview of the Colonial Office. Following multiple heated public debates for more than a decade about whether it was seemly to have the British East India Company rule in the name of the British Crown, the Indian Government Reform Act of 1784 established two entities that were supposed to develop good governance for India from two locales.[14] Public servants were divided between the Viceroy's council located in Calcutta, the seat of British governance in India, and the India Office in London. The idea was to have both local knowledge and British state connections, thereby improving accountability to the home country of practices in India, and to make sure that practices of good governance were being introduced—as much as was possible given the difficulties of the situation and the character of the people, that is. James Mill welcomed the appointment of T. B. Macaulay as president of the Indian Law Commission in 1835 with the comment that now India will become "the first country on earth to boast a system of law and judicature as near to perfection as the circumstances of the people will admit."[15] In practice, the division of committees between London and Calcutta produced the absolute bureaucratic chasm, particularly during a period when correspondence could take anywhere from three to eight months to reach one locale from the other depending upon the time of year and the weather.

The subject of Mantena's book, Henry Maine, was a legal advisor on the Viceroy's council from 1862 to 1869 and was presumably accountable to the rest of the legal committee within the India Office back in London. But he spent years pleading for resolution of particular principles to no avail.[16] In his correspondence he notes the lassitude on the part of the London branch, complaining to a friend that one of his compatriots flat out refused to issue a ruling on a particular matter: "I remember (Dekelt?, handwriting illegible) telling me once he would not answer a colonial case of some importance to me-because it was, in his opinion, too hard to rescue the expenditure of intellect which it would have required on his part."[17] Clearly, though some administrators devoted their lives to creating and upholding something akin to the rule of law in the Empire, others were completely disinterested in the project.

The Rule of Law

It is important to begin by teasing out the theoretical intricacies of the concept "the rule of law" before investigating how it was pruned to fit into the profile of the British Empire. Paul Brest noted, "Examining the 'Rule of Law'—even at the risk of discovering that is entirely illusory—is a necessary step toward a society that can satisfy the aspirations that make us hold to the concept so tenaciously."[18] Judith Shklar's essay, "Political Theory and the Rule of Law," provides an excellent place to start with such an examination. She points out two dominant models of the rule of law, and associates them with Aristotle and Montesquieu. She argues that Aristotle saw the rule of law "as nothing less than the rule of reason."[19]

> In Aristotle's account the single most important condition for the Rule of Law is the character one must impute to those who make legal judgments. Justice is the constant disposition to act fairly and lawfully, not merely the occasional performances of such actions. It is part of such a character to reason syllogistically and to do so his passions must be silent.[20]

Such dispassion is not within the purview of most people, which is one reason Aristotle had no qualms about constructing a society that had been parsed into inferiors and superiors, and giving those of superior intellect the responsibility to protect and administer the law. The rule of law is the administration of society by those who are governed by reason; it is not the view that all of society will be reasonable. As Shklar points out, Aristotle's rule of law is compatible with ancient slavery and also the modern "dual state." "Such a state may have a perfectly fair and principled private law system, and also a harsh, erratic criminal control system, but it is a dual state because some of its population is simply declared to be subhuman, and a public danger, and as such excluded from the legal order entirely."[21]

In many ways Aristotle's view of the rule of law creates a tautology, which is familiar to anyone who has read him. Those who can be reasonable are subject to the law; those who cannot be reasonable are not. Justice is treating those who are equal with equality, while those who are "by nature" not equal should be treated unequally. Large sections of life, and segments of the population, are excluded from the law because of their inability to live outside of their passions; their exclusion marks them as unreasonable. Power, inequality, and segregation mark this version of the rule of law, even as it establishes the ideal of authority limited in its exercise.

An analysis of the invocation of the rule of law in colonialism that emphasizes the racial aspects of administration would find much of Aristotle's theory resonant. The British were able to be reasonable; their colonial subjects were not. Hence, it is predictable that the British would guard the rule of law and claim that one day a significant transformation would occur within the population that would allow them to take on the roles of guardians of reason. Aristotle's irrational subjects had no chance to change; in contrast, the British could be regarded as progressive in one aspect, since they claimed to somehow transfer the capacity to reason to their subjects. Yet the problem of trying to govern unreasonable subjects with the law haunted the colonial enterprise. If the population could not respond to reason, then why write the law in the first place? If the population was reasonable enough to follow law, then why could they not write their own?

According to Shklar, Montesquieu's rule of law "really has only one aim, to protect the ruled against the aggression of those who rule."[22] Montesquieu was above all concerned with making sure that the power given to those who govern was not used against those being governed. He was unwilling to assume Aristotle's tautology, that those who rule will be those who deserve to rule and use their power to achieve the law. Instead he saw that the potential to abuse one's power was universal, and that the people must be protected from power through the law. Montesquieu's rule of law protects and applies to everyone, and requires virtue on no one's part. *The Spirit of the Laws* establishes the mechanisms of this regime: divided power to prevent consolidation and abuse of sovereignty.

> All that was needed for the Rule of Law in Europe, given its many fortunate historical and geographical circumstances, was a properly equilibrated political system in which power was checked by power in such a way that neither the violent urges of kings, nor the arbitrariness of legislatures could impinge directly upon the individual in such a way as to frighten her and make her feel insecure in her daily life.[23]

Yet *The Spirit of the Laws* also acknowledges that such a system had not taken hold everywhere, and that geography and climate determine whether such a system is possible.

Montesquieu's theory promotes all Europeans to a position of equality, but is able to establish its character through another exclusion in relation to what he terms "oriental despotism." Europeans have the rule of law, which means that authorities are prevented from preying upon their charges. The rule of law governs those within its purview, but this time the exclusions are not based upon "natural" characteristics so much as national and geographical ones. His exploration of the European rule of law in comparison to oriental despotism is brought to its height in *The Persian Letters.* Once again, a tautology rests at the heart of his theory—his European readers know that the unspecified "they" are "orientals" because they submit to despotism. Similarly, "they" rule despotically because they are oriental.

Remarkably, this version of the rule of law also makes a central appearance in British imperial thought. By invoking the rule of law, the British are able to distinguish the exercise of their own power from those of mere "despots." Thomas Metcalf observed, "Indeed the entire structure of the rule of law established by Hastings and Cornwallis can be seen in large measure as a way of containing British fear of their own complicity in Asian despotism."[24] Because they presumably imported the rule of law, the colonial regime was not despotic despite the fact that it had no local accountability.

Interestingly, the rule of law becomes its own despot, and the British begin to insist upon its omnipotence. Sir James Fitzjames Stephen remarked before the Viceroy's council in 1870,

> The establishment of a system of law which regulates the most important parts of the daily life of the people constitutes in itself a moral conquest more striking, more durable, and far more solid, than the physical conquest which rendered it possible. It exercises an influence over the minds of the people in many ways comparable to that of a new religion ... our law is in fact the sum and substance of what we have to teach them. It is, so to speak, a compulsory gospel which admits of no dissent and no disobedience.[25]

The rule of law emerges as the stated goal, means, and justification for British colonialism. Although they are not a chosen power sanctioned by constitution and the social contract, they are not a despotic power. Because they have accepted limitations upon themselves, and seek to implement and enforce bureaucratic procedures, consent is immaterial.

By the end of the nineteenth century, where the rule of law ends and where the British civilizing mission begins becomes indistinguishable. Albert Venn Dicey was a constitutional theorist who also argued that the mission of providing the rule of law to others was uniquely suited to the British nation. Shklar rues the central role that Dicey's combination of legal theory and national fervor has played over the past hundred and fifty years. "The most influential restatement of the Rule of Law since the 18th century has been Dicey's unfortunate outburst of Anglo-Saxon parochialism.... The Rule of Law was thus both trivialized as the particular patrimony of one and only one national order, and formalized, by the insistence that only one set of inherited procedures and court practices could sustain it."[26]

Shklar presents this as an unfortunate historical accident, that Dicey would come to have such an influence upon modern conceptions of the rule of law through his own personal proclivities. But I would argue that Dicey's view is an almost predictable culmination of his family's role in colonial politics. Dicey's extended family had been deeply involved in—one might even say exclusively in control of—the legal administration of the British Empire. James Fitzjames Stephen, responsible for codifying the laws of India and quoted on the previous page, was his cousin. Both men were descendants of the Clapham Sect.

Originally focused around the abolition of slavery, the central figures in the circle called the Clapham Sect were James Stephen (father of the

James Stephen known as Mr. Mothercountry), Zachary Macaulay, and William Wilberforce. Wilberforce was the smooth politician who provided the face of the Evangelical movement to abolish slavery. The other two also held seats in Parliament. Sir James Stephen was described as "James Stephen, who with gifts of speech far greater than Macaulay's, with the relentless logic of a great lawyer, with a fierce and terrible temper that all Macaulay's steadiness could scarcely keep in check, with fervor that did not, like Macaulay's, glow unchanged for years but rather flared intermittently into white fury, was another Clapham giant whom the enemy always recognized as one of their really formidable foes." Once when Stephen had burst into indignation at the inactivity of the government, Macaulay turned to a young George Stephen, as the elder Stephen left, and said, "In anger, your father is terrific."[27] Zachary Macaulay was one of the earliest governors of Sierra Leone, founded by the Claphamites to serve as a haven for emancipated slaves.

Their sons were equally impressive in achievement, and curiously focused in the realm of law. James Stephen's son began his career by writing the bill to abolish slavery and then went on to virtually single-handedly run the British Empire for more than twenty years as colonial undersecretary. His power led some critics to call him "Mr. Oversecretary Stephen." Zachary's son, Thomas Babington Macaulay, wrote the penal code for India that is still in effect and was a prominent historian. James Fitzjames Stephen finished implementing the Indian Penal Code in the 1860s, and then added the Indian Evidence Act and facilitated the circulation of the criminal codes around the world to places such as Canada. The last significant figure in the group to have law as his primary mission was Albert Venn Dicey. Following in the footsteps of his uncles and cousins, he articulated a theory of the rule of law and its export that went to heart of the civilizing mission.[28]

Shklar's genealogy helps establish the strains of thinking about the law that reappear and even contradictorily attach themselves to British colonial practices. But another way of approaching the topic is to consider three different aspects of a regime characterized by the rule of law. Though scholarly attention has focused upon the rule of law as a justification or alibi for colonial rule, during the 19th century, the rule of law was most often considered as a response to the problems of actually governing the colonies, such as the determining the relationship between British common law and indigenous legal systems, the need to control agents that were exercising state power, and the need to punish criminal actions consistently.

First, and related to the Aristotelian tradition enumerated above, is the idea that the rule of law creates a boundary of legal jurisdiction more generally. For instance, there is a division between secular laws and religious principles, and some aspects of life are not appropriately subject to law. Some people—for instance, children and the insane—cannot be subject to the same laws as others. The space in which the law operates is presumably bound, and officially so. These boundaries may be altered, but not without a legal process that is not arbitrary. This is exactly the notion that Carl Schmitt has so devastatingly critiqued in *Political Theology: Four Chapters on the Concept of Sovereignty*. "The tendency of liberal constitutionalism to regulate the exception as precisely as possible means, after all, the attempt to spell out in detail the case in which law suspends itself."[29] Paradoxically, regularizing the boundaries of the law is one way of establishing its totality. So even if the law is not always applied, by acknowledging this fact, the "rule of law" remains as a principle if not an invariable practice.

In the colonial context what this meant was establishing what aspects of life in the territory, protectorate, or colony would be administered by the British rule of law, and which would not. It also meant figuring out indigenous legal systems and determining the proper relationship between these and British law. This was an invariably messy exercise. In 1772 and 1773, the Parliamentary Committee set up to investigate the East India Company and suggest new methods of governance concluded that India was the proverbial blank slate to be written upon. Bernard Cohn summarized the committee's findings as follows: "It was argued that because there was no law in India, British law and institutions should be introduced into the vacuum."[30]

Warren Hastings, governor-general of the East India Company since 1772, protested vociferously. He composed a team of eleven local experts to compile the "Ancient" Hindu Constitution, which was translated from Sanskrit to Persian, and then from Persian to English. The reforms of 1772 were subsequently presented as a restoration of sorts: "The judicial reforms of 1772, according to the Committee of Circuit, were intended 'to recur to the original principles and to give that efficacy of which they were deprived by venal and arbitrary innovations' … Both Hastings and Cornwallis claimed they were restoring the 'ancient constitution' in justice, merely introducing changes which would ensure its impartial and effective application."[31] In 1783, Sir William Jones went to India and began his study of Sanskrit, and within three years was making pronouncements upon the correct interpretation of existing Hindu law. "Jones wanted to provide the British courts in India, the Crown, and the East India Company with a sure basis on which to render decisions consonant with a true version of Hindu law."[32] Such attention is notable even if the results were not particularly excellent. Later scholars determined that Jones ascribed more confidence to his Sanskrit abilities than was prudent. But the debates that followed about who was able to interpret and speak for Hindu law, and the fear that local authorities were gaining more power than the British believed to be desirable, point to the next aspect of the rule of law in relationship to governance.

The rule of law is also a method of limiting the exercise of power by those who are given it through political structures. Most charitably, we could say along with Montesquieu that the exercise of power is divided, so it cannot be concentrated into one set of hands. This means that the governed are protected from the abuse of legally established powers. It is a way of preventing the dogs guarding the sheep from becoming wolves. James Madison wrote about using "ambition to counteract ambition" to keep government from becoming despotic; pitting elites against one another is the best way of protecting those under their jurisdiction. Less democratically, one could also argue that this really is a way of elites protecting themselves from one another. Participating in government should not make one a target of others interested in increasing their power. In other words, "avoiding the concentration of power" can also be read as a power-sharing agreement.

Interestingly, the British claimed a goal of setting up a system of law that would end "oriental despotism," but the controversy over finding authentic "Hindu law" shows how fetishization of the rule of law can inadvertently empower local elites. Jones hoped that having a written code of Hindu law would mean "pandits, the Brahmans, and the Indian 'lawyers' henceforth could not deal out Hindu law as they please, and make it at reasonable rates when they cannot find it ready made."[33]

A subsequent legal scholar in India, Robert Colebrook, became convinced that the British had been duped into following false prophets; local elites had been peddling stilted versions of the one and true Hindu law. Henry Maine arrived in the mid-19th century and determined that any attempt to turn Hindu law into a written code inevitably would distort the tradition. This brings up yet another difficult point: Can one have the rule of law as a common-law practice or does it need to be written? This was the debate that was roiling Britain at the start of the 19th century, and it spilled over into colonial territories as well. Maine argued that it was better to start afresh and push forward with complete codification of the British laws in India as a way of curbing the power of local and potentially corrupt elites.

Hence, we can see how the rule of law in the colonial context was supposedly an attempt to distribute power equally, but the effort to implement it created new elites and amplified some voices. The continual failure to bound the power of local and native elites became a renewed cry for the rule of law. Colonial power abuses and the rule of law circulated in a relationship of codependency for more than a hundred years.

Finally, the rule of law provides procedures for its own failures, namely in the instance of crime. Dealing with those who fall outside the reason of the law demands clear criminal codes if a society is not to lapse back into a state of war. This aspect of the rule of law can be associated with John Locke's *Second Treatise of Government*, in which the criminal is seen as the test for the strength of government. In the face of the disruption of natural rationality, does society lapse back into a state of war, or does the social contract have provisions for those who fall outside the bounds of reason? Do we allow the practice of revenge to infiltrate society when crimes have been committed?[34] For Locke, and others, one central measure of the rule of law is the regulation of procedures to deal with crime—eliminating emotion in doing so. Law rushes in where reason has failed us; law—the product of reason—can eliminate any gaps in its own regime.

This may account for the disproportionate amount of energy and attention paid to criminal and penal codes in British colonial legality. Not only was criminality largely expected from indigenous populations, but demonstrating how to deal with irrationality, which is how the British regarded the crimes of others, was a central aspect of the colonial enterprise.

We can see that many of the most central ideas about power and powerlessness rest behind this term "rule of law." Shklar's discussion of the term's genealogy illuminates the fact that it openly divided populations and capacities at one point assuming that disparity in responsibility could be used to create equilibrium. The inevitably unequal distribution of power—whether it is perceived as natural as in the case of Aristotle or socially or politically constituted as in these other formulations—is the central problem of politics. Law is repeatedly conceived as the solution to this problem. The utility of the rule of law as a concept is that it allows fear, ambition, greed, power, and vulnerability to be "solved." Codification of law, ironically enough, pursued with greater success and vigor in the British colonies than in the homeland, providing the rationalization of the political landscape. "These codes mark the transition to the modern legal and political order; the abstract juridical subject is moved to the center of the law, and the relationship between the juridical individual and the constitutional state is coded as a finite and self-contained rendering of possibilities."[35]

While the intent in the colonies was to control the distribution and challenges of colonial power through the deployment of legal codes, the result was quite different. By trying to recognize indigenous codes, the boundaries of colonial society became affixed, and some individuals were held more accountable than others. Local elites were able to figure out how to use codes to increase their power, and colonial plunder was able to continue to avert accountability. As Chapter Five explores, the problems of power and accountability were not solved, but they were definitively shaped by British legal practices in their colonies.

You may protest that power and powerlessness and political and economic abuses persist in all regimes that claim to be governed by the rule of law—and you would be correct. This is where the unique aspect of the rule of law as a political ideology starts to become more evident. It is invoked as both an ideal *and* a remedy for political abuses. Would you not be wary if your doctor said your medicine was the same as your cure? This is why the rule of law as an ideal is never discarded, as its very failures are heralded to prove its necessity.

If we could just dismiss all this attention to the rule of law as merely a justification for colonial practices, it would be much simpler. But my archival research shows an inordinate amount of attention to detail and conscientiousness surrounded the application of law to British colonies. The details are worth examining not because these men—and they were of course all men—succeeded in doing what they thought they were doing. Instead, it is worth considering in detail because so many of the problems of power and the incapacity of the rule of law to deal with them become evident. Some administrators tried to use the rule of law as a way to neutralize colonial tyrants, yet the larger historical tide of colonial appropriation and the growth of the international system ultimately swallowed and fundamentally changed what the rule of law means in a global framework.

The following chapters try to capture this transformation by giving four different snapshots of how the rule of law appeared in colonial administration. Each vignette demonstrates a different aspect of the difficulties of administering the rule of law, the evolving philosophies behind it, shifting economic contexts, and particular colonial circumstances. Taken together, they illustrate a fundamental shift in the way the rule of law was practiced, and the ends to which it was deployed.

The next chapter, "Genealogical Explorations: The Rule of Law as Practice," takes up the personal and familial story of "Mr. Mothercountry." Recently Catherine Hall published *Macaulay and Son*, which examines the central roles that both Zachary and Thomas Macaulay played in the British Empire. Although Zachary and Thomas Macaulay both appear in this book, I focus upon the other central family of the Clapham Sect, the Stephens. Reflecting their grand sense of historical import, the Stephen clan produced a number of autobiographies and biographies, sons writing about fathers or brothers, several fathers addressing memoirs to their children and grandchildren. The last memoir in the series was written by Virginia Woolf to her nephew, and it includes musings about her affinities with her grandfather, Sir James Stephen, aka Mr. Mothercountry. These accounts have been instrumental in helping me piece together the relationships between these figures as well as their personal motivations for engaging in lives of public service.

The primary figure in this chapter is James Stephen, who almost single-handedly oversaw most of administrative aspects of the British

Empire for 20 years. He developed the colonial administrative apparatus and provided legal opinions on all laws and regulations passed in the British colonies as to whether or not they were consistent with the British understanding of "the rule of law." His approach toward the law was marked by skepticism; he believed that the law was frequently used as a tool for the powerful rather than for justice. It was his personal mission to uphold higher standards of justice, as opposed to mere legality, in his legal administration.

He was a tireless worker, but records of the family and his own diary suggest that he was driven to collapse from nervous exhaustion. Once his vision of the rule of law is explained, such an outcome is not terribly surprising. This chapter focuses upon the rule of law as Stephen's existential practice. Taking the rule of law as seriously as Stephen did can be an intense burden, and an exercise in continual frustration and perceived failure. However, Stephen's faith and humility were the source of his greatest success in administering the rule of law; these same factors meant that his career could not easily be replicated.

As an abolitionist, Sir James Stephen believed deeply in the project of Sierra Leone, and took an immense interest in the colony. Chapter Three, "Lawless Places and Placeless Law: Stephen, Sierra Leone, and Extraterritoriality," examines the establishment of Sierra Leone as a "Colony of Freedom" that was intended as an evangelical model for the rest of the British Empire. Achieving the rule of law was considered one of the colony's central missions, along with providing a location for freed and former slaves to achieve self-determination. Sierra Leone was the location of the world's first international criminal court, established to punish those who continued to participate in the slave trade.

The colony was very small, and its trade was unstable enough to continually threaten the future of the experiment. But as devoted as he was to the emancipation of slaves, Stephen also believed that Britain should make no more claims upon African Territory, even if this move would have made the economic survival of the colony possible. Sierra Leone became a flashpoint in the negotiation over territorial jurisdiction and colonial expansion. The British wanted to control ever larger reaches of the globe, even if they did not want to claim and then have to defend their exclusive sovereignty in these areas.

Ironically, increased instances of criminality on the part of British settlers led to a crisis of jurisdiction. Too frequently, British citizens were creating havoc by committing crimes outside of official colonial territory, and local colonial officials from all points of the Empire tried to invent new ways of managing the issue. What emerged was a proposal for "extraterritorial jurisdiction," whereby British law could be invoked and enforced outside of formal British territory. While particular arrangements granting such privileges were relatively common, this Act of 1843 proposed to make it an integral element of international law. It was a provision that would end the need for the series of exceptions that the British were negotiating.

It would be an understatement to say that Stephen was adamantly, even hysterically, opposed to this legislation. He argued that it would provide a veneer of "law for a place that shall remain essentially lawless," and even worse, detach the rule of law from any "positive" basis. He had spent thirty years of his life defending a very traditional conception of sovereign territory and common law, often to the advantage of oppressed populations and against the wishes of local colonial administrators. If law could be invoked by powerful entities wherever and whenever they chose, law could no longer be an instrument for the weak. Stephen's objections were prescient, and what emerged was the principle of extraterritoriality, which is central in international law today. Some nations are able to exercise more sovereignty than others as a result of this provision. Extraterritorial jurisdiction also provided a crucial step in creating the postcolonial power arrangements of the contemporary world. Now citizens, and corporations, can be assured that their own country's laws will travel with them; there is no longer any need to conquer and control a given territory in order to determine what laws your citizens will be subject to. Though of course, as I will explain, this only holds true for citizens of more powerful countries.

Though his father had tried to export common-law tradition to the colonies, Stephen's son, J. F. Stephen, saw what a jurisdictional mire this created, and determined that clarity of legal procedure should be the focus of the rule of law, both at home and abroad. J. F. Stephen was convinced that legal ambiguities led to abuse of power, and he was involved in the attempt to hold Governor Eyre responsible for the murder of protestors in Jamaica. Though Stephen eventually expressed some sympathy for Governor Eyre, thereby earning the lifelong animosity of

J. S. Mill, he determined his lifework as clarifying laws and procedures to curb excesses of both criminality and its punishment. J. F. Stephen set out to codify laws, and his codes were then deposited in locations throughout the British Empire, a stark contrast to his father's approach of respecting the particularities of each situation. Chapter Four, "Codification and the Colonies: Who's Accusing Whom?," examines his philosophy that codification is the best way to instantiate the rule of law as a response to the Morant Bay Uprising in Jamaica.

The context for J. F. Stephen's codification project reflects a historical and a generational shift. The father believed in the moral force of law; the son specifically separated the two. J. Stephen spent his career trying to use the law as a moral shield for the oppressed; J. F. Stephen believed that jurisprudence was social science that should recognize inequalities rather than protect against them. The shifting perspectives in regard to the law between father and son are revealing; however, the son's emphasis upon procedure is the crucial turn. Codification turns the process of making legal decisions—as opposed to the substance and effect of them—the sign of whether the rule of law is implemented. For instance, an election may have only one candidate, but if proper procedures allow the nomination and voting process, then the election would meet the standards of the rule of law. One race or an impoverished population in a country may suffer disproportionately in the administration of justice, yet if the proper procedures are followed, then this too falls within the purview of the rule of law.

Given the British nervousness about governing their Indian subjects following the Indian Insurrection of 1857 it is not surprising that writing a criminal code would become a central aspect of British colonialism. As Metcalf observed, "the transforming power of the 'rule of law' was never abandoned. It triumphed above all in the codes of civil and criminal procedure, proposed by Macaulay's Law Commission and finally enacted in the 1860s."[36] J. F. Stephen tried to bring regularity and increased discipline to the use of laws in India, thereby promoting the edification of the native as well as—it was hoped—his docility.

In Chapter Five, "From Macaulay to Malimath: Punishment and the Police in India," I focus upon the policing system that was an integral element of colonial rule from the very start and its relationship to the formal administration of justice. Why did the British importation of the rule of law come to be contingent upon policing?

This final chapter examines the current debate about criminal law reform in India given all the high-profile cases of police corruption and violence against vulnerable populations that continue to go unpunished. It is important to remember the colonial history that provides the context for these current debates. The Indian Penal Code was written in London in 1837, by one of Stephen's friends, T. B. Macaulay. It was part of the grand experiment to give the rule of law to the rest of the world in the early nineteenth century. It is one of the most rapidly visible legacies of this period, and hence an appropriate place to end this history of the present.

In contrast to the vision of Sir James Stephen explored in Chapter Two, Macaulay saw "the rule of law" as something that was abstract, and hence equally applicable in any environment or context. In many ways, his version of "the rule of law" is what I expected to find in my study of colonial legality. Both father and son saw law as the instrument for bringing enlightenment to the masses, and Macaulay's primary identification as a historian of the British nation helped him see the legal project as part of the country's destiny. He had little self-consciousness of the edges of his own perspective, often denying facts in favor of his tightly regulated world vision. Catherine Hall provides excellent descriptions of his manic relationship with India.[37]

There have been repeated attempts to reform the criminal code in India which was left intact even after independence. This chapter concludes by investigating the suggestions of the Malimath Commission, which issued a 600-page proposal in 2004. The commission wanted to increase conviction rates above all, because the Indian court system today estimates that it has a backlog of *thirty million* cases. Cases are more frequently resolved through natural death than any other means. The role of the police is one of the central aspects of criminal justice reform because of many complaints about abuses by the police. Yet the commission suggests increasing police power in the interests of achieving a "natural" justice that will restore the "common man's" faith in the Indian justice system. Discord about what exactly the rule of law means for India, and whether India should try and establish a system of justice that is "indigenous" rather than imported, are central questions in this debate. The colonial origins of the Criminal Code weigh heavily on the minds of reformers and legal practitioners.

2

Genealogical Explorations

The Rule of Law as Practice

TO SAY THAT I AM GOING to do a genealogical exploration of the rule of law in nineteenth-century British colonial administration may sound like a Foucauldian endeavor, revealing the "centralizing power-effects" of colonialism and legality.[1] My general impression of and antipathy toward colonial rule led me to such assumptions; hence my surprise when the historical facts led me to another sort of genealogy. Lo and behold, what I assumed would be codes of law produced by the anonymous, collective, and impersonal administrative genius of the British nation was actually a family project. The inquiry became genealogy in a much more traditional sense and is populated by fathers and sons, uncles and nephews, brothers and cousins of the Stephen clan. A brief overview of the family tree will help to situate the main character of this chapter, Sir James Stephen.

Naturally, the Stephen family, which eventually produced three generations of lawmakers, had its origins in an ancestral pirate. The earliest James Stephen (and there were many) of the lineage occupied a small farm in Aberdeenshire. "He was engaged in trade, and, though it is stated that smuggler would be too harsh a name to apply to him, he had no insuperable objection to dealing in contraband articles."[2] The scoundrel James Stephen met his wife when he was one of the only survivors of a shipwreck, washing up in her part of the world. Robust seafaring adventurer that he was (I like to imagine him meeting boats laden with contraband goods—the flotsam of Grotius's free sea—on the windswept and dark Scottish coast), he fathered nine children, and his third son shared his name. James Stephen (the son) studied law briefly before becoming an investor in a failed coalmine project and losing what little he had. Eventually, he was put into debtors' prison, where he resumed his preoccupation with law with renewed zeal. "Stephen, however, was not a man to submit without knowing the reason why. He rubbed up his old legal knowledge, looked into the law-books, and discovered that imprisonment for debt was contrary to Magna Charta."[3] Stephen put together a case that he argued before a judge who was much less persuaded than his fellow prisoners had been by his research. His son, yet another James Stephen, stood at his side in the courtroom as his appeal was denied and he was returned to prison.[4] His insistence upon the unjustness of his situation never faltered, and after choreographing and then calling off a jail break, and then surviving a courtroom riot, Stephen was freed from jail and his initial accuser agreed to pay the debt on his behalf and to give his wife a yearly stipend. Stephen's exoneration was complete, though poverty was still his companion. He became an eighteenth-century version of an ambulance-chasing lawyer, his renown for having talked his way out of jail serving as his occupational advantage. This career led to spending an inordinate amount of time in pubs to find and meet with clientele, and he succumbed to vices such as smoking tobacco (!)—and others that are only hinted at in the family lore. Reportedly, his wife was extremely pious and instilled deep religiosity in their children. Both husband and wife died relatively young, leaving their children no inheritance.

The next James Stephen—who stood in court and witnessed the rebuff of his father's case—was given few options due to poor family finances. He engaged in elaborate self-education, spending much of his youth diverted by romantic tales and poetry. Funds from a wealthy uncle working as a doctor in St. Christopher's eventually enabled him to study law in Aberdeen, and he was encouraged toward worldly pursuits. He worked as a legal reporter to capture a steady salary at one point, until a larger inheritance after the death of his uncle in the Caribbean allowed him to enter the bar. In 1783, he sailed for St. Christopher's to begin what should have been a very profitable career as a lawyer. But his ship stopped in Barbados on the way, and his reporter's curiosity led him to attend a trial for murder that was underway.

> Four squalid negroes, their hands tied by cords, were placed at the bar. A planter had been found dead with injuries to his head. A negro girl swore that she had seen them inflicted by the four prisoners. There was no jury, and the witnesses were warned "in the most alarming terms" to conceal nothing that made against the accused. Stephen, disgusted by the whole scene, was glad to leave the court. He learnt afterwards that the prisoners were convicted upon the unsupported evidence of the girl. The owner of two of them afterwards proved an *alibi* conclusively, and they were pardoned; but the other two, convicted on precisely the same evidence, were burnt alive.[5]

The episode is worth recounting here because it appears repeatedly in the different histories and biographies written by the prolific clan. It is the moment that this James Stephen found his life's work: to end slavery. As a boy, he had watched his father's pleas be rebuffed even when the facts of law were on his side. His story that places his awareness of the evils of slavery awakening in a courtroom, curiously echoes the earlier episode. Stephen went on to live in St. Christopher's and witnessed the horrors of slavery at close hand. Why would his outrage not come from that experience? Why does his awakening to the injustice of slavery happen in a court of law? Law is on the opposite side from justice in both primal scenes; the mystery is why he nonetheless embraced the law as his vocation since it would be just as—if not more—feasible to be utterly disgusted by the travesties of legal justice. Instead, he decided to try and curb the evil of slavery through the law.

Upon arrival in St. Christopher's, Stephen refused to avail himself of slave labor, and used his private funds to buy and then liberate slaves as he was able. He also took it upon himself to try and enforce the slave codes. St. Christopher's, as did other British colonies, had extensive regulations detailing the acceptable treatment of slaves. These codes specified how many blows to the head were acceptable for punishment; the minimum amount of food to be given to children, women, and men; and so forth. Stephen took on cases in which owners were accused of abusing their "property," in one case, girls of only six and seven years of age. His victories were so hard won and the fines given to slave owners for breaking the slave code so disastrously small that he found the work utterly discouraging. Slavery could not be tempered; it must be extinguished. He would attempt to triumph in court where his father had failed.

Stephen made a 1789 visit back to London where he met and made a lifelong alliance with William Wilberforce, who had emerged as a leading abolitionist in England. Stephen returned to St. Christopher's, determined to keep gathering information and evidence to condemn the slave trade and abolish it in Britain's colonies. Health difficulties pushed him to return to London permanently in 1796, and his first wife died shortly thereafter. He became even more connected with Wilberforce politically and personally; he ultimately married William Wilberforce's sister, thereby sealing their alliance. Wilberforce and Stephen, along with Zachary Macaulay and John Venn, formed the core of what came to be called the Clapham Sect.[6] They were evangelicals, politically powerful and unbelievably energetic. The families intermarried, and the reformist zeal and interest in lawmaking passed from generation to generation. In response to many of the critiques about the moral decay inherent in the British Empire by figures such as Edmund Burke, and the soul-searching that occurred with the breakaway of the North American settlement, this group rose to prominence during an era of what Catherine Hall has characterized as "Evangelical Imperialism."[7]

At the turn of the nineteenth century, Britain was looking to reform its Empire and governance in accord with the highest principles of English civilization. For instance, in 1832, Parliament passed a provision that created a body that would act as the Supreme Court for the British Empire, the Judicial Committee of the Privy Council.[8] Abolishing slavery was one method of dramatically changing the profile of the British international presence, a way that the country could assert to itself and the rest of the world that its administration was benevolent and goals lofty. Evangelical imperialism was a specific response to the first crisis of the British Empire, and its heyday was brief, as the British imperial mission came to be redefined along secular and liberal lines soon after the abolition of the slave trade was complete in 1835. During this window, the Clapham Sect was central to saving and recasting the imperial project, and radical reformers were set loose within the machinery of British colonial administration.

Though Sir James Stephen coined the Clapham Sect's name, when he wrote about the group in his *Essays in Ecclesiastical Biography*, it was not a large movement, nor was it ever actually sectarian. The circle never had more than twenty or twenty-five members. Their small numbers only add to the impressiveness of their ambitions, however. Ernest Howse wrote a breathy history of the group entitled *Saints in Politics: The "Clapham Sect" and the Growth of Freedom* in 1952. He recounts:

> When it is recalled that a space of twelve years, 1792–1804, saw the campaign for abolition, the organization of the Sierra Leone colony, the first East India charter struggle, the founding of the Missionary Society, the organization of Cheap Repository Tracts, the institution of the Christian Observer, the founding of the British and Foreign Bible Society, the establishment on a wide scale of Sunday Schools and other projects of popular education, and ... when it is recalled that all these things were accomplished as the extra labours of a group of men already occupied by important duties of political, commercial, and professional life ... no further reminder is necessary that the Clapham Sect wrought a most unusual day's work in England.[9]

In short, the Clapham Sect was driven to work for justice and grace in the world; their brand of evangelicalism did not move them away from terrestrial concerns, but animated them. In England, in order to provide for education, they founded and paid for Sunday schools for all children in five counties; their "Cheap Respository Tracts" gave lessons in morals and proved to be tremendously popular; and they founded *The Christian Observer*, a literary, philosophical, and political publication published every month with the intention to "elevate" the level of public discourse. It published poems such as one by Hannah More entitled "Slavery":

> Shall Britain, where the soul of freedom reigns
> Forge chains for others she herself disdains?
> Forbid it, Heaven! O let the nations know
> The Liberty she loves she will bestow;

Not to herself the glorious gift confin'd,
She spreads the blessing wide as humankind.[10]

In the deeply gendered division of labor in the Clapham Sect, More was the author of many Christian tracts meant to appeal to popular audiences, women, and children. The strategy was surprisingly successful and proved to be instrumental in mobilizing public opinion against slavery, essential for winning the battle against entrenched colonial economic interests. "Hereafter on the first of every month they had the ear of a large section of the religious public of the middle class, and was (sic) thereby enabled, as they could not otherwise have done, to win a favorable hearing for their many causes."[11] Their brand of evangelism was different than those more familiar in the twenty-first century; they disliked emotional fervor or displays of spiritualism that were anything less than rational and controlled. God gave humans reason, and they should invariably use it to achieve his will. Though driven by what they saw as the oncoming zenith in the battle between good and evil, they were not revolutionaries. Stephen characterized the Clapham Sect's strategies in the following manner, both mocking and observant: "Ours is the age of societies. For the redress of every oppression that is done under the sun, there is a public meeting. For the cure of every sorrow by which our land or our race can be visited, there are patrons, vice-presidents, and secretaries. For the diffusion of every blessing of which mankind can partake in common, there is a committee."[12]

Nonetheless, the abolition of slavery was their main occupation, and it gave a global outlook to their reformist zeal. They clearly saw the struggle against slavery as requiring full geographical and international mobilization, hence their involvement in and funding of the colony of Sierra Leone, advocating for changes in the British law, attempting to influence peace treaty negotiations with France and the United States, fighting to establish the right of Anglican churches to move to India, and accomplishing the distribution of Bibles around the world. Some of their critics complained about their omnipresence and the potential conflicts of interest that arose from their many activities:

> At the African Institution they impudently declare that they have no concern either with commerce or with missions; they step into their

> coaches and *presto*—they are the Sierra Leone Company—*hey pass* [*sic*] and they are the Society for Missions to Africa and the East; another transformation makes them the Society for the Suppression of Vice, a fourth carries them to the India House, and a fifth lands them in the House of Commons. This marvelous property of being everywhere is not one of their least dangerous qualifications.[13]

The rosters of their different organizations have the same coterie of suspects over and over.

It cannot be denied that they took up their endeavors with purpose and enthusiasm. The souls of others, both near and far, were their objects of concern. The Empire was perceived as the best method for achieving universal salvation, if only British souls could be enlightened enough to use the tools of empire properly and not be corrupted by the vices of power. To make sure this was the case, they would have to rule the Empire themselves.

James Stephen, the abolitionist, was known as the most radical of the Clapham Sect. Henry Adams described him as a "high-minded fanatic."[14] He had friends in high places who helped find him a seat in Parliament that he kept for a five years before resigning in protest in 1815.[15] He withdrew from office because the government refused to take up a law he proposed forcing registration of slaves in all the colonies in order to prevent new slaves from the newly illicit slave trade from finding their way onto plantations. His recorded statement on the matter: "I would rather be on friendly terms with a man who had strangled my infant son than support an administration guilty of slackness in suppressing the slave trade."[16] He never lost sight of his earliest life's lessons, which taught him that having a law was one thing, and its correct application was an entirely different manner. Though the slave trade had been abolished before he entered Parliament, he knew that ever more regulation would be required to eliminate the practice. He published an exhaustive two-volume set entitled *Slavery of the British West India Colonies*: one volume was dedicated to spelling out the slave laws in place, the next was devoted to describing the actual practices of slavery in the colonies.[17] His decade of work on the slave codes in St. Christopher's was spelled out clearly for the British public to consider.

However, it is his son, the next James Stephen, who serves as the focus of this chapter. Born in 1789, and raised in the bosom of the Clapham Sect, this James Stephen married Jane Venn, another offspring within the group. He was the third James Stephen to study law, and the first to have the luxury of family support to take it on with complete seriousness.

Sir James Stephen served as undersecretary of the colonies for nearly thrity years, earning the moniker, "Mr. Mothercountry." It was not a compliment. One of his colleagues, Sir Henry Taylor, reported in his autobiography, "For a long period, Stephen might better have been called the 'Colonial Department' itself than 'Counsel to the Colonial Department.' "[18] His influence was bound to attract animosity, and his most vocal adversary was Charles Buller, who coined his nickname. Stephen was reviled in the newspapers and accused of using his office for an entirely personal vision of politics. His critics were not entirely mistaken; recent scholars such as Russell Smandych have investigated his "obsessive attention" to the conditions of slaves throughout the British Empire.[19] In his career, musings, and legal decisions, we can see how he formulated his work as his personal mission as well as a continuation of his family's legacy. In a 1829 letter, Stephen commented, "The last ten years of my life have been very busy ones, devoted not exclusively but mainly promoting, as far as was compatible with the duties of my office, the extinction of slavery. This task devolved upon me by inheritance."[20]

It is remarkable that the son of the most radical abolitionist in England would come to hold this place in the Colonial Office. After all, the British Empire was economically dependent upon the traffic in humans, an argument that continued to hold sway in debates about abolitionism. One contemporary fumed over James Stephen's appointment as colonial undersecretary characterizing him as: "The person whom the colonists supposed to be their greatest enemy…to put him in an office in which every communication to and from the colonies must pass through his hands was 'highly objectionable.' "[21] Stephen's poor reputation followed him into the twentieth century. Scholars such as C. H. Currey disapproved that Stephen was so deeply involved in the process of judicial review and felt that he was "thwarting" the inherent rights of "Englishmen" in the colonies who saw "Mr. Mother Country's meddlesome interference with increasing hostility."[22] James Stephen's diaries reveal that he smarted from the publicity and felt that his authority was greatly overstated and misunderstood. "I passed a long and painful life in the Colonial Office as a kind of lightening conductor, bound in honor to suppress my own vindication against injurious censures when it must have disclosed (as it invariably would have disclosed) the errors of my superiors. I thus contracted an unpopularity far exceeding the measure of my official rank or personal importance."[23] Stephen's reputation has improved in recent years among those few scholars who have noted his career. He has come to be recognized for his efforts on behalf of the more dispossessed individuals within the British Empire.

But the essential question remains: Why did James Stephen *want* to run the Colonial Office for so many years if justice was his aim? He did not romanticize the power of the law, as evidenced by his statement about "the impotency of the law in a protracted contest with avarice."[24] He was also deeply cynical about the impact that the British had upon world affairs. In his diary he characterized the British colonial ventures as a combination of "Man the Baby and Man the Bulldog, thus conspiring to move onwards the tide of human affairs."[25] Yet he nonetheless told his son that "the defense of our laws as often and as so far as they can be defended is the best of all possible paths to follow."[26]

Stephen was a religious man who believed he was put on earth to stand for good against evil. He interpreted his calling as a mission to quietly make the administration of the British Empire as just as possible, thereby curbing man's impulse to avarice and protecting the weak. Richard Ely has claimed that Stephen developed a theology of empire by seeing the human race as interconnected through God's love.[27] But Stephen was not convinced that the forces of good were winning as history progressed. In fact, he predicted the rise of a great "military despotism," one that would come into existence to suppress the spread of knowledge and would be as powerful as the energies it had come into being to squelch.[28]

Against Ely's postulation that Stephen had a theology of empire, I argue that Stephen had a theology of legal practice. For him the connection between the two was that he envisioned himself as a servant of both, and he had a complete comprehension of neither. In a letter to his son, he acknowledged that he believed that the scriptures had unity, and just as firmly, he believed that such unity was beyond his understanding.[29] What he did know was that law was the best way of defending what is good in humanity. In his *Lectures on the History of France*, Stephen describes the triumph of the British nation as entirely a result of the rule of law.

> Our land has ever lived under the dominion of law. By that power the physical force of the many, the formidable influence of the few, and the arbitrary will of the monarch, have ever been controlled with more or less of energy and success.... In our own times it is exercised in our courts of justice and in our high court of Parliament. During more than a thousand years, our legal tribunals have been interposed between the various organs of the state, to vindicate the rights, and to arrest the encroachments of them all. Throughout that long course of ages, those legal sanctuaries have been at once the bulwarks of order and the strongholds of liberty in England; and to them it is to be ascribed that the English Parliaments have never fallen as the Cortes of Spain fell, and as the States-General of France silently disappeared.[30]

Rather than trying to save individual souls as the first generation of Claphamites had done, Stephen would try to create a legal code that would allow grace and prosperity everywhere by securing limitations on the powerful (in the colonies, the settlers and merchants) and rights and protections for the weak (in the colonies, freed slaves and natives). He thought generally that the law had been used as a weapon of the powerful; he wanted to interpret the law in such a way that it would become a weapon of the less fortunate in all of the British colonies and protectorates.

Claiming utter boredom with the political and social intrigues of his day, he was unusually depoliticized for a man completely committed to public office. He found gossip about political maneuvers "silly" and "tiresome." He outlasted twenty secretaries of state, and so saw little need to bend to political fashions. He saw himself above all as a bureaucrat whose sole aim was to explain the law, and improve it when given the opportunity. Yet he was animated by a genuine passion to improve the lives of others through the law.

Finding an administrator with a conscience does not somehow overturn the violence of colonialism generally, nor the frequent brutality of the British specifically. Just as important, it is unclear how much power Stephen actually possessed. Could anyone sitting in an office on Downing Street change the behavior of planters in Jamaica or settlers in Malta?[31] I cannot make any claims about the actual adherence to the rule of law in British colonies based upon the values, behavior, and rulings of James Stephen. What I *can* do based upon a close examination of the difficulties faced by Stephen is suggest why thinking of the rule of law as a practice that is never complete and always unsatisfied is more appropriate than invoking the rule of law as a summative judgment. The rule of law is constituted in struggle and lost as soon as it is regarded as a fait accompli.

Stephen's career provides a clear example of what it means to *practice* the rule of law. Stephen's personal morality led him to embrace the principle of the rule of law to a highly unusual degree; as this chapter will demonstrate, he could not be accused of taking the endeavor with anything but the utmost seriousness. I also explain how Stephen's position in the government provided him with an equally unusual opportunity to personally influence the interpretation and influence of the law in many different jurisdictions. He did not fail because of lack of opportunity or power. His career is an ideal case study: unquestionable personal commitment combined with considerable administrative power.

Achieving the rule of law in the British Empire was not only a matter of political will; it provides an example of the difficulties in realizing the rule of law. Stephen's reflections on his own successes and failures beautifully encapsulate the dilemmas of the rule of law; it is clear that Stephen could see himself trying to reconcile moral imperatives with the world as it currently existed. Like a practitioner of civil disobedience, Stephen's faith and strong sense of personal justice led him to critique existing laws even as he observed and administered them. The rule of law is best understood as a practice that is historically bound, contextually contingent, and invariably messy.

Two central ideas appear in many invocations of the rule of law today: that it is a universal value that can be achieved in every country on earth given the will to do so, and that it is a precondition of functional political and economic orders. Brian Tamanaha has argued that "The rule of law thus stands in the peculiar state of being *the* preeminent legitimating political ideal in the world today, without agreement upon precisely what it means."[32] The rule of law has also been accepted as a self-evident good, largely because it is assumed to curb abuse of power. The US Agency for International Development (USAID) has a program that extends through dozens of countries and spends hundreds of millions of dollars every year to bolster the rule of law in countries such as Haiti, Cambodia, and Burma. Tyrants who throw dissenting citizens in jail, police who extort from those subject to them instead of protecting them—these problems and countless others could be fixed by the "rule of law." USAID "rule-of-law expert" Wade Channell explained his perspective on their programs:

> Without rule of law, the system breaks down. With that said, the biggest challenge is getting people to figure out what we're talking about and what they mean when they say rule of law. There is an unhelpful tendency for people to hear that phrase and think about laws and to focus on rule of law as something to do with laws: good laws, better laws, enforcing laws. Rule of law is about rule and the underlying relational structure within a society that produces rules that everyone agrees to obey.[33]

Channell describes the rule of law as a pre-existing ground upon which economic and political activities rely. The rule of law is offered up in the international arena as a fix-all solution to power inequalities, just as civil society was the panacea of development work in the 1990s. The problem with these common conceptualizations is that the rule of law is conceived in binary terms. Either the rule of law is being met, or it isn't.

In contrast to the invocations of the rule of law as a general *principle* of governance or precondition of political order by policymakers, the theoretical literature provides some more detailed assessments of what implementing the rule of law looks like as a *practice*. But the actual practice that constituted the rule of law in the British Empire looked quite different than the absolutist rhetoric that accompanied it. The rule of law is understood as a largely depersonalized activity, but every law must have its interpreter. In the case of the British Colonial Office, for thirty years, one person judged the legality of different laws passed in the colonies. His statements, letters, and bureaucratic rulings display clarity, rigor, anger, confusion, and angst. It is his *practice* that concerns me here, because investigating practice allows us to move away from the cycle of trying to hold the rule of law accountable to its own rhetoric.

To understand the complexities of Stephen's practice, Philippe Nonet's essay "Is That the Rule That Was?" offers unparalleled insight into the psychology that animates discerning the rule of law. How would you know that a given legal system is not adhering to the rule of law? How would you reform a system so it more closely adheres to the rule of law? Clearly, the rule of law requires judgment, not just mindless implementation.

Nonet begins his argument with a citation from H. L. A. Hart:

> When a social group has certain codes of conduct … it is possible to be concerned with the rules, either merely as an observer who does not accept them, or as a member of the group which accepts and uses them as guides to conduct. We may call these respectively the "external" and the "internal points of view."[34]

The external point of view is reflected in Bentham's description of the legislator of the world and Rousseau's figure of the lawgiver; for both thinkers, laws must arrive from the outside of a society.[35] John Rawls and his original position is a well-known example of the internal point of view, when someone imagines what rules they would like to be subject to. Nonet rejects the idea that these are distinct positions and argues these perspectives inhere in all people, and that frequently the insider and outsider perspective are in conflict with one another. "In fact my organism, *id,* does not want either liberation from or submission to society; it is forever torn by its desires for both."[36] This struggle is played out in the moment when the person is forced to articulate what is right, or just, in a particular situation. We think of the rule of law as being self-evident, that it requires application. But Nonet emphasizes the act of invention that happens with every judgment.

> Only if this case exhibited exactly and only the features in existing statements of law, would the right action be one that exhibited exactly and only the features abstracted in these statements. But my problem is not to find and do what is right in general, or in the abstracted world of statements of law, but to decide and do what is right

> in *this* case, that is, to do the concrete act that is universally (not generally) right under these unique and concrete circumstances (which may or may not fit the abstract model).[37]

Nonet's description is remarkably close to the processes that Sir James Stephen used in determining the rule of law in the British Empire. Choosing what was legal and what was not in such a situation where there were a plethora of precedents, jurisdictions, and legal traditions and no clear application of them meant that virtually every day, Stephen made up what was legal and what was not. His commentaries provide a rich account of his involved internal navigation of what Nonet characterized as the external and internal points of view. He was both radical critic and perpetrator of the British Empire, just as he was critic and practitioner of colonial law.

Stephen's Position in the Colonial Office

> To me a colony is as turtle-soup to an alderman—daily fare and hardly palatable.
>
> —Sir James Stephen

From our perspective, the formation and implementation of British colonial policy during the early nineteenth century is simply shocking. We correctly think of colonialism as one of the most momentous events in the modern world. It is almost absurd, comical, to see how makeshift the British colonial apparatus often was. There were two entities—the India Office and the Colonial Office—that enforced and practiced British colonial policy. Although the Empire was of great economic import, it was given a relatively low status in the structure of British governance. The secretary of state was primarily occupied with affairs and intrigues with countries much closer to home. Colonial affairs were moved from the home secretary to the secretary of state in 1801, and not a single person was moved with department to manage the workload.[38] This lack of staffing meant little or even no oversight. "Colonial despatches went unanswered, colonial governors reported crises, complained of their wrongs, and even died, without the minister seeming to be aware of the fact."[39] The number of officials and clerks in the Colonial Office did not surpass twenty-five people until the 1880s.[40]

The Colonial Office was largely the fiefdom of one appointed undersecretary, who supervised several senior clerks who specialized in different regions, and junior clerks who kept track of correspondence from companies, settlers, and all other parties who decided to take interest in colonial affairs.[41] Starting in 1836, these junior clerks kept meticulous records, copying both sides of all correspondence, including the minutes of legal argumentation and all other documentation or rationale that was consulted in the formulation of given policy. This was the start of a more comprehensive bureaucratic system that sought to oversee colonial affairs.

Interestingly, the well-ordered records contrast with the locale of the office in houses considered too decrepit to consider refurbishing at 13 and 14 Downing Street. Medieval sewers regularly overflowed next to the property, leading those who ventured into the office to note the desuetude of the office environment. The undersecretary made all final decisions, although his judgment could be overruled by the secretary of state on the rare occasions he took interest. One senior clerk, Henry Taylor observed that "in ninety-nine cases out of a hundred" the undersecretaries and clerks offered opinions that were adopted by the secretary of state without any discussion.[42] Because the position as colonial undersecretary required a breathtaking expanse of information, it was held for long periods of time even as secretaries of state changed with the political winds. The rhetoric of empire was grand, and the ideal of the rule of law is even more grandiose, but the mechanisms for achieving them in combination were surprisingly small and mundane.

From the year 1813 when James Stephen became the legal counsel until 1847 when he resigned from his post to become a professor of history at Cambridge, he worked tirelessly, issuing anywhere from 140 to 422 legal rulings every year in relation to acts that were passed in the colonies. Virtually every act that was passed by a colony made its way to his desk, from a levy to improve sanitation or restrain dogs, to laws around migration and immigration, to plans about whether to plant bamboo or aloe, to tariffs on products. He looked to British law for precedent and objected when there was deviation from it in the colonies. He would also review judicial proceedings from the colonies and point out when, for instance, a missing coroner's examination might put guilt into doubt. No detail seemed too small for his concern.

His appetite for work seemed bottomless, and he spared no effort in mastering the details of the British Empire; his sons described their father's occupation in the Colonial Office as follows:

> His duties were of the most various kind. The colonies, as my brother observes, were a collection of states varying from youthful nations like Canada down to a small settlement of Germans on the rock of Heligoland; their populations differed in race, laws, religion, and languages; the authority of the Crown varied from absolute power over an infant settlement to supremacy over communities in some essential respects independent. My father's duty was to be familiar with every detail of these complicated relations, to know the state of parties and local politics in each colony, and to be able to advise successive Secretaries of State who came without special preparation to the task. He had to prepare drafts of all the important despatches and of the various Acts of Parliament which were required during a period of rapid and important changes.[43]

His business of running empire was conducted with maps, letters, and—most of all—personal accumulated knowledge. The amount of information Stephen brought to bear in making a ruling is dizzying at times. For instance, in considering a regulation in Barbados, Stephen referred to various similar laws—including ones in Nova Scotia, St. Lucia, and India—when rendering his decision.[44] Each colony had its own register, and every law, skirmish, and disagreement was recorded and filed away in the appropriate location. As the years passed, the record books were established with pre-existing categories—"supplies," "laws," "taxes," "budgets," "Navy"—and the figures and facts were then filled in as needed. By the early 1830s, in addition to all these categories, there was a pre-existing tab in all of the colonies' yearly records: one simply called "J. Stephen." His opinions were so central to the administration of the colonies that they finally demanded a separate category in the bureaucratic ordering.

In evaluating Stephen's career in the Colonial Office, R. B. Pugh observed he would be remembered as "the architect of West Indian emancipation and the originator of laissez-faire in dealing with the colonial Governments."[45] Stephen was reluctant to suggest overturning colonial legislation, continually asserting that it was his duty to enforce existing regulations and laws. He saw himself as a public servant, not a statesman. Yet this posture obscures the fact that maintaining colonial self-determination was in fact a policy of sorts that he was practicing even as official ministers moved back and forth on what they regarded as the appropriate relationship between home country and colonies. His reluctance to overturn colonial laws did not lead him to lassitude in review of them. Far from it. His assiduous attention to the smallest details of the law, criminal procedure, and regulations in the colonies made it clear that *someone* in London was watching what they did, and closely. The minimal supervision over Stephen put him in the mind-boggling role of being perhaps the sole guardian of the rule of law in the British Empire. In such circumstances one would imagine lassitude or personal idiosyncrasy becoming the practice. But Stephen's personality and political commitments led him to adopt this mission with alacrity.

What is most striking about the descriptions of Stephen is his extreme self-discipline. His wife observed of him that he was "a man without a skin."[46] One way of interpreting this is to say that he saw himself as inseparable from the world, hence his discipline in avoiding anything that he found distasteful or potentially corrupting. Leslie Stephen, his son, provided the most thorough description of Stephen, the private man. He acknowledged that the austerity of their home was truly evangelical, yet the difference was that there was no condemnation of others, only relentless self-examination. Leslie Stephen remembers a quip from his father: "He was, he said, one of the few people to whom it was the same thing to eat a dinner and to perform an act of self-denial. In fact, for many years he never ate a dinner, contenting himself with a biscuit and a glass of sherry as lunch, and an egg at tea."[47] Stephen never wanted anyone to remember, much less celebrate, his birthday, nor did he ever look into mirrors, banishing them from his home.[48]

Every family has stories that characterize the figures within them. James Stephen's involved cigars. Recounted by his granddaughter, Virginia Woolf, in her own memoirs, she sees a common sensibility between the two of them. "But I think my feeling of shame went a great deal deeper. I am almost inclined to drag in my grandfather—Sir James, who once smoked a cigar, liked it, and so threw away his cigar and never smoked another. I am almost inclined to think I inherited a streak of the puritan, of the Clapham Sect."[49] The description of Stephen resonates with Shklar's interpretation of Aristotelian administration of the rule of law. Stephen tried to hold himself to even higher standards than he held the rest of the world.

His children remarked: "We were, indeed, fully aware, from a very early age, of his feelings, and could not but be continuously conscious that we were under the eye of a father governed by the loftiest and purest motives, and devoting himself without stint to what he regarded as his duty. He was a living 'categorical imperative.'"[50] Though Stephen may have embraced Kantian self-examination, his religious belief led him to experience shame when confronted with the suffering of others. He was certainly not inclined to rationalize away his culpability in the sorrows inflicted by his countrymen.

Stephen considered abolition of slavery his highest calling, one that he inherited from his father. The Colonial Office records display multiple occasions when he needed to comment on the legality of different provisions in regard to slaves. Many of these regulations pass his review without remarks on, for instance, the width of sticks that can be used to beat disobedient female and male slaves respectively. He did not restrict himself entirely to the legalities of the matter and at times he was moved to make claims on behalf of "Natural Justice." For instance, in a memo about establishing public chain gangs in Tobago as a punishment, he remarks:

> It is difficult to understand why the same rules of Natural Justice should be inapplicable to the case of slaves in our last Indian Colonies. To say that daily labour in the public chain is a condition to be preferred to detention in the Gaol at Tobago, is in other words to give a description of prisons in that Colony the truth of which is difficult to believe. A place of confinement must be wretched indeed if more irksome that the suffering and disgrace that the Law has condemned the worst class of criminals; and even if it could be supposed that such a representation of the Goal of Tobago was well founded, it would be improper not to object to an Act recognizing the existence and virtually supporting the continuance of such establishment.[51]

Most noticeably, when presented with legislation, he would imagine its effects upon the most dispossessed population and think through the ramifications of the regulation from their perspective and situation. Usually, predictably, this person was an escaped slave. For instance, Bermuda passed a law requiring all negroes, mulattos, or trustees entering the island or moving away from the island for even a short period of time, to pay a tax of thirty pounds upon their return. His evaluation of the duty was that it was truly intended to make Bermuda less appealing to ex-slaves. His response demonstrates one of his most frequent methods of dealing with laws he found distasteful: to claim ignorance and place the burden of proof back on the colony.

> The effect of this duty is therefore to restrain under a penalty of 30lbs, any person, not being a White, from quitting the Bermuda Islands for any temporary purpose. As I do not understand the policy of the Law, it would not be in my power, even if it were within my province, to offer to your Lordship any opinion on that Subject. But I apprehend, that such a prohibition is very incompatible with that chance of residence within all parts of the Dominion of the Crown, which the Law has permitted to his Majesty's, free [emphasis in original] subjects in general, and while it is indispensable for many Mercantile Domestic purposes. The restraint may be rendered necessary by some peculiar local circumstances; but I conceive your Lordship would think it right, that a statement of these circumstances should be made before you would advise the Prince Regent to sanction an enactment which seems inconsistent with the general principles of Law.[52]

It is clear that the person entrusted with protecting the rule of law in the British colonies for thirty years truly believed that the law could be used as a force for good and equity. Whether he was successful in using it as such is another question entirely, and one can see that he was wracked by doubts about this as well.

> When I look on the last 24 years of my life, all of which have been passed either in the Colonial Office or in a close official connection with it, I cannot but be thankful for the innumerable opportunities which have been afforded me of contributing to the mitigation, if not the prevention, of the cruel wrongs which our country has inflicted on so large a portion of the human race.... I shall lay down

> my weapons, whenever that time may come, with a fervent hope that they may be taken up by some successor who, inheriting my own views, may have greater power to carry them into effect.[53]

The shame of overseeing the British laws that approved slavery led him to state that law was most often used as an instrument of the wealthy and powerful. In his memos, he visibly chafes at being forced to quibble over the particulars of slave treatment that were dealt with in the law in British colonies. In one memo about a Sierra Leone official who broke the law in trying to emancipate the cargo on a Portuguese slave ship, Stephen admitted the law had been broken, but rightfully so:

> Although such is my opinion upon the mere question of Law, it is impossible not to sympathize with the horror and disgust which the Officer administering the Government felt on the present occasion and which may perhaps have incapacitated him for considering the case dispassionately.[54]

Stephen bends over backward to reconcile the particularities of each colony with larger principles of justice. For instance, in a memo on land deed in Upper Canada, he commented, "It is however, to be remembered, that this is peculiarly a subject in which particular local circumstances may justify a very wide departure from the ordinary rules of legislation."[55] Yet local custom and desires alone were not sufficient for Stephen to dismiss his concerns at all times. In his ruling on a law in Sierra Leone penalizing members of the Koo tribe for coming and going without permission, or returning to the colony after being banished, he commented:

> It would be easy to multiply objections to the system in its present crude and imperfected shape, as indeed it would be hard to propose any subject of legislation requiring more exact and cautious deliberation. Yet upon this subject also, it is nearly impracticable to form a distinct opinion of the legal effect and propriety of the Law, without a full explanation of the local circumstances in which it has originated. It is easy to conceive a state of things in which justice and policy may alike require at least the temporary enactment of a law

> like the present , however widely it departs from European models of legislation and even from our own habitual views of Equity. In the absence of any such explanation, I am however of the opinion that this act is highly objectionable because apparently unjust.[56]

In his rulings, Stephen always distinguished between the letter of the law—referring to "mere point of law" or "legal precedent"—and what was right. Stephen's rulings often contained these double steps when he encountered something he disagreed with. He did not discard what the law said, but his rulings had the curious effect of upholding precedent while making clear exactly how wrong the precedent was.

He tried at one point to reconcile in writing his duty to the law and the sense of justice that came from his belief. The ability to even conceive of injustice came from God.

> From God we derive the light of our Judicial Instincts—that is, of conscience, the interior tribunal by which we are either approved or condemned, in the use we make of that measure of free will and free agency which is entrusted to us. This is the restraint which the Author of that awful power has imposed upon the improper, the capricious, or the arbitrary use of it. But the accuracy of all judicial sentences depends on the knowledge, the capacity, the patience, and the impartiality of the judge. Who will venture to claim for the judge within his own bosom, the possession of these qualifications in a perfect, or even in an eminent degree? In what tongue or language has not the blindness of self-love passed into a proverb? Who is the man whose mental vision is not obstructed by some beam, as often as it is directed to the survey of his own heart, or of his own conduct?[57]

Here we can see how he saw rationality and systemization as a way of honoring the divine. Each of us has an "interior tribunal," but almost no one takes the care to listen to the judgments being rendered. Yet even for those who do, like Stephen, try to use knowledge, reason, care, and reverence, fallibility is inescapable. The best hope is to erect a system of law that is better than the men entrusted to uphold it. But he knew from extensive experience that interpretation is also fallible, and that the best laws can do great evil. And this again, is where his faith had to sustain him. In a letter to John Austin's wife he remarked, "Nevertheless, I believe that the progress of the affairs of our world is slowly towards good, and take comfort in the question 'Is there evil in the city, and the Lord hath not done it?'—convinced that the evils which he inflicts as a Judge, He makes the instruments of eventual good as an Administrator."[58]

"Legislator of the World"

Jeremy Bentham's work has been, and is, taken to embody so many different meanings that its utility for this exercise of interpretation is inevitably fraught. Part of this is because Bentham himself changed over his lifetime, his views becoming more democratic in the first decade of the nineteenth century.[59] Another reason is that those who considered themselves his disciples did things in his name that were not necessarily in accordance with Bentham's own views. My research has turned up many references from correspondence in the nineteenth century, both kind and disparaging, about those who would like to "play Bentham" in India, in Africa, or in the Caribbean. One project taken on largely by Jennifer Pitts has been to rescue Bentham, in particular his views on colonialism, from the hegemonic interpretive lens of James and John Stuart Mill. She has argued that Bentham was significantly more cautious about the difficulties of civilizational advance than they were; hence it is wrong to say that they were faithfully fulfilling Bentham's project.[60] Then, there is the issue with John Bowring, the man who collated and published Bentham's collected works. David Lieberman recounts, "When Bowring, as literary executor, supervised the first attempt to collect Bentham's works, he produced an edition which even at its initial appearance was recognized to be an 'incomplete, incorrect, and ill arranged … monumental repository, in which the opinions of the writer are buried out of sight - typographically interred.' "[61] Some scholars have decided that a wholesale reinterpretation of his oeuvre is required, and the Bentham Project was founded in order to rescue Bentham from his series of irresponsible interlocutors.[62] Scratch the surface of Bentham scholarship and there is a busy hive of recriminations, disavowals, and recapitulations that seem a fitting tribute to Bentham's emphasis upon distinguishing the real from the imaginary. We may get our "real Bentham" quite soon. Or perhaps we will not.

Nonetheless, more than any other thinker of the period, Bentham's work touches upon the practical difficulties faced by Sir James Stephen in his administration of colonial laws. It is worth a dip into the seamy pool of Bentham interpretation to yield a more nuanced understanding of how Stephen was reading law, how his readings constructed the law, and the difficulties of transferring law in time and place. Due to the efforts of the Bentham Project, Bentham's essay, "Place and Time" is available to read in conjunction with the Colonial Office records. I am not claiming that Stephen modeled himself on Bentham, though Stephen was well acquainted with the legal developments of his time. For example, he was close friends with John Austin and his wife. My reading is driven by a series of convergences: both were largely disgusted with the state of the law as it existed but were nonetheless interested in the problem of improving the human condition through law, and both envisioned this as an international endeavor with themselves at the center of the project. However, there are important distinctions between Bentham's and Stephen's views of the role of the legislator.

To begin, both Bentham and Stephen considered law as largely corrupted and used to serve the interests of the powerful. The family details included in this chapter give some sense of why exactly Stephen would approach law with a healthy skepticism. Bentham's political positions evolved greatly over time, largely in response to the frustrations he encountered in trying to achieve his legislative goals. Bentham made his reputation by attacking William Blackstone, arguing that the common law in Britain was obscure, ineffectual, and needed to be discarded. "Bentham likened the statute law to 'a vast Battery, of which the greatest part of the Balls are shot in vain for want of being leveled [at] the object'."[63] The practice of judicial interpretation that Blackstone saw as the primary function of a judge was not an inevitability but rather a flaw of a shoddy legal system. Bentham pointed out that most British people could not see these flaws for what they are; "It was only the having been born and bred under this System of elaborate confusion that could have made the burden tolerable."[64] From Bentham's perspective, an unknown law with uncertain application utterly defeated the purpose of having law at all. Some commentators have ventured to guess that Bentham started to see politics, rather than ineptitude, at work in this disastrous design. Faced with continued resistance to codification in Great Britain, he started to see how the uncertainty of the law favored the interests of the powerful over the powerless.[65]

One reason Bentham's legal vision became an international one was because he saw how people become acclimated to their own practices, no matter how unfortunate or nonsensical they may be. He wrote a series of reflections called "Place and Time" that pointed out how the perspective of an outsider helped subjects and legislators see laws for what they are. "Would you see the worth of any established body of law in its genuine colours, transplant it into a foreign clime. The vitious parts of it, no longer veiled by partiality, will display themselves in their genuine weakness and impropriety."[66]

"Place and Time" is an extensive critique of Montesquieu's *The Spirit of the Laws*, and Bentham does not see ignorance or prejudice as the exclusive purview of any climate or culture. Instead, every nation has its own blindness that can potentially be overcome with the assistance of an outside legislator. Jeremy Bentham was available for the position. He had correspondence with James Madison and Alexander I, the emperor of Russia. He was employed to write laws for a new Portuguese regime that unfortunately collapsed before he finished, and also wrote codes for Greece, Latin American countries, and Spain.[67] José del Valle, a Guatemalan lawyer, politician, and economist collected all of Bentham's works and gave him the title "Legislator of the World."[68]

Nor do the ignorance or prejudices inherent in a population of a particular location mean that they would not be able to receive good legislation. Bentham provides a biting rejoinder to those who say that laws are good enough for an ignorant population: "It is a saying attributed to Solon that the laws he had given to the Athenians were not the best in themselves, but the best they were capable of receiving … There could not be a more convenient maxim for saving the credit of a legislator: and those who have had a legislator to defend have not failed to make the most of it."[69]

This does not mean that Bentham thought it simple, or even possible, to drop laws into any and every space and not meet resistance.

> The patience of nations under the abuses which are the growth of their own country, and their impatience under which they are imported from a foreign country, have their source in the natural and unavoidable mixture of ignorance and prejudice. They will endure

> abuses they have been accustomed to, but they will not endure new ones; they will sit easy under the yoke of their own prejudices; but they will not sit easy under the prejudices of another people.[70]

Changing the expectations and practices of a people is difficult. The key here is noticing that Bentham says they will more likely be ruled by their own *prejudices* rather than the *prejudices* of another. If enlightened, rational, and clear lawmaking is imported and its utility is clear, Bentham implies the response will be much better. And it is tempting to think that James Stephen, sitting in his office on Downing Street was culled from Bentham's vibrant imagination to become just this enlightened legislator of the world. Yet the two men's approaches to the law were diametrically opposed.

In fact, Bentham made a case for a system of international code of law, one that would be universally applicable and called the "the Pannomion." David Lieberman has extensively reviewed Bentham's ideas on codification and uses Bentham's own words to describe the universality of the code that Bentham envisioned, a legal system in which "there are no terrae incognitae, no blank spaces; nothing is at least omitted, nothing unprovided for."[71]

"Place and Time" can be read as a thought experiment for the person who would write the Pannomion, outlining the perfect position from which to create a law that would be all-inclusive and timeless. The legislator was to see what was particular to a given time and place, and conceptually separate it from what is general. Expediency should be resisted at all costs, and the legislator should "raise his imagination to that elevated point from which the whole map of human interests and situations lies expanded to his view."[72] It would take a global view and local knowledge in order to distinguish what efforts would create the greatest happiness and which laws would achieve the maximum utility. "Place and Time" takes an example, not at all random, of trying to transfer a code of law from Britain to Bengal.

Bentham makes it clear that the legislator of the world needs to keep both local context and the larger issue of utility in mind in his deliberations. In other publications, Bentham argued the legislator of the Pannomium should be singular, known (for transparency), and foreign. "The hand of a foreigner, not only admissible but preferable. Reason. Exemption from local sinister interests and prejudices; deficiency in local knowledge being easily amenable by native hands."[73] Jennifer Pitts has argued that Bentham was particularly encouraged by the possibilities of legislating from afar—otherwise known as colonial rule. "Bentham's awareness of the widespread hostility to reform among the ruling classes of Europe contributed to what seems to be his almost gleeful sense of the political possibility latent in the peripheries. In many of his letters to non-European correspondents, whether in India, Muslim countries, or in the new states of South America, he conveys his sense that real innovation may come from such newer polities."[74]

But perhaps this optimism developed because Bentham was not as familiar with the international elites entrenched in the British Empire as he was with the forces against his version of progress at home. James Stephen became acutely aware of how settler and native elite interests drove colonial legislation, and used his position from afar to try to circumvent the more egregious of their actions. Here is where his ability to demand a clear and reasoned explanation for any divergence from the British common law became important. In maintaining British common law as his standard, he could be accused of blindness to the particularities of the contexts he was facing. This is the primary divergence between Bentham's vision and Stephen's practice. Bentham would have never taken English common law as the starting point for any laws that were to attain universal justice. But it can be argued that this was Stephen's way of fighting back against the particular power struggles and prejudices of local populations. For example, planters in Jamaica will have fairly defined views and practices according to race, but transporting those laws for review based upon English common laws yields them as legal anomalies.

But the men have a similar conception of law as an anchor for democratic empowerment. Stephen envisioned his office as a stopgap in the degeneration of the Empire. The mobilization of public opinion had been instrumental in the fight against slavery. But there was no way to raise public concern over small issues in places the British public had never heard of or planned to go. Seeing the relationship between law and democratic virtue was another convergence between Stephen and Bentham. Jennifer Pitts has observed that

> Bentham had a keen grasp of the social psychology of empire. Colonies, he believed, exacerbated the pathologies of European power politics. And they produced an exaggerated form of a more general danger in

> international politics; that although ordinary people could be trusted to defend themselves against "sinister interests" at home, the same public could not be counted on to rein in abusive colonial rulers because people are complacent about violence and injustice carried out at a distance.[75]

Stephen would have agreed. However Bentham saw the Pannomium—a code that was clear enough to be enforced by anyone—as the answer to the lack of public approbation. Stephen saw himself more as a benevolent dictator, using his unique office and accumulated personal knowledge to work the current legal order to its best possible end. Bentham saw the fragility of this system and had tried to develop a legal system that would deliver virtue and happiness, regardless of the character of those who administered it.

Bentham assumed that the judges tasked with upholding common law would be blind to the inconsistencies of such a system. But Stephen's personal faith gave him an outside voice and perspective, which he used to critique existing law. Here he would have found accordance in this practice from Bentham who divided the consciousness of the legislator into two parts. "To the province of the Expositor it belongs to explain to us what, as he suppose, the Law is; to that of the Censor, to observe what he thinks it ought to be."[76]

Bentham's legislator of the world needs a global scope in order to continually see what is truth and what is fiction. The universal perspective allows him to overcome local knowledge and local suspicions, as well as particular investment in any outcomes. In *A Fragment on Government* he argued, "The Expositor, therefore, is always the citizen of this or that particular country: the Censor is, or ought to be the citizen of the world."[77] One could argue that Stephen's position as critic of empire and receiver of thousands upon thousands of dispatches from every corner of the British Empire gave him such a perspective. He could see the patterns of abuse, greed, and suffering. He tried to build the law as a protective fence to create greater happiness. He did this, not exactly in the name of his country, but as an atonement for his country's sins. Colonialism did not bring the rule of law to unenlightened nation; instead, colonialism heightened the need for law to protect humanity.

The contrast between Stephen's and Bentham's visions of the legislator of the world is pointed. Bentham wanted to set in place a code that would make virtue unnecessary. But Bentham never completed the Pannomion. Bentham was able to articulate what could make a perfect, universal, and timeless code of law, but he was never able to write it. Nor can anyone who is human.

Stephen embraced the limitations of his knowledge and saw implementing the rule of law as a daily grind, one that was invariably frustrating, imperfect, and incomplete. Stephen saw progress driven by self-awareness and self-criticism and the continued implementation of the insights garnered from this process. Like Bentham, he was worried about the semblance of knowledge passing for the law and sought to avoid this trap. His version of improving the law required extreme vigilance, suspicion of one's own motives and thought processes in making decisions. Stephen had to drive himself to become more virtuous, but simultaneously resigned to the fact that he would never achieve virtue definitively. Complacency above all needed to be avoided: "If there be any one habit of mind which I should especially desire to discourage in men entering into the business of life, it is the habit of substituting a shabby plausibility for sound knowledge."[78]

Bentham and Stephen provide mirror images of one another. Bentham saw himself as a clock maker spending his life envisioning the perfect machine. Stephen was a Sisyphus resigned to repeated failure. Bentham devoted his entire life to distinguishing fact from fiction by studying the world and trying to overcome his particular perspective and fears.[79] Stephen also spent his life trying to distinguish true and false justice, but his journey led him deep within himself to investigate his faith in God and mankind. Bentham was never able to finish his life's work, while Stephen's led him into nervous exhaustion and early retirement. Creating the rule of law in a global framework was a task that ultimately overpowered both men.

Conclusion

In his history of Andrew Jackson, *Fathers and Children: Andrew Jackson and the Subjugation of the American Indian*, Mike Rogin makes the following observation:

> Ordinary men rely on cultural myths, but their entire personalities are not at stake in them. The leader, by contrast, experiences

> widely shared social tensions as personal traumas. What is ideology for the mass of men is psychology for him. He breaks through cultural defenses, illuminating material better-defended men keep buried. The hero is distinctive not merely for what he suffers but for what he achieves. He transforms his problems into national political solutions.[80]

Here then, is another way of understanding Sir James Stephen. For the British, exporting the rule of law through the Empire was an ideological position, the endorsement of a principle that many repeated and very few considered. For Stephen, adopting the responsibility for serving inhabitants of the British Empire through the rule of law became an intense personal problem, and an all-consuming practice. But simply administering the law as it was written was not enough, since he knew how it had been abused in the past. He did not believe that the law was an end in itself; after all, slavery had been legal. At the same time, he did not believe in simply disregarding the law and implementing what he saw as justice. The rule of law became a redemptive project for him, one that in the end became curiously self-defeating since what he knew was justice was not always law, and achieving justice meant rewriting, not following, the law. Stephen regularly referred back to "his duty" in administering the law as he found it, but he was driven to this duty only as a manifestation of his calling to serve the less powerful. The struggle played out over and over, as he reviewed what settlers were doing in the name of Britain and found their actions lacking.

Stephen's practice also led him to clearly distinguish between different kinds of knowledge, and the limitations of abstract reasoning. After he retired and became a professor of history at Cambridge, he prepared several lectures on Grotius. In a letter he commented, "I have this morning come to the end of the Letters of Hugo Grotius (one of the saints of my calendar) and I have laid them down with the conviction that a man who knew 1000fold more of books than I do could at the same time by 100fold more mixed up with the way of the inhabitants of the world than I ever I have been."[81] For Stephen, judgment had to be specific in its application in order to be meaningful. Judgment disconnected from the world was of little use. This understanding was essential in helping him continue to approach the rule of law as a struggle to reckon with the realities of British colonies as opposed to simply applying laws in an abstract plane. This kept the tension in the practice—a dialectic if you will—between the principles of British law and the realities of British colonialism. He tried to understand both, not use one to negate the other.

Stephen claimed that he could not judge his efforts successful, and this was perhaps the most essential attitude he could have brought to practicing the rule of law in the Colonial Office. Nonet offers this observation about the need to balance the individual's intellect with the arena of action in the rule of law.

> If the intellect is to exercise its theoretical powers (as indeed it should; practical reason invites us to this reflection), it must have objects upon which these powers actually can be exercised ... In order to flourish the intellect must acknowledge its own dependence upon a practical knowledge of which it can form at best an incomplete and tentative representation. Unfortunately, as we know, the intellect is at times affected by self-destructive hubris. It is at times tempted to usurp the supreme authority of practical reason, that is to claim for its own assertions, statements of law, an authority that can only be vested in Law.[82]

Stephen's humility was the key to his practice. If he would have thought that he had found the perfect formula to achieve his purposes, he would have stopped grappling with the limitations of British colonial law and the problems of British colonialism. Because he saw himself failing, he never stopped trying. Despite the scope of his authority, he never claimed to speak for the Law, or even for justice itself. He admitted his incomplete understanding repeatedly, and explained that when making judgments, he never confused his actions with the realization of principle. He noted, "I am living, or trying to live, more under the guidance of an invisible Hand, and under the impulse of undefinable motives, than in submission to any logic, or body of evidences, or weight of authority."[83] Stephen never succumbed to the temptation of seeing himself as all-knowing, thereby trying to submit the law to his own reason or ends. Instead, he remained servant of both law and God, convinced to the end that he failed to achieve the majesties of either.

3

Lawless Places and Placeless Law

Stephen, Sierra Leone, and Extraterritoriality

SIERRA LEONE HELD A UNIQUE place in the consideration of James Stephen while he was in the Colonial Office. He overturned a greater percentage of the legal decisions made in Sierra Leone than in any other colony during his tenure. This is not terribly surprising given the fact that Sierra Leone was a special project of the Clapham Sect. Granville Sharp, the founder of the settlement, and Zachary Macaulay, one of its first governors (1794–1799), were close friends of Stephen. In 1817, he commented upon the particular importance of Sierra Leone to a colleague: "I need not remind you that the settlement of Sierra Leone was established upon the express and avowed principle of advancing the cause of justice and humanity, by studiously respecting the rights of native inhabitants, till then perpetually violated by all the nations of Europe and emphatically by this country."[1] Sierra Leone was an idealistic venture amid the sea of economic ambitions driving British colonialism, and was quite pointedly intended to supply a penance for—not just an alternative to—British exploits.

Perhaps it was the charge of the colony to bring enlightenment to Africa that led its governors to be particularly committed to upholding the law. Many of the yearly reports to the Colonial Office during the early nineteenth century are tinged with a sense of mission that is absent in many other such documents.[2] Granville Sharp's founding constitutional document is centered around a rigorous adherence to the rule of law and the principle of self-determination (*Short Sketch of Temporary Regulations (until better shall be proposed)*, 1786). Despite these intentions, legal ambiguities defined and often threatened the settlement from the very start, as would be expected when a small organization without sovereign authority sets up shop on the coast of Africa. Granville Sharp made a treaty in 1787 with Chief Tom of the Sherbro/Temne for permission to settle on the peninsula. However, Tom was not the authorized chief of the Sherbro/Temne; the true leader was Naimbanna who had moved to his compound inland at Robana. Naimbanna refused to honor the treaty and burned the settlement down the next year. A Captain John Taylor helped Granville Sharp negotiate the next treaty with the Sherbro/Temne in 1788, but Taylor was a private citizen, not an authorized member of the British government able to sign treaties with foreign powers, so the legal status of this treaty was always suspect. To compound the difficulties, in the Treaty of 1788, the British thought they were acquiring ownership of the land permanently, while Naimbanna did not recognize ownership of land and believed he was agreeing to temporary use of the land by the Sierra Leone Company.[3] These interpretational differences came to blows by 1807, when the parties warred. The new Treaty of 1807 was grounded in conquest. In British colonial administration, different legalities were created through cessation as opposed to conquest, and therefore the Treaty of 1807 compounded the legal difficulties as opposed to resolving them. It is small wonder that Stephen was often frustrated at the difficulties of Sierra Leone's jurisprudence.

The mission attached to Sierra Leone did not mean that Stephen was sentimental in his assessment of the colony and its challenges by any means. And he was nothing if not assiduous in *all* of his administrative duties, so it is difficult to argue that he held the governance of this colony to a higher standard. In this chapter, I argue that particular circumstances of Sierra Leone provoked legal innovation at the end of Stephen's tenure. Many of these circumstances were geographical; Sierra Leone was a tiny settlement of twenty square miles surrounded by as-yet-uncolonized territory, and it was never able to sustain itself economically. Stephen argued against the expansion of the British territory in West Africa consistently; his opinion was either lauded or dismissed according to the current economic aspirations driving British policy.

Sierra Leone was destined to an economically fragile existence. Settlers were continually moving outside of the formal boundaries of the small colony, and Stephen was adamant about protecting indigenous sovereignty in spaces that had not been formally ceded to the British. Other circumstances that led to legal innovation were political in nature; Sierra Leone was in the midst of the French and British struggle for dominance in West Africa, a dynamic that became more pressing by the middle of the nineteenth century after the slave trade collapsed. There was a fundamental tension between the British desire to control the volatile region and Stephen's mission to adhere strictly to the rules of sovereignty, territory, and legality. Explaining this tension and its ultimate resolution is the endeavor of this chapter.

In the end, it was British criminality in the regions outside of Sierra Leone that provoked a crisis of jurisdiction. In this phenomenon, Sierra Leone was not unique, and the rise of British criminality around the globe was notable in the 1830s and 1840s, as explored by Radhika Singha in *A Despotism of Law: Crime and Justice in Early Colonial India* and Elizabeth Kolsky's *Colonial Justice in British India*.[4] A series of trails in Malta also brought national attention to the problem that British subjects were trampling the law in locales around the world instead of importing civilization.[5] The solution developed for controlling British criminality was the Foreign Jurisdiction Act of 1843, which stated that British citizens would be subject to prosecution under British law even though they were outside of Britain's formal territorial jurisdiction. The principle came to be known as extraterritorial jurisdiction. Though specific arrangements for a form of split sovereignty were an integral element of British colonialism before 1843, the Foreign Jurisdiction Act sought to obviate the need for special arrangements and instead offer a blanket principle. It was a systemic solution for a series of problems in specific locales.

James Stephen vociferously resisted the idea that British law could be enforced outside of British territory and insisted that it would be the end of "positive law." His attachment to the traditional understanding of legal jurisdiction was defeated by a combination of commercial interests and a desire for prosecutorial certainty. If the British could have their own law in other countries, this would facilitate the expansion of their economic endeavors without the need to control ever-larger portions of the globe. In many ways, this particular innovation was key in facilitating economic expansion outside of formal colonization. The effect of this innovation was to detach British law and hence sovereignty from British territories and, I argue, to give birth to one of the central elements of contemporary international legal practices whereby some countries seem to have "more" sovereignty than others and can enforce their laws outside of their national jurisdiction.

To establish how this episode of British colonial administration promoted the deterritorialization of law, the story of Sierra Leone will have to be recounted in detail. But first, I shall explain the legal system established by colonialism that was based upon the traditional linkage of sovereignty and territory. To see the importance of law's deterritorialization as it unfolded in Sierra Leone, it is crucial to understand the territorialized legal regime.

Carl Schmitt and *The Nomos of the Earth*

A Schmittian reading of the rule of law in the colonies based upon *Political Theology* would view Great Britain as the sovereign who spins the norm but also makes the decision when the norms apply. "Here, too, it is always asked who is entitled to decide those actions for which the constitution makes no provision; that is, who is competent to act when the legal system fails to answer the question of competence."[6] Colonial rule offered many examples of the difficulty of applying norms, and both the Colonial Office archive and the India Office records provide ample evidence of legal advisors trying to decide whether particular laws apply to British citizens, "natives," non-British Europeans, naturalized citizens, and so on. Yet focusing on the Schmittian exception emphasizes the inherently politicized status of the law, particularly its founding and maintenance. The argument derives strength from our expectation that the law is *not* politicized. It is interesting to study colonial legalities precisely because they are so evidently determined by the interests of power. But this is not the entire story to be told. The shape and rationale of the law changes, however constant the relationship to colonial power remains. Let us not neglect the import of shifting away from territory as the basis of law.

Though a complete explication of this complex argument is out of the scope of this chapter, Schmitt's *The Nomos of the Earth* provides a basis for understanding the expansion of international legal regimes through European colonialism. He elaborates on the relationship between the era of European hegemony and the development of international law, a regime he calls *jus publicum Europaeum*. This legal regime replaced the *rayas*, which were the agreed-upon spheres of influence by Spain and Portugal during the height of their power. "For a raya to obtain, two princes, both recognizing the same spiritual authority and the same international law, had to agree on the acquisition of land belonging to princes and peoples of another faith."[7] The problem with international law was (and is) the lack of a higher agent to guarantee it; the Pope could serve that function for Catholic empires but not for others, so the system broke down with the development of non-Catholic colonial powers.

Schmitt argues that *Landnahme*, or "land-appropriation," is the basis for international law. Schmitt makes it clear that the system is dynamic; the structure of international law changes according to spatial political practices. "The many conquests, surrenders, occupations, annexations, cessions, and successions in world history either fit into an existing spatial order of international law, or exceed its framework and have a tendency, if they are not just passing acts of brute force, to constitute a new spatial order of international law."[8] From the practice of land acquisition, negotiation of spheres of influence, and relationships with indigenous legal systems and peoples, international law slowly emerged.

What is particularly illuminating about Schmitt's discussion is that he notes that the rules of law followed by the established players in Europe were different than they were between European powers in other locales. There was an agreement to in effect suspend the rule of law in places that had not yet been colonized.

> The core of this nomos lay in the division of European soil into state territories with firm borders, which immediately initiated an important distinction, namely that this soil of recognized European states and their land has a special territorial status in international law. It was distinguished from the "free" soil of non-European princes and peoples open for European land-appropriations.[9]

Schmitt's description is evocative in that he takes the assumption of an international legal regime and overlays a topographical map; the *nomos* may have been all encompassing, but that does not mean it was the same everywhere. The jurisprudential history of colonialism from the sixteenth through the nineteenth century was in deciding what parts of the globe fell into which legal category. European powers had particular codes of conduct in their own territories, slightly different rules in their colonies and protectorates, and yet other codes for spaces that had not been claimed by any European power.

The spatial order described by Schmitt required a great deal of laborious administration to determine the movement and assertion of the boundaries between different categories of firm earth. He acknowledges this as an essential aspect of maintaining this order: "If the common spatial order, despite such a territorial change, is not to be destroyed, then this change must remain within the total spatial order, must proceed in a certain manner, and must be recognized accordingly."[10] Schmitt seems to think that as long as this administration was managed, the spatial order could be maintained, but my account of Sierra Leone will suggest otherwise. Regulating the boundaries between different spatial orders placed far more strain on the inherent logic and claims of the legal system than Schmitt acknowledges in his book.

Schmitt's focus in *The Nomos of the Earth* is both earlier and later than the mid-nineteenth-century investigations of this chapter. He does not dwell upon the emergence of extraterritoriality. He claims that conditions in the Western Hemisphere made it possible for Europeans to simply "take" the land and claim sovereignty, putting their new lands in the second and third categories of firm land above. Because of the inherent conditions in the Eastern Hemisphere, Schmitt claims that "in the non-Christian Old World of Asia and Islamic Africa, it was possible only to establish subjugated regimes and European extraterritoriality."[11] This makes it seem that extraterritoriality was a compromise position, one that implied a weaker assertion of power. Schmitt assumes that control of territory was always preferable within the colonial paradigm. In fact, seizing and controlling territory started to be considered a burden in particular circumstances, as the discussion of Sierra Leone reveals. I agree with Schmitt's notion that colonialism created an international legal order with European states in a privileged position, and that they developed spatially distinct gradations of legality. However, Schmitt sees the breakdown of this spatial order as a waning of European power, while I see it as an acceleration. Extraterritorial jurisdiction provided a way of exerting control over particular actors and contractual terms in any space, rather than having to control all actors and contractual terms in a given space. The first arrangement has far more flexibility and has supported the expansion of markets with fewer political and military costs.

Schmitt calls the end of the *jus publicum Europeaum* the breakdown of a "concrete spatial order" that protected the unique privileges of the European states that originated this hegemonic system. He characterizes the new form of international law that emerged after the end of spatial order: "From the standpoint of special technical materials, it was nothing more than a series of generalizations of doubtful precedent, most based on transitory or heterogeneous situations, combined with more or less generally recognized norms, which, the more generally and more spiritedly they were 'recognized,' the more contested was their application in a concretely disputed case."[12] Schmitt clearly sees this development as the end of a functional international legal regime; however, a strong case can be made that deterritorialization created a more cohesive and efficient legal system from the point of view of colonial interests.

Schmitt points out the emergence of a new form of universalism that was distinct from the concrete interstate order that preceded it: "The prevailing concept of global universalism lacking any spatial sense certainly expressed a reality in the economy distinct from the state—an economy of free world trade and a free world market, with the free movement of money, capital, and labor."[13] Because the system lacks clarity, he believes that it is less functional. But Schmitt's statement above points to the advantages of this new version of international law: the free movement of money, capital, and labor promoted the economic interests of European powers even if it strained the political conception of sovereignty beyond anything recognizable. As colonial outposts grew in size and complexity, and settlers engaged in more appropriation—both legal and illegal—controlling and regulating this economic activity became more difficult given the territorial uncertainties and uneven forms of sovereignty. Exceptions and problems with the legality of settler appropriation started to swallow all of the energies of the Colonial

Office. A new system of understanding territory and sovereignty would have to be invented in order to bring regularity back to administration. I turn now to the history of Sierra Leone to illustrate the compounding difficulties of upholding Schmitt's spatially based legal order, and to detail how an alternative to this order emerged.

The Founding of Sierra Leone

> We must therefore turn our views to Sierra Leone, from whence will probably emanate any degree of civilization which may be attained by the adjacent parts of Africa in the south-east quarter.
>
> —Ludlam and Dawes[14]

Sierra Leone was central to the Christian abolitionist vision in a number of ways. Most obviously, it would harbor former slaves and provide them a space of freedom. Second, it would be a starting point for evangelical aspirations to spread the gospel in Africa—hence religious educational institutions were always central in the settlement. "Sierra Leone was imagined as a new world, a society to be made from the beginning, a laboratory for how Africa might be reconfigured, how freed Africans might become new subjects of empire."[15] While the Claphamites believed all human beings were descended from Adam and Eve, they also believed worldly circumstances and lack of education created a hierarchy between those who were superior and inferior (more or less Christian) by their calculations.

Zachary Macaulay was unable to complete formal schooling past the age of fourteen and was instead sent to be a bookkeeper on his uncle's plantation in Jamaica. Here he personally witnessed the horrors of slavery, but was also disturbed at the rapidity with which he grew accustomed to viewing them. Upon his return to England, he began fervent Bible studies and was welcomed into the Clapham circle. He decided that religious instruction had lifted *him* out of that state of semi-barbarism in which he had become accustomed to the scourge of the earth: slavery. He determined to devote his life to providing religious instruction to lift slaves out of their even deeper physical and spiritual subjugation. As someone who had already lived in the tropics and came from a rougher background than many others in the influential Clapham sect, Macaulay was a natural choice for the governorship of Sierra Leone. He was one of their own, but his personal transformation made him even more avid in his pursuit of the civilizing mission through education.

Zachary Macaulay's diary during his governorship reveals an obsessive concern with the spiritual practices and beliefs of the settlers, whom he viewed as his personal flock. He expressed dismay at the reluctance to attend Sunday school by some families because it required a long journey on what was a day of rest from labor. Alternately, he was also alarmed at the vehemence with which they expressed their religious enthusiasm:

> Some Methodist preachers returned this morning from Granville town, greatly rejoicing in the work that God was carrying on there, and saying that many had proven obedient to the heavenly calling. An Inquiry found that the wildest extravagances had been committed there. People falling down as if dead and remaining in a trance for some time. Others bellowing with all their might, pretended that the Devil overpowered by their preacher was wrestling with their spirits.... It is much to be wished that some sober minded and authorized Methodist preacher might come out who might introduce more discipline and regularity among that people, and correct the extravagant ebullitions of their spirit.[16]

Macaulay's vision of what *authorized* religious training could do for Africans encapsulates the vision the Sierra Leone Company had for their residents. The colony would demonstrate that freedom, education, economy, and Christianity could transform "the sons of Ham." The project of Sierra Leone would provide the ultimate confirmation of the justness of their long struggle to abolish slavery, what Stephen described as "a pestilence over Africa; that monster iniquity ... converting one quarter of this fair earth into the nearest possible resemblance of what we conceive of hell."[17]

Catherine Hall has argued that education became central to the British Empire at the start of the nineteenth century, and with the abolition of slavery, policymakers were thinking about new forms of control and power.[18] Education became central to the new vision of a British-led global order, and Sierra Leone was a proving ground for these educational aspirations. As befitting its position as the center from which improved African society would emanate, Sierra Leone was the primary source for students trained in the "African Academy" back on Clapham Common in London from 1799–1806. After countless missionaries died trying to bring the word of God to Africa, Reverend John Campbell proposed to bring Africans to London, train them in Christian ethics and European methods, and return them home.[19] Half of the students of the African Academy returned to Sierra Leone. Sierra Leone ultimately became an educational center on the West Coast of Africa, and many local leaders sent their sons to be educated in Freetown.

Finally, Sierra Leone was intended to be a proving ground for the assertion that colonialism could be profitable without slave labor. The colony was unsuccessful in this regard and was plagued by the threat of bankruptcy from its inception. The land area was tiny since the British only claimed the peninsula that Freetown was located upon. The peninsula is mountainous and only thirty kilometers long (see Figure 3.1). Despite the efforts of philanthropists such as William Allen, the colony produced no exports and yielded no economic prospects. Between 1840 and 1850, it briefly became a source for "free labor" in the Caribbean

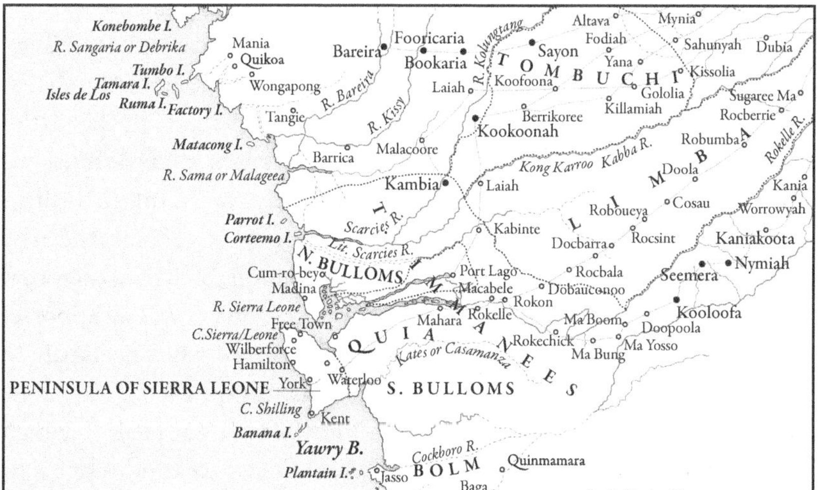

FIGURE 3.1. Map of Sierra Leone 1843

Source: John Arrowsmith, 1790–1873, "Map of the west coast of Africa: comprising Guinea, and the British possessions at Sierra Leone, on the Gambia and the Gold Coast, together with the countries within the courses of the rivers Senegal, Gambia, and Kowara."

following emancipation of the slaves in the British colonies there. As I will briefly explore in the following chapter, labor for sugar plantations became very scarce after slavery was abolished and the transport of 11,000 recaptives—slaves seized by the British from slave merchants and settled in Sierra Leone—were intended to demonstrate the superior power of free labor and save the rapidly sinking fortunes of the British planters in the Caribbean. Sierra Leone failed even in this economic endeavor however.[20]

The contrast between the ideals behind Sierra Leone and the population that came to inhabit it are stark. Granville Sharp founded the settlement which he initially called "The Colony of Freedom" (contemplate that moniker!) in 1787 by transporting a number of the "Black poor" from London. The Black poor were former American slaves who were awarded their freedom in exchange for fighting on the side of the British during the American War for Independence. Many of these former slaves were moved to Nova Scotia, and others were transported back to London. The population was not welcomed into London society, and hence the group became destitute and dependent upon public relief. A Committee for the Relief of the Black Poor determined that sending them to Sierra Leone would be the best solution, and made alliances with Sharp to help him populate his new settlement.[21]

Many of the black poor had never been to Africa and feared reenslavement, but were persuaded to move nonetheless. Sierra Leone historian Christopher Fyfe recounted that as the ship carrying the settlement's new residents left London's harbor, there was a late addition of forty-one white, female prostitutes who were promptly married off to partners on the ship. Unbowed by the prospects of settling the new beacon for humankind with the castoffs of London, Sharp insisted that Sierra Leone should be an independent country. Sharp was a supporter of the American War for Independence and believed wholeheartedly in the principle of self-determination. His constitution for Sierra Leone was based upon the old English system known as "frankpledge" which created small groups of collectives that would pay taxes and select representatives for governance.[22] Because it was not a formal state colony, the project was supported by funds raised by missionaries.

In addition to the difficulties making treaties that have already been sketched, the project was further imperiled by the fact that half of the original settlers died on the voyage or within four months of landing on the Sierra Leone peninsula. The reputation of West Africa as "the white man's grave" would become a central aspect of the mercurial British imaginary about West Africa. In 1791, Sharp refounded the settlement with the assistance of Stephen's good friend William Wilberforce under the auspices of the newly formed Sierra Leone Company. The Company rebuilt on the former site (called Granville Town) and named the city Freetown. The number of settlers was extremely small until 1,190 of the Black Loyalists that were in Nova Scotia agreed to fortify the settlement after being promised free, large plots of land upon their arrival.

These promises generated a great deal of conflict between the settlers and the Sierra Leone Company after 1793, when war between the French and English led to France burning down the entire settlement for the second time in its brief existence. The Company, short on funds, decided to charge the settlers a tax for use of their lands even though they had been promised it for free. Soon the Company and the settlers moved into an adversarial relationship, which was further exacerbated by the arrival of Maroons, Jamaican rebels who had also been sent to Sierra Leone with the permission of the Company. All semblance of self-government was driven from Freetown, and the Sierra Leone Company positioned itself as a benevolent dictator of the varied populations that now resided in the tiny area. This is when Zachary Macaulay was governor, and his tenure was characterized by his desire to develop the character of all settlers in accordance with his personal religious views, a project that gained no love between the population of the colony and its ruling body.[23]

A war with the Koya/Temne tribe broke out in 1802, and peace between the settlement and the Koya/Temne was not achieved until the treaty in 1807. The Sierra Leone Company was at this point bankrupt from the continuing wars and the fact that the peninsula was so small that external trade was desperately needed. Conflict with local tribes made trade impossible, and conflict between missionaries, Nova Scotians, and Maroons made life in the tiny settlement turbulent at best. Given the gritty realities of the grand experiment, the settlement would have been abandoned if Parliament had not abolished the slave trade in 1807.

The Act of 1807 specified that the owners and crews of slave ships captured by the British would be tried before a British court. Presumably, the cargo would also be freed. Because of its close proximity to the slave factories on the west coast of Africa and the routes of the slave ships, it was determined that Sierra Leone would be an ideal place to set up the British court for adjudication of slavers and the freedom of their cargo. The British government formally took over the settlement and it became a Crown colony that housed a vice-admiralty court to try captured slavers. Interestingly, the court became one of the most reliable sources of revenue for Sierra Leone. "Captors who brought ships before the Vice-Admiralty Court had prize agents in London to collect bounty money and in Sierra Leone to prosecute cases ... The Court also brought the Colony employment and wealth in the form of court officials' fees, fees for ship-minding and admeasurement, and small contracts for ship's stores and carpentering."[24]

In 1808, the newest British colony had only two thousand inhabitants. By 1815, they had been joined by six thousand "recaptives" or "Liberated Africans"—the terms for the cargo captured by the British from slave merchants. This population formed a relatively distinct society within Sierra Leone, as they had not been enslaved long enough to start to inculcate Western traditions and habits as the settlers from Jamaica, London, and Nova Scotia had. Hence, the settlement remained a distinctive gathering of cultures that did not necessarily mix. The British used one group to quell the rebellions of the others. This practice created a strong animosity between the Nova Scotians and Maroons; the British used "recaptives" to stifle protests by Nova Scotians and Jamaicans against the levied taxes for land use. The result was general acrimony amongst the population and towards the British, not at all what Granville Sharp had imagined for his grand experiment.

The colony was founded by the idealism of the abolitionists, but it persisted largely to serve the pragmatic necessity of the vice-admiralty court. Recaptives were haphazardly placed into decrepit settlements on the outside of Freetown, and reports of the colony's vices and astonishingly high mortality rate meant that every year the governor of Sierra Leone had to beg for continued funds. The project of Sierra Leone became subject to debate among the small population in the United Kingdom who followed colonial policy. In a letter to Undersecretary of State R. W. Hay printed in the *Edinburgh Magazine* in 1826, James M'Queen charged that

> A studied system of deception, imposition, and delusion, has been practiced upon this country by those connected with Sierra Leone, and who also assumed to themselves the whole direction and control of African affairs during the last thirty years. The length to which this system has been carried almost exceeds credibility, and yet it can be substantiated by undeniable facts. It is time the veil was torn asunder.[25]

M'Queen is referring to the notorious influence of the abolitionists in foreign policy, and charging Stephen in his complicity in obscuring the sordid truths about Sierra Leone. The attacks against the missionaries in Sierra Leone had started almost as soon as Sharp's first ship landed; the ostentatious idealism behind the project was bound to be disappointed by the realities of colonial administration. The colony had been under a great deal of scrutiny, at least in terms of its finances, for quite some time since the British did not want to pour funds into the project and the colony was never self-sustaining. It did not help matters that Kenneth Macaulay, Zachary Macaulay's cousin, had been found careless in his task of accounting for recaptives and the funds provided for them, and had to be removed from his official position. It was suspected that profit, not humanitarianism, motivated the Sierra Leone settlement.

It was not until lumber mills were established and wood export tariffs were lifted that the colony was able to find any economic attraction for continued British investment. Timber is a finite resource, and though it became the largest export from Sierra Leone, by the end of the 1830s supplies were running low, and a new wave of businessmen were seeking ways to make West Africa profitable.

Sierra Leone and the Challenge of Lawless Places

Although James Stephen was accused of ruling according to his political sentiment, he was remarkably unblinkered when it came to the prospects for West Africa. Frequently, new projects would be advanced to expand British presence in the region. For example, T. F. Buxton, a wealthy brewer and idealist who had worked for emancipation in the West Indies, proposed that further expansion into and trade with West Africa could definitively eradicate the slave trade in the interior of the continent. He had become the leader of the Christian abolitionist sect in Parliament after the retirement of Wilberforce, and it is safe to assume that Stephen had every sympathy with his political aims. Buxton's hypothesis was that further permeation into the territory would provide alternative economic prospects for slave traders and hence end the practice. But Stephen was invariably dismissive. About the prospects of developing trading relations through the expedition, he remarked:

> I may very possibly be wrong, for I am certainly very ignorant about the internal state of Africa, but it seems to me (with the most sincere deference to the very high judgments which are ranged on the opposite side) that few schemes could be more unpromising or hazardous than that of sending Ships many hundreds of miles into the heart of that Continent, there to make compacts which apparently at least we have not the slightest power of enforcing, and the breach of which by the Native Chiefs may be regarded as almost a certainty. They will take our presents, and sign what we like, and then do just what they like; and who is to prevent them?[26]

What motivated Stephen's lack of enthusiasm for conquest was his familiarity with the difficulty of asserting sovereignty in a convincing fashion in remote territories. He was ideally situated to be able to foresee the problems with enforcing treaties where there was no clear jurisdictional authority. Unless Great Britain was ready to invade or settle Africa, Stephen pointed out the foolishness of trying to create any more entanglement of the Crown's government. "If we could acquire the dominion of the whole of that Continent, it would be but a worthless possession."[27] No trade agreements could be enforced, no settlements could be protected, no laws could be implemented given the current capacities of the British.

Stephen had come to see that colonists were trying to invoke British law as a way of creating sovereignty, or at the very least, creating personal entitlements in new areas of the globe. Antony Anghie has noted the strong relationship between practices of colonialism and the development of sovereignty in his work: "Sovereignty cannot be accounted for as an example of the application of sovereignty; rather, sovereignty was constituted and shaped through colonialism."[28] Anghie sees the broader historical shape of this practice, but this particular case is slightly different because Stephen was absolutely unsympathetic to these attempts. Here he points out the hubris of British citizens venturing into distant areas and expecting the government to provide for them in the manner to which they had become accustomed:

> If some 50 or 60 of the Queen's subjects will settle themselves as a distinct Community in a settlement some hundreds of miles distant from any other British Colony, they have no fair right to expect the advantages of the Institutions, Legislative, Judicial, and Financial of the other parts of the British dominions. They cannot afford to pay for them; and the British Treasury ought not to afford it. In the very nature of such an enterprise it is implied that all parties will submit to the inconveniences of living under a very rude system of Law and Judicial administration.[29]

The geography of Sierra Leone was bound to provoke these questions, since the small area of the colony provided little outlet for profit-making. Naturally, settlers started to engage in more trade, and attempt expansion outside of the formal boundaries of the colony. This fact combined with competition with the French would push the situation to a crisis point.

In 1842 the newly installed Governor George MacDonald, in his annual report (called the Blue Book) to the Colonial Office, explained a number of developments. Laws allowing the British to prosecute the Portuguese (Order of the British Council of 1839) and a Treaty with Spain had temporarily increased the population of Liberated Africans in Sierra Leone. In 1840, Captain Joseph Denman destroyed the last two great factories for processing slaves on the west coast of Africa, freeing 841 slaves and providing a great victory for the abolitionists.[30] This had the impact of pushing the slave trade further from Sierra Leone to the eastern side of Africa. This movement had meant a serious decline in immigration into the colony, and also a significant reduction in the court fees that were cycling into the colony through the vice-admiralty court. At the same time, the business of transporting emigrants from Sierra Leone to the West Indies had increased, and hundreds of people were abandoning the colony and moving across the Atlantic.[31] Timber was running out. The population and income of the colony were down, and the expenses were up. One can imagine the nervous tone of MacDonald's account to the Colonial Office.

MacDonald also reports continual difficulties with the settlement of Liberated Africans into adjacent territories. They would settle and farm in these territories, not understanding the limits of the colony's boundaries. Local chiefs would be angered by the encroachment, leading to many skirmishes, continual violence against property and crops, episodes of enslavement of natives by Liberated Africans (!), and instances of the re-enslavement of Liberated Africans by local tribes. Adding to these problems, there had been a series of incidents with local missionaries and European settlers committing crimes in the region just outside of the colony. To prevent a full-scale war, the governor decided they needed a way to adjudicate those guilty of criminal activity.

In his note to Lord Stanley (then secretary of state), Governor MacDonald explains the necessity of controlling British subjects outside of the defined territory of Sierra Leone. A law was passed on March 15, 1841, providing for a tribunal, which would be assembled to conduct proceedings against those accused of committing crimes outside of the colony. MacDonald describes the frequency of "petty delinquencies, in which our vagrant population is too apt to indulge, when they consider themselves beyond the grasp of British law, and yet protected from the effects of native vengeance by their condition as British Subjects." But there were also instances in which British subjects did find themselves tried by "cruel and oppressive measures, by which under the name of 'country law,' the lives and liberties of offenders, are at times placed in jeopardy, such as trial by 'red water,' 'witchcraft' etc."[32]

To prevent the mistaken assumption of impunity on the part of British subjects as well as their subjection to such "raw" justice, the governor and council had passed a law declaring that subjects of Sierra Leone would be accountable to the laws of the colony, even when they were outside its formal boundaries. When a case of criminal activity would arise outside the colony, a special commission would be formed which would adjudicate the case, and then be extinguished at the end of the trial. Because the commission would be temporary and only British citizens would be subject to its rulings, the Sierra Leone government determined that this would be a satisfactory solution to the problem. But for safe measure, the law also included the following clause:

> And be it further enacted, That nothing herein or in any such commission or commissions contained, shall extend or be construed to extend to invest her Majesty, her Heirs, or Successors, with any claim or Title whatsoever to Dominion or Sovereignty, over any such territories as aforesaid; or to derogate from the rights of the tribes or people inhabiting such territories, or of the Chiefs or rulers, to such sovereignty or Dominion.[33]

In order to solve the problem of British impunity, the Sierra Leone government decided to simply declare that it could prosecute crimes committed by its own subjects in other territories. They assumed that expressly stating that this did not entail sovereign claims on the part of the Crown, or limit sovereign rights of the local leaders, could make it so.

In his letter MacDonald assures the Colonial Office of the soundness of the system as well as the amenability of everyone to the solution:

> A question may arise, as to the mode in which such enactment would be regarded and received by the natives; in his reply I affirm, with much confidence, that the natives entertain a high respect for the equity and Justice of British law. Moreover the Act by its very passport and terms comes recommended to them by its providing for the sure punishment of delinquents, without the risks of involving them (the natives) in disputes and controversy, with the Government and authorities of Sierra Leone.[34]

The final clause of the legislation makes it clear that Liberated Africans are subjects of the British Crown, and hence subject to the provisions of the Act.

The Colonial Office, represented by James Stephen, was most unhappy with this news. After scolding MacDonald for taking a year to convey the news of this legislation to him, he proceeded to strike it down.

> They (the laws) both proceed on the assumption that it was competent to that Legislature to make Laws for the Trial and punishment of offences committed beyond the precinct of the Colony itself. But this is a power that cannot be properly ascribed to the Legislature of any British Colony. The authority of such bodies is entirely local and from the nature of the case could not be otherwise. If any one Colonial Legislature could impose on the Queen's subjects penalties for actions done in Foreign Countries, every such Legislature must have the same right, and thus there might arise a variety of Laws concurrent yet inconsistent with each other, and all alike simultaneously binding on these for the Government of whom they had been passed. This functional inconvenience, though little to be apprehended in the immediate cases in question, illustrates the objection to the principle on which such legislation proceeds.[35]

In this memo, Stephen mentions similar legislation in South Africa that he struck down, and refers to recent cases in other colonies. While the problem of British criminality was serious, the solution of having colonial, or even British, jurisdiction exceed the boundaries of the colonies would create more jurisdictional muddles. What would happen when two colonies had different provisions that were invoked? He calls this a "functional inconvenience," but it is clear that he is still thinking about law in a territorial fashion, while colonial governors were moving toward thinking about law as linked to particular populations. But linking law with territories had been one of Stephen's primary tools during his tenure in the Colonial Office. He used spatial designations as a way of using law to promote greater individual freedom. For instance, an escaped slave would be just another immigrant in a territory that did not allow slavery. Former slaves could be given the same rights as those who were never enslaved by attaching law to particular spaces.

However, his method of using territory to anchor and insist upon particular laws was under strain by this juncture. The British did not want to claim sovereignty over larger and larger parts of the globe and be forced to defend it against encroachments by others. Instead, they wanted their citizens to be able to circulate throughout the globe, and be able to have the force of British law support or constrain them as needed. The movement from seeing law as linked to sovereign territory understood in its traditional form to seeing law as a tool that could be detached from sovereignty and used to support commercial ventures would continue to unfold.

Stephen's judgment in overturning the law in Sierra Leone was not questioned, but the question of legality and territory would reassert itself in the same area just a few months later in relationship to the newly abandoned slave factories and forts on the West Coast of Africa. At the start of 1843, the French arrived and took over the fortress there. Captain Maclean reported:

> The French have commenced operations at Assineé. They will encounter various difficulties in the establishment of their settlement, but these they will of course overcome, and when they shall be once more firmly established they will prove, I fear, troublesome neighbors to us. I have heard also that they have purchased the Danish forts. I sincerely hope this is not true, if it be, our Government is really much to blame.[36]

Established Colonial Office policy had been to abstain from acquiring new territories on the West Coast of Africa. But private merchants, including Matthew Forster, MP (member of Parliament), wanted to expand his trade from its current base in the Gambia. He proposed that the British take possession of the Gambia and the two Gold Coast forts. During what would become contentious hearings on the matter, Joseph Denman—the captain who had destroyed the slave factories and was familiar with the coast—testified in opposition to the expansion. An outraged Forster in turn said that Denman's actions that destroyed the slave factories were illegal. His outburst had the end result of encouraging the Spanish to sue the British for damages against their property, and a cessation of Britain's more aggressive actions against the slave trade. Forster wanted the Colonial Office to annex these territories for his business purposes. Maclean urged the British government to action before they were outflanked and potentially cut off from vital supplies by the incursion of the French:

> The advantage the French would derive from possessing Christiansborg and its dependences; they would have the command of a fine territory extending from Christianborg to Pope. 140 miles along the coast in which there are four forts exclusive of Christiansborg Castle … this territory reaches 60 miles in a northern direction—in which are reared all the livestock for the supply of the English, Danish and Dutch settlements.[37]

A Parliamentary committee was established to try and figure out the problem of the forts and settlements on the West Coast of Africa in 1842. A few possibilities were offered: the territories be annexed and considered part of Sierra Leone, they could be founded as independent colonies, or they could be ceded to other nations. The first solution had been tried half-heartedly, as the Colonial Office had included the Gold Coast forts under the political jurisdiction of Sierra Leone and the arrangement had failed; additionally Forster presented the Sierra Leone "as a sink of corrupt jobbery" and wanted no affiliation.[38] The department of State was loath to have the French establish a foothold there, but not sufficiently excited to incur the expense and difficulties of establishing new colonies and overturning the long-standing principle of avoiding additional sovereign claims in West Africa. The ideal option, as far as they were concerned, was not to claim it as a colony but to simply try and occupy it. To protect the interests of the British who were occupying the forts and establishing commerce, a judicial officer would be appointed. This is remarkably similar to the proposal to curb British criminality posed the previous year—to have British law outside of British jurisdiction.

In a memo Stephen comments upon the plan:

> The Judicial officer who is to extend beyond the precincts of the Queen's Dominions Justice rather than Law, would be encumbered

> rather than aided by any form of legal appointment. There is no apparent good reason why a Juridicature, which in its exercise is to be independent of all positive Law, should in its institution seek a legal basis. All the manuscripts and seals which legal subtlety could bring together would of course be unavailing to legalise the appointment of an English Judge beyond the Queen's Dominions, except indeed as an Act of Parliament might be said to render it legal within the local range of the authority of Parliament. But how to frame such an Act is, I suppose an insoluble problem. We are about to make an usurpation which the goodness of our motives, and the necessity of the case are to justify, and I suppose that such a mortification would not be improved by an abortive attempt to give a semblance of the Law to that, *ea hypothesi*, is to be lawless. If the arbiter judge is fit for the employment, he will not be critical about his Commission.[39]

Stephen clearly contrasts justice and law in this memo, just as he had earlier contrasted the two in relation to the seizure of cargo from slave ships. In that case, he was on the side of "natural justice" in the "illegal" liberation of slaves. Here, he sides with law against the presumption of exporting "justice" into realms he felt were being commandeered for commercial interests. It could not have helped that Forster had challenged the legality of destroying the slave factories during his testimony, exposing himself as linked to a purely commercial form of British expansion as opposed to the more idealistic variant of colonialism espoused by Stephen.

Stephen points out that appointing a judicial officer for a non-British territory would detach British law from its "positive" origins. From his perspective, the command of law was difficult enough to maintain under the obscure circumstances of territory, multiple citizenries, and thin institutional veneer. Invoking "a semblance of law" would only risk muddling the tenuous distinction between law and lawlessness that Stephen had spent the previous thirty years upholding.

Stephen's rage spills onto the page as he addresses James Hope concerning the proposed changes. Stephen knows that he has already lost the battle, and that the shifts are forthcoming. To serve commercial interests, the British government is going to sacrifice the "positive" basis of law in territory and sovereignty.

> It could answer no good purpose to trouble Lord Stanley, or you, with an argument to prove that the recommendations of the Committee are wrong, not in details, but in their essence. Yet such is the only opinion which I could express on the "advisability" of these changes, if I wrote what I really thought. I would not be deterred from doing so by the dread of appearing arrogant if there could be the slightest prospect of any advantage from the attempt. But to what end trouble you with a disenssion (sic) to prove, that the value of these African Settlements to our Commerce, or that their utility as preventatives of the slave trade is enormously exaggerated, that in fact they are nothing else than Factories kept up at the expense of the Nation at large for the profit of half a dozen inconsiderable merchants, who avail themselves of our national sensibility on every subject on which the Commonwealth or the national importance of Great Britain are concerned—that the trade of all of them all put together is of less value to us, present or prospective, than the trade with the Isle of Skye—that we are recklessly increasing and dispersing our Colonial Empire in all directions and creating a demand for Naval and Military force which there are no means of meeting, except by weakening that force where its presence is most needed—that in short neither the Gambia nor the Gold Coast are worth retaining.... Such being the notions which I entertain, I think you will fully agree with me, that it would be a mere waste of time to say anything more about them.[40]

Stephen foreshadows the solution to the British conundrum, an act of Parliament could potentially offer legal cover for the assertion of legal authority outside of political sovereignty. In a few months, the same James Hope would write the memo on behalf of the Foreign Office to explain the Foreign Jurisdiction Act of 1843. Stephen had struck down the Act of 1841 that had been passed in Sierra Leone, but there were others in a dozen other locales. Hope explains the presence of "foreign jurisdiction courts in Turkey, Egypt, Tunis, Morocco, Persia, China, Japan, Western Polynesia, the Eastern and Western coasts of Africa, in

Madagascar, Zanzibar, Cyprus and other places. And they continue to be established wherever new countries are opened up by British enterprise, and the conditions of civilization necessitate the exercise of the Queen's power and jurisdiction for the protection and good government of her subjects resorting to new regions."[41]

One of the interesting sleights of hand in this memo is that Hope is presenting the Foreign Jurisdiction Act largely in commercial terms. New countries are "opened" by British "enterprise"; however, the Colonial Office record shows quite clearly that such courts were put in place in order to curb British criminality, not to ensure commercial success. In fact, in the subsequent investigation into the impact of the Foreign Jurisdiction Act, the Foreign Office asks for reports from outposts around the world as to its impact. The records contain hundreds of reports from officers attesting to the dramatic decrease in British criminality. From Brussa, the judicial officer reports: "It tends greatly to the repression of crimes and offences by parties ranking as British subjects, that they are now made amenable to punishment with increased certainty, and under legal powers of jurisdiction, before wanting."[42] And from Smyrna, "Offences which were formerly of frequent occurrence have of late become so rare it may fairly be presumed that the knowledge which the lower classes of British subjects residing here now possess, that I am invested with jurisdiction in criminal matters, has inspired them with a wholesome fear of punishment."[43]

British criminality remains the unacknowledged background necessitating foreign jurisdiction. Even in the confidential memo, Hope instead paints it as a matter of clashing legal norms to his Parliamentary audience. "But whether any other important jurisdiction of this kind may at present exist or not, it is plain that intercourse between Christian and Infidel, civilized and barbarous nations, must at all times tend to create them; and it seems, therefore but prudent that a country whose colonial and commercial relations are so extensive as those of great Britain, should be provided with settled principles by which to decide every new case as it may arise."[44]

Hope's strategy in arguing for the Foreign Jurisdiction Act is that there are no new powers being created; it is only formalizing a common practice. Of course, this position makes sense given the common-law tradition in Great Britain. Hope cites the foreign jurisdiction courts in place around the world and points out that they suffer only from an ambiguous legal status that can be corrected by Parliamentary action.

> And whereas doubts have from time to time arisen as to the exercise of such jurisdiction, and it is expedient to remove the same ... it shall be lawful for her majesty, her heirs, successors, to hold, exercise, and enjoy such jurisdiction or authority, according to the nature and extent thereof, and to perform all acts necessary and expedient for the due administration of the same, in as full and ample a manner as though such jurisdiction and authority were a territorial jurisdiction or authority acquired by cession or conquest from a foreign power.[45]

Of particular interest here is his analysis of the origin of extraterritorial right referenced in the last sentence "acquired by cessation or conquest." Hope points out that a country would only give the right of extraterritoriality if it was already compromised. He uses the example of *The East India Company v. Sandys* to start his explanation. Most of the time a country would not cede its power to another in this way. But in unequal power relationships, it would be forced to do so. These are "the peculiar circumstances," which make such a capitulation "consistent with safety and dignity."[46]

Hope's logic is applied to the pending negotiations with China, in what would become the Treaty of Nanking.

> Let us assume by the pending Treaty China concedes an island, and that by the same Treaty she concedes a jurisdiction over British persons and causes within her own ports.
>
> How are these two cessions distinguishable? As it would appear, only be this: that the former is supported by the natural and most secure, but not the only basis of jurisdiction, viz. territory, and the latter is without it.
>
> In both cases the Emperor parts with his sovereignty; in both cases Great Britain acquires it. The difference between them is not so much one of kind as of degree and strength. In the island our authority extends to everything not specially exempted in the cession; on the continent we have also power, but only in excepted instances. In the island we can command physical force to give effect to the

> jurisdiction; on the continent we have an equal right to make it effectual, but we may need foreign assistance to do so. In the island the territory helps to maintain itself, and by a maintenance of the territory we maintain the jurisdiction; on the continent our arms and negotiations may effect the same result, only they have a less secure base of operation.[47]

Hope's memo points out that the condition creating and the exercise of legal right is the same: "Our arms and negotiations may effect the same result." Before conquest and cessation had created different legal rights; now the basis and exercise of extraterritorial jurisdiction are acknowledged as a fact of the superior strength of British sovereignty. This is a risky move, because the British were still waiting to see if China would indeed assent to the Treaty of Nanking. When the treaty was signed, *The Illustrated London News* reported that it was very favorable for Great Britain but there were doubts "whether it will be observed after the force to which it was conceded is withdrawn."[48]

Hope is taking a practice that was hard won in China and expanding it as a policy more broadly. The broadness of the legislation has been noted by others: "It is clear before this act was passed, laws took account of particular situations."[49] The contrast is stark, because the act takes what was won in the conflict with China and applies it as a blanket principle: "A British subject was subjected to British law, no matter where he (or she) might be, but subjected as an individual, not based on territory."[50] Would other countries simply assent if the British assert this principle as a right?

Placeless Law

> The time will come when we and the French will have to tell the Sultan that it is not a privilege we are seeking but our right.
>
> —Lord Hardinge[51]

The episode in Sierra Leone provides an example of the old spatial order described by Schmitt in *The Nomos of the Earth* coming under pressure from the unfolding complexities of settler activities, and ultimately breaking down and being replaced by a much more direct system. Detaching British sovereignty from territory, while a sea change in understandings of sovereignty and territory, created a legal path for the British to assert their sovereignty as they would like. Before then, colonial legality was, as Schmitt describes in detail, occupied with keeping territorial jurisdictions straight and determining which laws applied where. As this book has recounted, Stephen was largely the person who was occupied with this mission in the first half of the nineteenth century on behalf of the British. Eventually, maintaining legal jurisdictions based upon territory became onerous, especially given the ever-increasing circulation of British subjects seeking profit. Schmitt blames the emergence of the United States as a global power on the breakdown of the land-based system. But I believe this chapter demonstrates how the contradictions of maintaining the system while pursuing British economic interests ultimately led to its collapse.

It was as if the tensions and difficulties of maintaining one legal system finally led to a break with old ways of thinking, and a new legal system was born. It should be evident by now that Sierra Leone was never an "average" colony in the British Empire. But it does provide a very clear lens into the processes of administering Schmitt's spatially ordered system of law. Schmitt's view is from a long distance, and *The Nomos of the Earth* paints broad strokes. Taking a specific case study such as Sierra Leone allows us to see the legal entanglements that arose from this presumably clear system.

Obviously, power or force was needed to defend the exclusive exercise of sovereignty over a given space. Processes of conquer and cessation formally transferred aspects of sovereignty—or sovereignty in its entirety—to another power when the current regime was unable to defend its claims. These capitulations led to a muddied exercise of sovereign authority in British colonies, as I have discussed previously. The most important aspect of this system of territorially based legality was an assumption that sovereignty was *exclusive*. In fact, the link between exclusivity and territory was the way that sovereignty was defined.

Once the practice of extraterritoriality became established, the detachment from territory also meant a fundamental shift in the understanding of sovereignty. James Hope did not set out to redefine practices of sovereignty. Indeed, in his memo explaining the Foreign Jurisdiction

Act of 1843, he says that he is merely making law what already existed as a practice. British sovereign claims, backed by warships, cannons, and the mighty sterling, did mean more than the claims proffered by the current inhabitants in virtually any place on the globe. As a practice, power did create sovereignty, even as the legal framework was built around the assumption of sovereign claims as zero-sum.

However, the practice of extraterritorial jurisdiction created a different underlying assumption about sovereignty: some sovereigns are less equal than others. Some sovereign powers have the right to claim extraterritorial jurisdiction; others are forced to submit to the asserted right. And from this moment international law shifted from being a system that sorted out and tried to monitor claims of sovereignty in given spaces to being a system that sorted sovereign powers into the greater or lesser categories.

The rush to claim extraterritorial privileges in China demonstrates this process clearly. I have presented James Stephen's objections to the detachment of law from defined space. But in the United States, there was a similar belief in the absolute convergence of territory and sovereignty. In 1812, Chief Justice John Marshall 1812 stated, "The jurisdiction of a nation within its own territory is necessarily exclusive and absolute ... being alike the attribute of every sovereign, and being incapable of conferring extraterritorial power."[52] Yet in 1844 in the Treaty of Wanghia, the United States demanded the right of extraterritoriality in China. "Although the United States continued to reject the British model of territorial imperialism (at least in China, except for some erratic interest in Taiwan), it adopted, with a vengeance, the key form of British nonterritorial imperialism: the cultivation and elaboration of the privilege of extraterritoriality."[53] The point was to assert their membership in the company of nations who could demand this right.

> By taking on the practice of extraterritoriality, America took on a form of imperial sovereignty that rendered it *Britain's* equal in extraterritorial imperialism in China.[54] Ultimately, there were nineteen different countries who demanded and received the right of extraterritoriality in China, thereby asserting their first-class membership in the international system.[55]

Once the right of extraterritoriality was asserted, the rationale supporting it was not long in coming. As Gerrit Gong has argued, using different measures of civilization to measure whether or not a country could gain entrance into the company of nations on equal terms developed in the late 19th century.[56] The existence of different legal systems, once a problem for British legal administration to try and accommodate (as in the development of Anglo-Hindu law discussed in Chapter One), was redefined. Now the presence of non-Christian legal systems was a disqualification from the full exercise of sovereignty. In a memo in regard to the newly established extraterritorial privileges in Turkey, Lord John Russell insisted that they originated from "the principle that Turkish rule and justice are so barbarous that exceptional privileges are required."[57]

Ruskola summarizes the development of extraterritorial jurisdiction that "had neither a coherent territorial referent nor a constitutional one." He argues, "It was a placeless law that was justified, ultimately, by the Orientalist axiom that China itself was a fundamentally lawless place."[58] China of course did not see the agreement to extraterritoriality on the same terms. When advising the emperor about whether to sign the Treaty of Nanking, three commissioners argued, "Should we fail to take advantage of the present situation by soothing the barbarians, they will run over our country like beasts."[59] Little did they know that their capitulation would be construed as evidence of their own status as an "uncivilized" country in a few decades.

Stephen's career in the Colonial Office ended very shortly after he lost this battle. Arguably, there was much less need for someone with his specialized legal knowledge of the particularities of every colony after the Foreign Jurisdiction Act was passed. And though the impetus for foreign jurisdiction courts was British criminality, the utility of such courts for British commercial activity was already self-evident in the hearings over the expansion of the British presence on the West Coast of Africa, and the appointment of a judicial officer intended to enforce contracts made by British merchants. As Johnston points out, the Gold Coast was the first place the British asserted their newly minted right of extraterritoriality after the bill had passed.[60] Commercial conquest did not have to be backed by jurisdictional sovereignty if it could be backed by extraterritorial privileges. Individuals would be given rights according to their affiliations and nationality, regardless of their location. This would open a world of possibility for commercial expansion for any British citizen.

But the development of a bifurcated system of sovereignty from this episode is just as important. Even as the modern form of international law emerged, it made it clear that not all countries would be able to exercise sovereignty in the same way. It was a double movement. As the criteria for inclusion into the company of nations were articulated upon Anglo-American norms, legal practices awarded extraterritorial privileges and made it clear which countries were less than equal. Consider Lord Russell's pronouncements to Turkey in 1859 that would allow them greater autonomy "in proportion to improved government and to an 'impartial and regular administration of justice.' "[61]

This dynamic remains in place today. The rule of law is taken as a measure of a country's worthiness, even as some countries are not allowed to exercise their sovereignty in the same way as more powerful regimes. Is it any wonder that we continually find a mismatch between norms and practices? As colonial powers exported the rule of law *for their own citizens* through extraterritorial privileges, they took it away from the citizens of other countries.

4

Codification and the Colonies

Who's Accusing Whom?

MANY SCHOLARS HAVE EXPLORED THE role of the Indian Insurrection[1] of 1857 in changing British imperial practices; less well known is an event that followed just seven years later. While the widely publicized horrors of the Indian Insurrection served to numb the British population to the violent reassertion of British rule there, an incident in Jamaica known as the Morant Bay Rebellion caused international scandal and embarrassed the Crown. Morant Bay caused a round of finger pointing: Jamaicans accused the governor of despotism; the governor accused the colonial subjects of wanton disrespect for order. No real punishments were issued as a result of British misdeeds; new practices of criminal accusation and law in the colonies were the end product of this rebellion. Succinctly put, codification was a project to enlarge the disciplinary function of the law in the colonial context. This was a movement from vague promises of eventual self-rule for colonial subjects to clearer guidelines for their self-regulation through the criminal codes.

"Eight Miles of Dead Bodies"

Since the abolition of slavery in the colony in 1834,[2] Jamaica had become an increasingly troubled location in the Empire. Plantation owners who specialized in sugar crops faced steep competition from European beet sugar and newly opened sugar cane fields in Brazil and Cuba. To compound the difficulty, the British ceased giving preferential status to Jamaican sugar, forcing plantation owners into the wilds of global free market competition. Freed slaves refused to work on larger plantations, where wages were low and paid irregularly. They preferred instead to move into the Blue Mountains and pursue small-scale farming for subsistence and export, though with mixed success on this latter front.

> The British government, unfortunately, … preferred to think of this development not as a healthy adjustment to the decaying Jamaican sugar economy, nor as a natural reaction to large areas of unoccupied land. Rather, they bemoaned the fact that the lazy Quashee preferred to grow his own food rather than work for the low, irregular and uncertain wages of the frequently absent estate owners.[3]

The Jamaican economy was faltering at every level, and predictably, all parties blamed the colonial administrators. Hence, from the perspective of the Colonial Office in London, the governorship of Jamaica was considered a vital, if difficult, post. Edward John Eyre had gained some notoriety in Australia for his connection to and advocacy for indigenous populations, bringing him into the eyes of the Colonial Office, which appointed him "Protector of the Aborigines." His heroism and success on the colonial frontier and reported partnership with different tribes recommended him as a choice that could inspire disgruntled plantation owners and former slaves alike. In 1862, colonial undersecretary Frederic Rogers pushed through Eyre's appointment as interim governor general of Jamaica; it became permanent two years later.

The census of 1861 placed Jamaica's population at 44,000 individuals, 13,000 of whom were white. There were 26,000 Jamaican Baptists, and they served as a numerically powerful core constituency that could be mobilized into political action. Jamaica had three rebellions in the previous century, and Baptist abolitionist activists were implicated in helping slaves foment revolt.[4] The Baptists were a strong force that opposed the planters and their interests. A legislature was in place, but high property qualifications meant that only 1,903 Jamaicans were qualified to vote in the 1864 election. In 1865, Jamaica was a rapidly failing plantation economy run by an oligarchic assembly and a British-selected governor general.

The temptations to despotism were great. Governor Eyre began his increasingly unpopular reign by awarding a large contract for construction of a local tramway to an incompetent engineer. The tramway construction failed spectacularly, but Eyre refused to admit his mistake. Locals suspected he had somehow lined his pocket in the deal, which was never proven and most likely not true. He was simply unable to admit his failings, instead falling into the unfortunately common cycle of wielding his power more heavily and thereby hastening its depletion.

Eyre identified George William Gordon as his most powerful enemy. Gordon was a self-educated former slave who became a successful produce merchant. He bought his own and his mother's freedom before abolition was passed. Remarkably, after his white father's plantation collapsed following abolition, he rescued his father and white half-sisters from certain economic ruin. Gordon was a leader within the Jamaican Baptists, and followed in the tradition of being inspired by faith to use power to help the less powerful. He was elected magistrate of Morant Bay, a small city, and had proposed to repair horrific jail conditions there. The jail was so decrepit that, as in some other British colonial outposts, it had emerged as a clear symbol of the bankruptcy and corruption of the colonial enterprise altogether.[5] Gordon's request to upgrade the jail was ignored by Eyre upon his arrival in Jamaica.

Eyre was irritated at this Jamaican gadfly and threw some fuel on the fire by summarily removing Gordon from his office in Morant Bay. Gordon wrote to the Colonial Office to protest, and doublespeak on their part ensued, demonstrating the ambivalent impulse to keep orderly colonies but do so according to proper procedures. The Colonial Office privately reprimanded Eyre for overstepping his authority but decided to keep a unified front behind the struggling governor by supporting him publically. Gordon subsequently ran for the National Assembly and was elected, demonstrating his support among the emerging middle class of Jamaica who formed a part of the small group of property-qualified electors. Eyre had cast his lot with the planters. Gordon was able to take his war against Eyre to the Assembly. In a speech on the floor, he pronounced,

> When all over laws are put at defiance, the populace will break out from discontent, and the Governor will be unable to allay their

> feelings ... When a governor becomes a dictator, when he becomes despotic, it is time for the people to dethrone him ... I have never seen an animal more voracious for cruelty and power than the present Governor of Jamaica.[6]

Eyre's sense that Gordon was an enemy to be reckoned with obviously had merit. More importantly, the fact that Gordon took care to ally himself on the side of law while casting Eyre on the side of despotism proved prescient.

Where else then, would the troubles begin than a courtroom? On October 7, 1865, a young boy was fined for assault in the court of petty sessions in Morant Bay. The court ordered the boy to pay the court fees for the trial, a total of sixteen shillings, in addition to paying for damages. An observer rose and shouted to the boy to pay the fine but not the court fees. The suggestion was a form of civil disobedience whereby the offender would accept the penalty but refuse to support the travesty of justice being offered by the court system. Officials tried to seize the man, but other observers beat them back, and the man—Geohagen—escaped. One of the courtroom observers who helped Geohegan was Bogle, a well-known and popular Baptist preacher. The court issued an arrest for Bogle the following Monday for disrupting the administration of justice, and the next day six policemen and two constables (who were all black) were dispatched to arrest him. Reports estimate that anywhere from three to five hundred members of Bogle's church responded to his cries of alarm and mobilized to save their pastor from arrest.

The men then organized and decided to storm the courthouse in Morant Bay.[7] The courthouse was burned, and reports of atrocities committed by angry mobs against British administrators reached Eyre. Fearing a local version of the Haitian revolution, he declared martial law in Morant Bay and told his generals to spare no mercy in the suppression of the insurrection. The organized "army of rebels" could not be located however, and had apparently dispersed after burning the courthouse. Any black residents who failed to flee from Eyre's army were labeled "rebels" and shot. Under martial law, almost five hundred people were killed immediately and hundreds of others were wounded or maimed by the troops.[8]

Eyre, certain the rebellion was suppressed, returned to Kingston where he was presented evidence that Gordon (in Kingston because of his duties in the National Assembly) had led the rebellion from afar. Eyre immediately ordered his arrest, and Gordon gave himself up promptly to be examined by the courts in Kingston. Instead, Eyre ordered the prisoner transported to Morant Bay where a military court found him guilty upon flimsy evidence and refused to let him speak on his own behalf during the widely scorned trial procedure. He was hung two days later. Eyre wrote in the report to the Colonial Office, "Considering it right in the abstract, and desirable as a matter of policy, that whilst the poor black men who had been misled were undergoing condign punishment, the chief instigator of all the evils should not go unpunished."[9] Eyre framed Gordon's execution as a matter of fairness in regard to all those that had already been killed.

London heard sensational news about violent colonial rebellion, which quickly turned into suspicion after no traces of the rebel army could be found. The initial reports in which Eyre's generals described taking revenge upon the bodies of their victims in order to deter any potential recruits to the rebellion were met with increasing horror. Reports slowly arrived from Jamaica, and public opinion turned decisively against Eyre. The *New York Herald* published a sensational headline, "Eight Miles of Dead Bodies," describing the carnage of the British in suppressing what was characterized as a minor rebellion. Two thousand Jamaicans had been killed over the month of martial law. The Crown was embarrassed; the people outraged. "The Jamaica insurrection gave rise to a three-year long controversy as to whether Governor Eyre ought to be treated as a hero who had saved Jamaica for the Crown, and the lives of 13,000 white men and women in the bargain, or whether his repression of the uprising had revealed him as not only stupid, cruel, and incompetent, but a murderer."[10] His presumed crimes were brought to the center of British political debate, highly unusual for controversies in the colonies. There were a series of meetings, called Jamaica Meetings, in towns such as Lambeth, Brighton, Liverpool, and Bristol. They were attended by as many as a thousand people. In an increasingly fractious political landscape, the pointed question was whether there was any limit to the actions a government could take to suppress revolt among its citizens and subjects. R. W. Kostal aptly observed, "If Gordon could be hanged by martial law in Jamaica, John Bright could be hanged by martial law in England. In the space of just more than two weeks the Jamaica affair had been transformed from a narrative about the salvation of Jamaican colonists into a narrative about the destruction of the English constitution."[11] What was called "the Governor Eyre controversy" put the principles of the rule of law on trial. Usually public opinion assumed that rabble-rousers deserved what they got, but in this instance, those who wielded the power of law incurred a surprising torrent of accusation upon themselves.

The trial of Warren Hastings in the previous century served to catalyze a debate about the British mission in India and propel Edmund Burke into the spotlight. The Governor Eyre controversy provoked a national discussion about British colonial governance, and whether it would infect British rule of law more broadly. In 1865, a body called the Jamaica Committee was formed. It was headed by J. S. Mill, who demanded that Eyre be tried for the murder of Gordon. James Fitzjames Stephen was hired as the barrister for the group that included nineteen members of Parliament. Whose accusation should be believed? Geohagen's condemnation of the colonial legal system? Eyre's case against Gordon? Mill's against Eyre? The honor of the Empire was at stake, but so was the position of the rule of law in the colonies and at home. Who is at fault when regulation of a population becomes force, brute force? The governor who ordered suppression of foment by all means, or those who burned the courthouse down? Should the law be used to protect the citizens against the rulers, or the rulers against unruly citizens? Remarkably, the position of the angry colonial mob was given credence; sometimes the governors were in the wrong and the governed were in the right.

A royal commission was formed, and the members spent three months in Jamaica collecting thousands of hours of testimony from hundreds of residents. First, they managed to determine that the gruesome reports of Eyre's generals had been greatly embellished. Thankfully, the generals had not committed all the acts they had reported to Eyre. Nonetheless, there was still plenty of evidence that they had suppressed the rebellion with a zeal that made many British officials—including J. S. Mill—uncomfortable, if not outraged. The peculiarities of colonial sovereignty were exposed by the bloody event, and it followed all too closely on the heels of the Indian Insurrection. It was one thing to assert control over what had been assumed to be hapless populations; it was another matter to have to violently assert—and reassert—the right to rule the expansive territories and populations of the Empire.

In April 1866, the commission issued its findings both praising Eyre for his rapid response to the insurrection but also that martial law had been extended beyond absolute necessity. The royal commission concluded:

> That the punishments inflicted were excessive. (1) That the punishment of death was unnecessarily frequent. (2) That the floggings were reckless, and at Bath positively barbarous. (3) That the burning of 1000 houses was wanton and cruel. All of which we humbly submit to Your Majesty's gracious consideration.[12]

The statement is a masterpiece of British euphemism, asserting the rule of law in principle while acknowledging that in practice its maintenance is not always possible. The Jamaica Committee was not convinced by this resolution and instead developed a plan for their own inquiry to gather enough evidence to place Eyre on trial for the murder of George Gordon.

In response to the report, Eyre was removed from office permanently and the Jamaican Assembly (in existence for more than two hundred years) was dissolved since it harbored the potential of political fragmentation within the changing colonial state. Jamaica became a Crown colony legislated entirely through the Colonial Office. In short, the British decided to endorse clearer despotism in the hopes it would eliminate future conflict. During his year as barrister for the Jamaica Committee, James Fitzjames Stephen came to have a certain amount of sympathy with Eyre, arguing that excessive force may have seemed necessary at the time.[13] In his application submitted in April 1867 to bring Eyre to trial, Stephen praised Eyre's suppression of the rebellion but said that, legally, he had nonetheless committed murder by hanging Gordon. "The governor … had been guilty of an 'outrageous stretch of power,' and had hanged Gordon, not because it was necessary to keep the peace, but because it seemed to be expedient on general political grounds."[14] Stephen's distinction between morality and legality outraged the other members of the Jamaica Committee who saw Eyre's crimes as above all moral, and only secondarily legal. Stephen resigned from his post and the life-long animosity between himself and J. S. Mill began.

Stephen's investigation into the Morant Bay Rebellion, particularly his distinction between laws and morality, was crucial for Stephen's subsequent career as legal scholar and practitioner. For Stephen, force and law were essential elements in any government. When a regime rules over people of impeccable morals and similar values, the force of law is largely instructive rather than explicit. Stephen judged that power inequalities and a diversity of morals make the necessity of explicit force unavoidable. The best that could be hoped for was that everyone would recognize the advantages of order, and get along with it. The less developed technologies of power are, the more force is necessary to create authority. Later in his career, Stephen observed that "questions of sovereignty can be determined only by force."[15] Hence, his sympathy for Governor Eyre, whose hold upon sovereignty seemed tenuous. In a country such as India, which had vast cultural differences between ruler and ruled and extreme power imbalances, the more benign exercise of the force of law would be impossible. Stephen's self-appointed task was to build a framework for law whose exercise would be more tempered than the notorious oriental despots who preceded the British in India (and other colonial territories) but that would nonetheless recognize the character deficiencies of colonial subjects and their masters. Codification was his method. Colonial subjects would be rendered automatically suspect by the legal codes that separated Indo and European populations into different procedures; in exchange, they would experience a less violent colonial rule.

Sovereign violence could be replaced by a clearer disciplinary apparatus articulated by the criminal codes. Being reminded of the historical context that propelled this program displays that it was a deeply *defensive* move. The actions of colonial subjects were illuminating the British inability to live up to their own rhetoric of enlightened rule. The British colonial system stood accused of brute force as opposed to exporting the rule of law as it claimed. Modernization of the technologies of law were intended to put suspicions about the nature of colonial sovereignty to rest. If the British were going to be successful in their civilizing mission, they would need to straighten out their laws. Codification was intended to illuminate the moral character of the rulers, just as much as it was intended to mold colonized subjects.

James Fitzjames Stephen: The Rule of Law as Social Science

Sir James Fitzjames Stephen wrote the Indian Evidence Act, drafted a codification of criminal laws for England that was debated twice by Parliament, completed seminal works on evidence and criminal law, and wrote a three-volume history detailing the history of criminal law in England, in addition to writing one of the most influential rejoinders to J. S. Mill's *On Liberty* called *Liberty, Equality, Fraternity*. Naturally, his career has attracted a great deal of academic attention.[16] Here, I am focusing rather narrowly on his ideas about codification. Codification, it has been observed, is a dry topic. However, we should care about it precisely because it emerged at a point of changing public opinion, growing democratic sentiments, and the evolution of the colonial mission. Radhika Singha has observed that codification was "a ripening" of the colonial project in India to consolidate rule by the state rather than the East India Company, and to create the conditions for sustainable economic extraction.[17] Stephen saw law as a dynamic element in the relationship between colonized subjects and their rulers. Examining his codification project in the colonies is an excellent way to see what the British thought about their colonized subjects, including their aspirations for molding them, as well as their beliefs about inherent characteristics that could not be changed. There is an implicit accusation of the character of the colonized embedded in the codes, and a profoundly ambivalent one since colonized subjects could presumably not rule themselves, yet the code of laws was intended to teach them how to.

As might be expected from a country that embraced the common-law tradition, the British were interested in maintaining at least some modicum of respect for indigenous legal traditions and practices. When J. F. Stephen's father, Sir James Stephen, was undersecretary of the colonies, maintaining the rule of law meant following the particular practices of each colony. This created significant confusion as the British tried to determine the content and character of pre-existing traditions and laws that were to be honored and incorporated into British colonial rule. For instance, they tried for several decades to locate the one and only "Ancient Hindu Constitution," despite the fact that none of the British colonizers could read Sanskrit.[18]

To compound this ambiguity, the British also had divergent legal arrangements based upon the origins of different colonies. Did the colony enter the Empire through conquest, agreement, or some other method? In every case, different legal arrangements were made. For example Madras, Calcutta, and Bombay all had a different legal status in the 1830s. In Bombay, the British East India Company exercised sovereignty on behalf of the British Crown because sovereignty was formally ceded by the Portuguese. "All Inhabitants, whether English or Indian, were presumably subjects of the British Crown." In Madras, the English exercised sovereignty, "subject however to Indian superiority shown by the payment of quit-rent."[19] In other words, the British controlled the territory presumably on behalf of the Madras feudal lords, and could be asked to give it back at some point in the future. Calcutta was the most complicated of the three main areas of control. The British bought their way into the traditional feudalist system of tax and order, buying itself the position of "a minor zamindar under the local faujdau."[20] K. J. M. Smith has described the state of law in India before the Reform Act of 1833 as "a mind-numbing jumble of Hindu or Muslim law generously overlaid with a mixture of English law and East India Company administrative 'regulations.'"[21]

Predictably, there was much confusion about who was subject to which laws, where, and why. The answer to these questions was different all throughout the British Empire, and this is not to mention the complex negotiations between Britain and other European powers in contested territories and border regions. Sir James Stephen was invaluable in the Colonial Office because he had mastered the details and history of the colonies under his jurisdiction and was able to navigate the historical, political, and legal morasses associated with each of them. During his career, administering the rule of law meant combining singularities and traditions with overall principles whenever possible, and pushing back against settlers and interests that wanted to put personal advantage, geopolitical strength, or economic strategy over this combination.

If it could be said that Sir James Stephen, father, dedicated his life to attempting to reconcile overlapping legal precedents and transcendental justice in the Colonial Office, you could summarize his son's lifework as an attempt to regularize, clarify, and modernize the law. The generational shift is stark; it reflects developments in colonial economy, potential technologies of administration, and a growing understanding of the need for new forms of population control and policing because of events such as Morant Bay. Stephen did not resist these new forms of population control; instead he saw the opportunity to use the law to make them more palatable than the alternatives: despotism or anarchy.

Curiously, all of these factors could be articulated in a new vision of British rule of law. While the idea of civilizational advance persisted, the steps along the way could be measured by the route of the law. The interpretation of what was required to uphold the rule of law changed significantly, while the commitment to the rule of law in the colonial context persisted. To reverse the popular adage: it was new wine in old bottles. Stephen surveyed the legal complexities that attended colonial rule due to distinctive institutional arrangements, local histories, struggles, indigenous legal practices, and British imperial history, and correctly determined clarity was missing. In 1871, Stephen pointed out that "nearly every trial which had taken place in Bengal and the North-West Provinces since 1829 was irregular."[22] Anglo-Indian Law was a jumble of local inclinations (often erroneously interpreted, but that is another matter) and British traditions. Stephen articulated the particular failings of this arrangement as follows: "A good deal may be said for an elaborate legal system, well understood and strictly administered. A good deal may be said for unaided mother-wit and natural shrewdness; but a half-and-half system, in which a vast body of half-understood law, destitute of arrangement and of uncertain authority, maintains a dead-alive existence, is a state of things which is by no means easy to praise."[23]

Stephen's view of the law was dominated by his philosophy of law as a social science, an instrument which could produce relatively predictably human behaviors. If grandiose visions of British largesse and wisdom had previously guided ideas about "the rule of law," the codification project of James Fitzjames Stephen intentionally discarded the idealism and instead embraced the gritty realities of one people dominating another.[24] For Stephen, the question was how to govern increasingly empowered subjects whose education and morals were not necessarily the same as those who governed them. He did not believe in a future in which all would rule themselves; instead he envisioned a future in which everyone would understand the benefits of behaving, which included less need for the violent assertion of authority. The need to avoid the backlash from sovereign violence was perhaps more evident in the colonies, but Stephen saw codification as an equally pressing issue in Great Britain. For J. F. Stephen, the law was an instrument of social control distinct—though not entirely separated—from notions of right, ethics, and morality. Good, clear laws could regulate governance even in times of political uncertainty and moral plurality. Stephen developed a science of law, which emphasized the distinction between laws and morality for precisely this reason: laws can hold firm in the midst of social upheaval in a way that morals would not.

Clearly, Stephen was influenced by Bentham, as anyone who embraced the project of codification would be. But Bentham saw codification as a key to the democratization of society through eliminating the excessive power of the bench and lawyers. Stephen defined a science of jurisprudence as "classifying and describing the relations with which the law must deal, and the limitations placed upon it by the nature of human affairs."[25] Stephen published a series of articles in *Cornhill Magazine* and *The Edinburgh Review* that argued how to properly understand the goals of the social sciences; they were not intended to eliminate free will as many initially assumed but, instead, to surmise patterns of human behavior.

Law could be envisioned as a bridge between human nature, common morality, and the state. If the law veered too far from human nature, it would lose its importance as an expression of human will. If it moved too far from common morality, it would lose its credibility, and its utility. Stephen's biographer, K. J. M. Smith, noted, "But although, for him, the law had nothing to do with notions of absolute truths, the relationship and interaction between the criminal law and morality was still of extensive importance."[26] Here the relevant morality was the contemporary or "positive morality of our time and country, that which as a fact, is generally regarded as right or wrong by people of average education and sensibility."[27]

One of Stephen's main concerns was about this "positive morality" of his time, and he spent considerable amounts of his energies contributing to the *Saturday Review*, and the *Pall Mall Gazette* in order to bolster the level of historical knowledge and moral and intellectual engagement of the British public. So it is perhaps not surprising that he seemed to think that law doesn't only reflect the popular morality; it can also build it, but only if it is clear enough to be ascertained by the general population. He approached the law as a text to be read and debated, a tool to instruct and move "the positive morality" of the population. A morass of legislation could only lead to muddled debates, and a greater division between the state and its subjects. If the law could inform common morality, it was also a reflection of that public opinion at a given time. "The sentence of the law is to the public sentiment of the public in relation to any offences what a seal is to hot wax. It converts into a permanent final judgment what might otherwise be a transient sentiment."[28]

Codification and the Colonies

In 1869, two years after he resigned from the Jamaica Committee, Stephen was offered and accepted the post of legal member of council in India, replacing Sir Henry Maine. Though separation from his family would be a hardship, Stephen had long been fascinated by India, stating that Macaulay's essays about Hastings and Clive had been particularly influential in his intellectual development. His acceptance of this office could also be framed as an inheritance of sorts. His brother commented, "He was pleased to recollect that the post on its first creation had been offered to his father. Among his earliest memories were those of the talks about India which took place at Kensington Gore on that occasion, when Macaulay strongly advised my father to take the post of which he soon became the first occupant."[29] During his years in India he finished the implementation of the penal code that his friend Macaulay had written thirty years previously, wrote the Indian Evidence Act and the Indian Contract Act, and revised the Code of Criminal Procedure. Like his father, he was devoted to curbing the abuses of the powerful. Unlike his father, he was uncertain of the potential for grace and morality within his fellow men and instead saw the fact of power relations as completely unalterable. In *Liberty, Equality, Fraternity* he observed, "Power in whatever form is the essential thing. Anarchy may be mischievous in civilized as well as uncivilised life, and the only way out of it is by coercion. To direct that power aright is, I think, the principal object of political argument. The difference between a rough and a civilised society is not that force is used in one case and persuasion in the other, but that force is (or ought to be) guided with greater care in the second case than in the first."[30]

For Stephen, law was the answer to providing "greater care" in guiding force. It is important to emphasize that he saw law itself as a manifestation of force, and that law needed to *regulate* rather than eliminate force. Stephen decided that it was the ambiguities of British common law at home and the jumble of colonial jurisprudence that led to law's failure in curbing the use of force. Hence his response to the conundrums of colonial authority and violence that he encountered in the Morant Bay Rebellion led to the project of codification. "Clear, short, and simple laws are absolutely indispensable to a vigorous form of government which is to produce lasting effects."[31] This vigorous form of government would be the balance of law and force, or law would curb the use of force in highly detailed ways. Stephen claimed, "Force is an absolutely essential element of all law whatever. Indeed law is nothing but regulated force subjected to particular conditions and directed towards particular objects."[32] The coexistence of law and governance is contrasted to the mutual exclusion of law and despotic power: "To suppose that law and despotic power can subsist side by side, is to show complete ignorance of the very nature of the law."[33] This is equivalent to a definitional stop; the mere presence of law means that governance, not despotism, is at hand. This position had clear utility in the context of British colonial policy.

In India he renamed his position as legal advisor "Benthamee Lycurgus," which required he square the following equation: "Given corrupt natives, incompetent civilians, and a sprinkling of third-rate barristers, how to get perfect judges."[34] He had given up on the civilizing mission that had occupied earlier imperialists, and argued that the influence of law was similar to religion and more transferrable than religious beliefs ever could be. While the Clapham Sect had initially found cause in spreading the gospel in India, J. F. Stephen found that "our law is in fact the sum and substance of what we have to teach them. It is, so to speak, the gospel of the English, and it is a compulsory gospel which admits of no dissent and no disobedience."[35] Stephen argued that codification could prevent many abuses of governmental power and create clear guidelines for citizens to follow. Thus British rule could persist without violence, coercion, common culture, or virtuousness. Instead, clarity in regard to who had authority and who did not was needed to eliminate conflict and avert violence, particularly as more traditional forms of authority were crumbling in both India and England. Stephen explained,

> Laws must be based upon principles, and that it is impossible to lay down any principles of legislation at all unless you are prepared to say, I am right, and you are wrong, and your view shall give way to mine, quietly, gradually, and peaceably; but one of us two must rule and the other must obey, and I mean to rule.[36]

The most telling aspect of this statement is the "quiet" and "peaceable" aspect of asserting hierarchy through law. Codification was uniform, but it did not create equal legal subjectivity; instead it asserted the necessary hierarchy of colonialism in an orderly fashion. Stephen was not equivocating on the colonizing mission or the superiority of the British in relation to their colonial subjects.

For Stephen, the contrast between the way law operated in England and in India was crucial in developing and presenting his ideas about codification. In two extended essays, "Legislation under Lord Mayo" and "Codification in India and England," he develops his argument for the centrality of his codification project in maintaining order and perpetuating the regimes, both home and abroad. Both essays were intended for domestic consumption as Stephen prepared his audience for his draft of the criminal code for England. He assumed that showing the benefits of codification in India would convince others of its utility at home. Furthermore, he presented the debates about the place of law and power in India as examples of logic that could be transferred to other continents.

The first argument against developing the rule of law in India was that British laws could not be transferred to another locale. This was one of the primary arguments against employing principles of the rule of law in the colonies in the nineteenth century (not to mention one of the arguments against international law today). Stephen replied,

> To wish to put an end to legislation because some laws are not wise, is like wishing to put an end to tailors because some clothes do not fit. To argue that, because some English laws are unsuited for some Indian populations, law in general is not the instrument by which India ought to be governed, is to assume that law is not that which a legislator enacts as such, but a mysterious something which is found in England, and which must be introduced bodily into India, if India is to be governed by law at all.[37]

Stephen then proceeds to illuminate the real reason for the resistance to codification in India. Local officials want to keep power for themselves. He points out that local officials claim populations are ungovernable; officials need maximum discretion in order to keep order. In a variant of this argument, others say that India had always been ruled despotically, and that as inheritors of the previous regimes, the British also should rule despotically. This is an interesting twist on the impulse to honor local traditions, but one that Stephen dismisses as also self-interested. Following Bentham, Stephen argues that having a complex code of laws that no one could understand only empowers lawyers and obfuscates the responsibilities of authorities.

Stephen believed that the population to be governed would be greatly improved by codification as well. First, the code could become a central part of national identification. In "Codification in India and England," Stephen points to the prominence that the US Constitution and the Bill of Rights had in American discourse, and notes a similar dynamic in Scotland. "The whole national character of Scotland is moulded by the Westminster Confession. Its system of divinity gives a complete account of things, human and divine, and a large proportion of Scotchmen used, at all events, to be able to repeat it by heart from end to end, together with its Scripture proofs. What are these but cases of codification?"[38]

Codification allows a country to popularize a knowledge of the law, and once codes are accessible, Stephen argues that they become the subject of argument and discourse, similar to the Kantian idea of judgment. "When the law is divested of all technicalities, stated in simple and natural language, and so arranged as to show the natural relation of different parts of the subject, it becomes not merely intelligible, but deeply interesting to educated men.... I am very much mistaken if that Act is not carefully studied by a large proportion of merchants of the Presidency towns with a definite reference to their daily affairs."[39] Hence the code works to educate the population more generally, a central concern for British elites looking at the entrance of the working classes into the political process. The law is a healthy occupation of public discourse, inculcating robust understanding of the public's need to obey.

Stephen had a vision of a small technocratic elite whose job it would be to construct the legal codes, and also maintain them. The small group was needed in order to promote transparency above all; Stephen wanted codification in order to provide accountability for the exercise of power, but he was not about to endorse a process that would obfuscate the production of law. "We are often told that laws grow and are not made. In fact they are made in a way which has a certain analogy to growth. If we are to use metaphors at all, I should say that laws grow best in the light, and worst when they multiply like mushrooms in a cellar."[40] Once the codes are made in public and with the greatest possibility accountability, they will still need to be maintained. This maintenance would also need to be public. "I would protest against the supposition that the work of codification can ever be final. To suppose that any code will go on by itself forever is like supposing that a railway can be built which will not want repairs. You must have an engineering staff to keep your works in order, when they are made, as well as to make them in the first instance."[41]

The technocratic vision of neutralizing power is decidedly not romanticized. Yet for Stephen it is the obvious solution to a system of government in which the governed and governing classes have little in common. For that reason, it is equally applicable in India and England. If obedience and order is the goal, then codification is the method. When asked to summarize the state of Anglo-Indian Law after the process of codification, Stephen commented:

> If it is asked how the system works in practice, I can only say that it enables a handful of unsympathetic foreigners (I am far from thinking that if they were more sympathetic they would be more

> efficient) to rule justly and firmly about 200,000,000 persons, of many races, languages, and creeds, an in many parts of the country bold, sturdy, warlike ... The Penal Code, the Code of Criminal Procedure, and the institutions which they regulate, are somewhat grim presents for one people to make to another, and are little calculated to excite affection; but are eminently well calculated to protect peaceable men and to beat down wrong-doers, extort respect, and to enforce obedience.[42]

What exactly does it mean to extort respect? Enforce obedience? Law becomes the dictator here, but a depersonalized one that would not engender resentment in the same way as an embodied authority. His codes will rule as despots.

The Codes in India

If Stephen's view of codification was that it needed to reflect and imprint current moral beliefs and practices, it should be no surprise that the codes he implemented worked to cement the racial hierarchies of Indian society, deepen religious distinctions, and ultimately, continue the impunity under which Europeans could act in India. Stephen correctly pointed to the jurisdictional confusion that would lead some to literally get away with murder; codification did little to fundamentally change this fact.

Elizabeth Kolsky's *Colonial Justice in British India* details the violence of white settlers not associated with the Company or the Crown in India, a violence that grew along with their numbers in the nineteenth century. Multiple jurisdictions meant that "non-official Britons" had "practical impunity" from punishment even for egregious crimes. As instances of violence grew, officials correctly perceived the predominance of overt violence could put the entire colonial enterprise at risk. "With law far and London even further away, nonofficials in the India interior posed a persistent threat to the lives of local people and to the stability of the government precisely because of the legal vacuum in which they operated."[43] (I discussed the response to settler criminality in West Africa in the previous chapter and the development of extraterritorial jurisdiction.)

Stephen took the criminal code as his starting point, precisely because of his observed gap between morals and law. Stephen assumed that there was a higher chance of general regard for the laws of the public realm such as forbidding murder, as opposed to provisions about marriage that differed according to religious practice. Regulating the public sphere was the necessary first step before codes could be developed to regulate other arenas of life.

The important thing to realize about Stephen's project of codification was that it was focused above all upon procedures. Certainly, given the status of Anglo-Indian Law, this focus was needed. But the outcomes of the system of justice worried him less than the methods by which they were derived. Bentham's version of codification was to arrange an entire legal universe from scratch that would be consistent, orderly, and just. Stephen's version of codification was to eliminate redundancies or inconsistencies in existing laws and to clarify definitions, procedures, and logics. Far from Bentham's legal idealism, Stephen approached codification with the spirit of a rigorous editor. He developed the Indian Contract Act and the Indian Evidence Act, and finished the Native Marriage Act started by Henry Maine, his predecessor.

In 1855, the second Indian criminal law commissions suggested making one system of trial and jury for all inhabitants of India regardless of race or nationality, but this proposal was defeated by the logic of racial superiority. In fact, the rule of law in this case meant having the best possible judge placed in the position of power. Having Indians serve as judges would *defeat* the rule of law: J. M. Macleod argued that placing a native on the appellate court would rob Indians of the benefit of the rule of law, "the benefit of the integrity and intelligence of the gentlemen sent from England to rule over them."[44] Emerging even before Plessy v. Ferguson (1896) was a doctrine of separate but equal in British India. The idea was that British citizens had long been accustomed to liberty and equality, but Indians were products of oriental despotism and would thereby need to have different legal provisions. In a country accustomed to caste, ideas of equality would be dangerously out of step with the "general morality" of the population. One early Indian nationalist observed, "The Goddess of British Justice, though blind, is able to distinguish unmistakably, black from white."[45]

Stephen accepted the diversity of moral aptitude among European settlers, Indian natives, and official British representatives as a scientific fact, and created a code to separate the three. For instance, the Code of Criminal Procedure ascribed different procedures for Indian and European populations. Sure enough, the procedures were unified into a singular code which was clearer, but the distinct protocols remained.

> The amended Code of Criminal Procedure (1872) barred Indian judges and magistrates from trying European British-born subjects in the *mofussil*. No magistrate, Sessions judge, or justice of the peace was permitted to inquire into a complaint or try a case against a European British-born subject unless he himself was a European British-born subject.[46]

Interestingly, the logic behind this prohibition was that Indian judges would certainly take the opportunity to exact vengeance upon the conquerors of their country. "He [the Indian magistrate] might not designedly give an unfair judgment, but I believe that with many, the bias would be against the European, and that when placed in a position of momentary power over him, they would feel pleasure in asserting that power to his disadvantage."[47] Even judges were not exempt from the accusation of irrationality leveled against Indians. Stephen's code ultimately reflected and reinscribed racial hierarchies and tensions over power disparities *within* its clear procedures. When he left India in 1872, he congratulated himself on having completed the codification of Indian law.

The public debate around the Ilbert Bill of 1883, eleven years later, shows how deeply entrenched racial privilege was in the legal arena after Stephen's tenure. The Ilbert Bill was an attempt to eliminate some of the racialized provisions in the criminal code and bring more equality to the proceedings. In response to the idea that Indian judges who had been educated in England might be able to pass judgment on Europeans, others countered, "Do you think that Native judges will by three or four years' residence in England become so Europeanized in nature and in character, that they will be able to judge as well in false charges against Europeans as if they themselves were Europeans?"[48] Equality was an empty ideal in a country with a caste system; it was utterly meaningless as a legal aspiration. Taking jurisprudence as a social science meant including current hierarchies within codification.

Ranabir Samaddar has investigated the implications of the Indian Evidence Act as it was written by Stephen. He argues that the seemingly simplistic categories of personhood, proof, and fact articulated by the Indian Evidence Act "achieved a stupendous feat: they succeeded in setting up the individual as a legal category to be inspected, monitored and judged on the basis of a code by a new form of power, judicial power, from then on."[49] This statement corroborates entirely with Stephen's vision that his codification would replace the violent despotism of colonial rule with a procedural system, based upon rules, self-interest, and rationality. It is important to recognize that even as the codes separated different populations according to contemporary racial hierarchies, the codes were all-inclusive. In order to achieve stability of colonial rule, all subjects needed to be constituted as rational agents who could identify and enact their self-interest. To have a criminal code indicates that even those who refuse to operate within the norms of the society can be considered rational agents who engage in calculations of self-interest. Samaddar proclaims,

> Thus came into operation on 1 January 1862 the Act XXV of 1861, better known as the Indian Criminal Procedure Code. Reason henceforth ordained equality before the procedure of law: the peasant could now approach the law; the procedure became detailed and, hence, time-consuming and expensive; fear of god now gave way to fear of law. All in all, the age of rule of law in coping with criminality had begun.[50]

The important aspect of Samaddar's observations are that *procedure* created the rationality then ascribed to everyone who appeared in the court. Outcomes and assumptions were not the basis of this form of equality. Rule of law came to mean equality, hence inclusiveness, of legal proceduralism. Furthermore, facts, evidence, and proof could only be produced and recognized through proper procedures. British rule was finally modern, and thoroughly legal.

Codification, the British Empire, and International Law

Codification in the colonies was a project largely undertaken in the last half of the nineteenth century, which was also the start of a new era of law in the international context. The international legal system played an essential role in the colonial enterprise, as Gerrit Gong has explained in *The Standard of "Civilization" in International Society.* Gong's argument is an interesting inversion of Carl Schmitt's legal geography in *The Nomos of the Earth.* Schmitt points out how colonial powers divided the world in order to demarcate where rules regulating conquest, the conduct of war, and respect for sovereignty would be obeyed and where they would not. Schmitt points out how originally these spatial logics made it possible for powers supposedly contained by law to rape, pillage, and slaughter in places that existed outside the "civilized world." Gong's argument focuses on a later period, the second half of the nineteenth century, when the international legal order was moving toward a universally inclusive vision of legality. Once again, the globe was partitioned, this time in a taxonomy developed by James Lorimer, into three categories: civilized, barbarous, and savage. Accompanying this taxonomy was a largely juridical codification of what made a country eligible to be placed into each of the categories. The alteration is crucial. Before, laws were suspended or followed based upon the territory; by the end of the nineteenth century, territories were defined by the laws that they followed.

Gong points out part of this transformation had to do with the increased circulation of European colonizers throughout the globe. "The first step of the standard's emergence was the codification of its requirements, for example, the assumption that the life, liberty, dignity, and property of European nationals would be protected in non-European settings. Initially implicit in the customary practice of the European states-system, these assumptions were not necessarily shared by all non-European countries."[51] As an examination of the jurisprudence of the Colonial Office in the early nineteenth century demonstrated, there was a great deal of confusion about what laws were applied to which populations in which colonies, so the ambiguity that Gong points out is not confined to non-European powers.

Schmitt was certainly right that the suspension of laws made colonial primitive accumulation "legal," even as international rule of law provided protections for European powers from one another.[52] But other commentators have observed how British colonial ideology in the eighteenth century developed in such a way as to both condone and even encourage disparate practices at home and in the world. David Armitage has precisely detailed the emerging conceptualizations of the British Empire in the eighteenth century. "Protestantism, oceanic commerce and mastery of the seas provided bastions to protect the freedom of inhabitants of the British Empire. That freedom found its institutional expression in Parliament, the law, property and rights, all of which were exported throughout the British Atlantic world. Such freedom also allowed the British, uniquely, to combine the classically incompatible ideals of liberty and Empire."[53]

This bifurcation of practice and beliefs according to location started to break down in the nineteenth century, causing the larger crisis of British authority that was reflected in the Hastings trial and later in the Governor Eyre investigation. These cases made it clear that the British would suspend laws in one arena and follow them in another. Of course, there were concerns about hypocrisy. But there was a larger sense that the workable dualism of British freedom at home and empire abroad was becoming more difficult to manage. Some critics articulated the fear that the despotism either inherent in the Empire, or the connections that the Empire made with more despotic societies would come to infect British freedom. Richard Cobden asked in 1860, "Is it not just possible that we may become corrupted at home by the reaction of arbitrary political maxims in the East upon our domestic politics, just as Greece and Rome were demoralized by their contact with Asia?"[54]

So we could say the realities of empire started to catch up to its ideologies. There was no longer any neat division between British subjects and those others subject to British rule as the increasingly complicated legal entanglements testify. But there is another argument, that at this juncture of colonization, the lack of legal clarity was becoming a hindrance, not an aid, to the imperialist project. Law was needed to develop more certainty for advanced forms of colonial appropriation and the actors who were engaged in it. The reaches of the Empire were expanding, and a universal code needed to emerge in order to serve the imperialistic project. Their rule of law needed to be transparent and routine, *particularly* in the colonies where economic possibilities were dizzying but still tenuous. Smith has argued that the 1833 Charter Act "functioned as the legislative foundation for the British government's policy of transforming the subcontinent from being a source of land rent revenues and some trade into a huge market of traders and consumers, capable of absorbing much of the vast manufacturing capacity generated by Britain's accelerating Industrial Revolution."[55] The colonies were also the proving ground for how codes of law could be moved from one locale to another, providing the example for other countries to fall in line. Before they could accuse other countries of being barbaric because of their codes of law, they themselves needed to fulfill the legal practices that would characterize them as civilized. This was the start of developing a global system with recognizable, predictable legal practices supporting capital accumulation.

Stephen played a crucial role in developing this universalistic vision of a code of laws, both at home and abroad. The ghost of Bentham accompanied him. What does it mean that his schemas for codification succeeded in British colonies and failed at home? This fact should tell us much about the political subtexts of something as dry and procedural as legal codification. Though I have emphasized the economic context which made achieving codification appealing at this point in colonization, I cannot overlook the modernization of political institutions. Lindsay Farmer, historian of English codification debates, observed, "These codes mark the transition to the modern legal and political order; the abstract juridical subject is moved to the center of the law, and the relationship between the juridical individual and the constitutional state is coded as finite and self-centered rendering of possibilities."[56] In England, codification was conceived as a way of guaranteeing the rights of individuals who would no longer be subject to the whims of judges or dependent upon lawyers. It was the law's intermediaries that needed to be eliminated; let individuals meet the law on their own defects or virtues.

If codification was really about empowerment of individuals and curtailing elites, it is puzzling why it succeeded in India and failed in England. In her study of Henry Maine, Karuna Mantena describes the Indian Penal Code "as a peculiar anomaly."[57] Indeed, why would the

British want to empower Indians more than themselves? There must be another way of understanding what was at stake in codification.

Codification, particularly of the criminal law, treats all subjects as potential criminals. The logic of codification assumes that rational actors will decided to avoid criminal violations, but in every society not everyone will be rational. Criminal codification then implies an inevitable ungovernability of part of a population. But codification, particularly in the words of Bentham, also points out the unreliability of the rulers, the judges. While the colonial criminal codes give the initial impression of native populations as criminal, further investigation shows that colonial powers are also being accused of improper behavior. For James Fitzjames Stephen, the tyranny evidenced in the colonies was part of what drove him to embrace codification as his life's work. He used the example of India to try and shame the British public out of their complacency and embrace modernization of British rule.

> To compare the Indian Penal Code with English criminal law is like comparing cosmos with chaos. Any intelligent person interested in the subject could get a very distinct and correct notion of Indian criminal law in a few hours from the Penal Code. I appeal to you to imagine the state of mind of a man who should try and read straight through the very best of English books on criminal law.[58]

Codification, so the hope goes, will make virtue, reason, and power irrelevant for both ruler and ruled. However, its claims for universalism and omniscience point to the inability to simultaneously control populations *and* government representatives. Codification reflects a cycle of accusation, one that moves dialectically between unruly subjects and tyrannical rulers. Yet it attempts to solve this same dynamic by developing a system of misrecognition of colonial subjects. All Indians were suspect; even those who were trained as judges. All British subjects needed to be given the benefit of the doubt, which is why codification did not succeed in passing in England while it did in the colonies. In short, the British modernized the law by creating an implicit accusation of the colonial subject; they were unwilling to do so in England because they themselves could be captured by this apparatus.

To understand why codification became central in this moment in British colonial history, we can reflect upon the importance of law in the development of the United Kingdom during the eighteenth century. With industrialization came social change, and the ruling class needed new definitions, processes, and procedures in order to maintain order and—not inconsequentially—their own privileges. E. P. Thompson's classic study *Whigs and Hunters: The Origin of the Black Act* concludes with a rumination upon the rule of law during this period of change. Just because the law remained an instrument of the ruling class does not mean that it exists only as an ideological scrim. Because of changing social relations, law was needed to bolster the legitimacy of the ruling class to a whole new extent. As Thompson argues, only to the extent that law does upon occasion serve justice can it act as an ideological front for the powers that be. Bolstering political order during times of economic and social change requires that the political elites also appear to be at least marginally bound by the law themselves. The British learned this lesson at home, and exported it to the colonies. Economic shifts in British imperial practices and concerns about the legitimacy of British rule meant that visible commitment to the rule of law was necessary.

I agree with Thompson that the presence of the law exceeds its ideological purpose. "It is true that in history the law can be seen to mediate and to legitimize existent class relations and mask ulterior injustice. But this mediation, through the forms of law, is something quite distinct from the exercise of unmediated force. The forms and rhetoric of law acquire a distinct identity which may, on accession, inhibit power and afford some protection to the powerless."[59] Codification in the colonies was a response to British recognition of the need to bolster their ideological claims that they were importing the rule of law to their colonies. James Stephen's version of serving the rule of law that included respecting local traditions, overlaying jurisdictions, sources of sovereignty and very distinct populations was a messy enterprise that, ironically enough, most likely undermined the *ideological* position of colonial law. James Fitzjames Stephen's embrace of the rule of law as codification made the law clear, accessible, and hence more available for ideological deployment. The father strove and failed for the reality of the rule of law, the son embraced the utlity of appearance.

This movement did not make the colonial rule of the British any more substantially just. In fact, the emphasis upon codification is a subterfuge in many ways, because it focuses exclusively upon procedures rather than outcomes, traditions, or genuine complexities. Yet, just as Thompson pointed out that the law has an existence beyond ideological façade with sometimes surprising impact, we can see that Stephen's codes took on a life of their own as they were scattered around the globe.

Epilogue

Stephen's claim that the codification effort would serve to educate the population seemed absurd and far-fetched, but perhaps this was more of a success than one would assume. Sayijat Ray's 1956 film, *The Philosopher's Stone*, begins with a portly bank clerk in his fifties receiving a layoff notice from his firm. Pushed off the crowded streetcars of Calcutta, unable to afford a taxi, he walks home in the rain becoming drenched under his tattered umbrella. In the park where he stops for a respite, he finds a shiny, black, egg-shaped stone that has the ability to turn any metal into gold. The clerk discovers this wondrous capacity and soon is living in a mansion at the edge of town and delivering large gifts to different charities who fete him for his cultural contributions. Ray's film retells the Midas story, but an interesting subtext appears in the film. Though the clerk is a devout man, his initial concern is not that he might anger the gods by taking some of their magical powers. Instead, he worries what the police will say if they find out he is creating gold. At one point in the film, he cites two different numbers from the Indian Penal Code in a conversation with his wife about the consequences of his use of the stone. When the former clerk gives the stone to his secretary as he hastily flees town, one instruction accompanies the gift: "The most important thing is—if the police ask for it, you must give it to them."

Ray's film is largely a fable about the fantasies of middle-class enrichment, but it also demonstrates the centrality of law and policing in newly independent India as the self-evident limit on the powers of man—whether acquired through supernatural means or not. Even something as intangible as the vicissitudes of fate or the whims of deities could be controlled—had to be controlled—by the penal code. Ray was surely involved in gentle satire here, that even the force of the Gods needed to be bound by law. Yet even as satire it reflects the centrality of law in organizing the newly independent India. The film reflects the ideological success of Stephen's project, to turn the penal code of law into a "compulsory gospel, which allows no dissent." Stephen's project was more successful than he could have dreamed; even the divine could be subject to the disciplinary regime.

As reflected in the film, Stephen's codification in India was marvelously successful in some regards, as opposed to his efforts at home. And yet, as difficult as it was to write the code for Indian law, it was impossible to foresee exactly how it would work.[60] Of course, this was supposed to be the strength of codification, to provide distance between the confusing jumble of colonial reality and the imperative to order. "Colonial governments assumed that the regulatory power of law was a significant means of taming, disciplining, and rendering legible cultural practices inscrutable to colonial officials on the ground."[61] Law was to be constant, and unwavering when colonial officials could not be.

Yet there was a flexibility included in the codes as well for executive discretion. J. F. Stephen had not forgotten the lessons of the Jamaica Committee, and his sympathies were firmly in line with the colonial officials and their difficult task of creating order. Law and force were not incompatible in his view—quite the contrary, law is only effective because it was backed with an enormous reservoir of executive power. Stephen observed, "To say that the law of force is abandoned because force is regular, unopposed, and beneficially exercised, is to say that night and day are now such well-established institutions that the sun and moon are mere superfluities."[62] Stephen did not think that law was going to eliminate the need for colonial violence, but rather that colonial violence was a necessary underpinning for the codification of law. Furthermore, as Radika Singha has recently observed, within the structure of Stephen's codification there remained a large purview for executive discretion.[63] Ideally, colonial officials would not have to resort to violence as occurred in Jamaica, but they would also remain in some essential ways above the regular procedures of the law.

But ultimately, perhaps it was the system of evidence put into place by Stephen that has proven to be just as problematic as anything else. After all, having proper procedure in a court means that it produces what is considered facts, evidence, and proof. But what happens when there is an increasing gap between the facts that are produced by the courts and the experiences of those who live in the country? "The problem, of course, begins with the day-to-day expediency which dictates the rules of governance to the extent that great crimes may pass unpunished or waves of murders produce no 'evidence' before the courts, and therefore remain unaccounted for through ages; where disorders reappear with food riots, communal riots, excise riots, militia orgies, gang robberies, endemic and often violent smuggling."[64] The accusatory finger now points at cumbersome legal procedures and rules of evidence, the legal system that cannot "see" the world it is supposed to regulate. This is the observation that has led to more recent attempts to restructure the penal codes in India, the subject of the next chapter.

5

Macaulay to Malimath

Punishment and the Police in India

> It is not torture of the high European sort ... Indian torture is ready, impromptu, ingenious, cheap, annoying, disgusting, revolting and petty in the extreme.
>
> —*The Times*, September 3, 1855

THE ABUSE OF POWER ON the part of the police in India is a consistent theme throughout the country's colonial and postcolonial history and includes, most notoriously, the suspicion that the police chose not to pursue the group attempting to assassinate Mohandas Gandhi.[1] This sense of impunity on the part of the police, in combination with the fact that almost 70% of prisoners in India's jails have not been tried for any crime, suggests that the rule of law is only sporadically enforced or utilized in punishment.[2] There appears to be a fundamental separation between the stated values of the legal system and the police, so much so that David Arnold claimed that "the 'rule of law' is, therefore, an inappropriate context for an examination of police power."[3] On the contrary, I argue that the disjunction between the stated support for the rule of law and the continuation of police impunity is worth attending to.

It is easy to draw a direct line between the colonial implementation of the rule of law and its accompanying system of policing, and contemporary debates about policing and the rule of law in India today. The last chapter explained the movement to codify the laws and procedures in the British Empire in the 1860s and their subsequent dissemination across continents and locales. Though the traces of these codes remain in place across the globe today, few former colonies have left the British colonial legal codes in as undisturbed a state as India. Given the centrality of the codes in the Indian imagination, and their relatively unaltered state, India is an excellent place to examine the contemporary legacies of the colonial origins of the rule of law. Admittedly, the notorious violence and corruption of the police in India is in some ways a uniquely spectacular example of the rule of law failing to curb the abuse of state power. Nonetheless, the debates about criminal justice reform in recent years allow a consideration of the residue that remains attached to the rule of law in postcolonial contexts. There are many places in the world where attempts to use the rule of law to curb abuses of state power have failed. But India is one of the only cases that actively debates the criminal codes with a sharp awareness of their colonial origins. As my later discussion of the Malimath Report will demonstrate, the fact that the codes are a "foreign" implant deeply influences perspectives upon them.

The argument of this chapter builds upon the excellent, extensive, and growing research about policing and colonial power in British India, as well as investigations of current problems of policing in India. The basic facts established by these other researchers provide the background for this inquiry, which is focused upon investigating contemporary experiences, perceptions, and invocations of the rule of law as it was established under colonial administration. It is the simultaneous presence of a discourse of the rule of law and the routine abuse of police power that interests me. It would seem that two forces—police violence and the rule of law—have reached an impasse for at least 150 years; their theoretically incompatible co-existence is firmly entrenched. I would argue this tension is one instance where we can see how the circulation of the rule of law via British colonialism inflects postcolonial political regimes.

This chapter will explore this tension between law and policing in India, both as it originated during colonial rule and in the attempts to reform policing in contemporary India. As the last chapter indicated, I believe the British project to codify laws within their colonies was largely a defensive move in response to well-publicized abuses on the part of colonial administrators. But policing was an integral element of the British colonial system before this time. Furthermore, the use of the police force in India became a model for other colonies in the Empire.

The deployment of police to create order as opposed to investigate crimes was a system that was "perfected in India."[4] What this means is that the police were largely removed from enforcing and employing the rule of law through criminal investigations and the collection of evidence. Instead they were used to extort obedience.

The colonial police were considered necessary agents of coercion to maximize British control, and the fact that they were drawn from indigenous populations only created an additional logic for the necessity of British rule. The British used the police to find criminals, extort confessions, raise revenue, and enforce British rule. When the police were "caught" engaging in interpersonal violence—that is, when their actions were made publically visible—their violence was considered just another proof of the need for British rule. The instantiation of this cycle in early British colonial rule through the criminal code written by Macaulay and implemented by J. F. Stephen is the subject of this chapter. The Police Act of 1861 and the Indian Evidence Act were the companion pieces of legislation that were intended to render India "governable" through modern methods. Yet older forms of direct physical coercion were also incorporated into the system through policing.

This inquiry will conclude by examining some of the recent attempts to reform the Codes of Criminal Procedure and how postcolonial political dynamics inflect these reforms. The Malimath Commission suggested a number of systematic reforms to the Indian Criminal Code in 2004. Many of these reforms attempt to resolve the lacuna between law and police practice, but do so in a way that is particularly troublesome and, I believe, have an odd resemblance to the gaps between policing and law that were evident under British rule.

Colonial Legacies: The Indian Penal Code of 1860

> The true secret of government is to give absolute power to a vigorous man, and leave him to be a law in himself.
>
> —James Fitzjames Stephen

Liberal individualism takes the rational judgment of individuals as its central axiom, and offers the law as a clear marker of what behaviors shall be rewarded and punished. Importing this worldview into a region that was perceived as decisively lacking in rational individualism and what would have been recognized as moral judgment is a well-documented problem of colonialism.[5] Do you establish clear laws and then punish transgressors until their behavior falls in line? In other words, can order be used as a precursor to the larger goal of self-regulation? Or do you attempt to teach individualism and judgment in the hopes that the population will ultimately become self-legislating and self-regulating and follow the patterns of governance outlined as an ideal by Stephen in the passage above? The British, like other colonial powers, lacked any coherent approach to their project, as evidenced by the colonial observers at the time who varied greatly in their characterizations of the Indian capacity for regulation, of themselves and one another. (They were fairly consistent in their rejection of the possibility that Indians might be able to regulate Europeans, however.)

Sir Thomas Munro embodies some of the conundrums of how to understand British law in India: Is it a tool to educate the population toward the aim of self-rule, or an instrument to impose colonial order, which ultimately produces the wealth, class consciousness, and social structure to support what will eventually become indigenous governance? The former vision has a faith in the capacity of individuals to immediately comprehend and begin to abide by the rule of law once they are exposed to it; the second vision assumes that certain educational, social, and economic preconditions must be established before self-governance and the rule of law can be generated from the local population. In a statement from 1824, "On the Ultimate Aim of British Rule in India," Munro, then governor of Madras, stated that the British need to look at their presence in India as a permanent arrangement "until the natives shall at some future age have abandoned most of their superstitions and prejudices and become sufficiently enlightened." Yet he also rails against the policies of the regime that refuses any administrative capacity for the local population, seeming to believe that the natives will never become sufficiently enlightened unless they are given more responsibility. It should be noted the amount of trust placed in the local population is measured by whether they are allowed to administer punishment.

> With what can we talk of our paternal government if we exclude the natives from every important office, and say, as we did till very lately,

> that in a country containing 150,000,000 inhabitants no man but a European shall be entrusted with so much authority as to order the punishment of a single stroke of rattan?[6]

If punishment is to teach self-regulation, it is not surprising that the penal code and its administration becomes an important element in understanding the inherent tensions in the stated goal of "bringing" self-government to India.

When the British came to India, they found that Muslim criminal law had replaced Hindu criminal law everywhere the Muslims had been successful in establishing control. One might expect that as soon as the East India Company arrived, they would begin to alter the criminal code, but not until 1790 was there a concerted attempt to change the criminal code of India, though Warren Hastings, the administrator in Bengal, did make some reforms of the existing codes. In 1793, the Cornwallis Code modified Muslim criminal law, and the code was adopted initially in Bengal, then in Madras and Bombay—the presidential states in India. Traditional Muslim law remained intact in all other areas. Interestingly, in 1832 the British argued that because not all Indians were Muslim, it was unjust for everyone to be subject to a code of law that was linked to the Islamic faith. From this point, Hindus could demand to be tried for crimes under an alternative code, as could Europeans. Once the standard of a singular criminal code was broken, during the next thirty years, the presidential regions—Madras, Bengal, Bombay, Punjab—saw a greater divergence between regional punishment codes and practices that were largely adopted to suit the local groups' religious codes. Hindus, Sikhs, Muslims, and Europeans contributed to a legal pluralism that one observer commented was "utter chaos and confusion."[7] George Campbell commented, "Our criminal law is very much a patchwork made up of pieces engrafted at all times and seasons on a ground nearly covered and obliterated … the general result is that all the worst and most common crimes are satisfactorily provided for by special enactments but that there is a very great want of definition, accuracy and uniformity as to the miscellaneous offences … it wants remodelling, classification and codification."[8] In short, the British created the chaotic criminal code which some observers blamed upon the indigenous population, but then ultimately offered a solution.

The project of codifying the Indian legal system developed over a great period of time and was reluctantly taken on as a project, in contrast to the image of English genius descending upon the subcontinent like a flashing vision. James Fitzjames Stephen commented in 1872:

> It has often been said, and with more truth and sincerity than many people suppose, that political power, and especially the responsibility of all direct government of India, was forced on the Company, and afterwards on the Crown, by the course of events, and to a great extent against their will. It is quite certain that the whole history of empire shows the greatest reluctance on the part of its rulers to interfere with the laws, the habits, and the daily life of their subjects in any case in which they could possibly help it.[9]

Into this breach came Lord Macaulay, who was made chair of the first Law Commission of India in 1834.[10] For the next three years, he and his committee labored to produce a unified code of law, providing absolute unity for the subcontinent. The code was hailed as brilliant; however, the draft languished under opposition to such a drastic change. The forces of inertia won out until the Insurrection of 1857. The bloodshed revived English interest in law and governability in India. Sir Barnes Peacock made some slight amendments, and the code was finally adopted as law in 1860.

The Indian Penal Code is complete, yet concise. It elaborates different types of crime and criminals, providing clear guidelines for distinguishing the circumstantial, habitual, and career criminal so punishment can be tailored to either reforming and reintegrating the offender into society or segregating the criminal from society. Yet even though the Penal Code of 1860 is elegant enough to be applicable to cybercrimes in the twenty-first century, it was judged to be unable to deal with the burgeoning independence movement at the start of the twentieth century. In response to mass organizing, the Indian Sedition Committee was formed and recommended the normal judicial procedures in the Anarchical and Revolutionary Crimes Act of 1919, otherwise known as the Rowlatt Act. One commentator has noted, "The Rowlatt Committee ... arrived at the conclusion that the ordinary criminal law was not adequate to deal with the cases of revolutionary crime."[11] It is important to consider the modifications of the Rowlatt

Act, as they are similar to some modifications recently suggested by the Malimath Committee in 2004. The normal mechanisms of trials were suspended and three judges working together formed a tribunal that could rule on cases, and more lenient rules of evidence were allowed. There was no right to appeal any decision in cases of sedition, though all three judges had to unanimously agree for a death sentence to be administered. In cases of sedition, legal counsel was no longer a right, and suspects could be held for a period of up to three years with the approval of a committee of three commissioners. The Rowlatt Act made it possible for the British to jail all known Indian Congress Party members after they proclaimed the "Quit India" resolution in 1942.

Macaulay's criminal code and the Rowlatt Act were adopted in toto in the Indian National Constitution. This is a particularly interesting contrast with another postcolonial case study that I presented in *Punishment and Political Order*: that of the United States. Punishment and colonialism have a very particular history, as transport of convicts was one of the ways that Great Britain sought to populate their colonies with those of Anglo heritage. The penal code of England during the seventeenth century was harsh, and offering transport as an alternative to death was seen as convenient for purposes of peopling territories, as well as being more humane, more thrifty, and far easier than reforming the entire criminal code. It was horror at what they called "the sanguinary criminal codes" of Britain that led the Quakers to prioritize reformation of the criminal code in Pennsylvania. It was in fact, the first task of the new Pennsylvania legislature to suspend the existing criminal code. What emerged is the well-known Quaker experiment of the penitentiary.

It is important to recognize this in its proper postcolonial context: the new penal code and its penitentiary clearly established that the United States was going to be a regime that respected individual rights and human dignity. In *The Rights of Man*, Thomas Paine argued, "Lay then the axe to the root, and teach governments humanity. It is their sanguinary punishments which corrupt mankind."[12] Not only did brutal state punishment reveal the untempered exercise of sovereign prerogative, it also created a population that was denied the capacities to self-govern through the criminal code. Excessive punishment only encouraged rebellion against authority without generating the capacities for self-regulation.

Early democratic theorists wanted a form of punishment that would actually promote self-regulation rather than demonstrate its limits. Reforming the penal regime was then considered an essential part of developing a truly democratic society; this was an impulse that was shared by France, as evidenced by the fact the government sent Alexis de Tocqueville to the United States to study its penal system.[13] While it is evident that the United States has not maintained this commitment to democracy through its penal system today, it is an interesting moment of founding whereby the instruments of law and administration of justice were reimagined and thereby transformed into tools that became part of the new nation's self-conception.

The contrast with India's movement into independence could not be any greater. The fact that there was no perceived need to amend this aspect of the law after independence is even more striking given Gandhi's bleak assessment of the structure of English law and governance: "Parliaments are really emblems of slavery."[14] Both leaders of the Nationalist movement, Gandhi and Nehru, were trained as lawyers and might be expected to perceive of the relationship between legal codification and political rule.

Furthermore, both Gandhi and Nehru spent long periods of time in prison under the auspices of the Indian Penal Code. Nehru spent more than ten years of his life in prison. Like Gandhi, he seemed to find his time in prison accommodating for personal growth. Nehru wrote several long volumes while in jail, including a history of India, his lengthy autobiography, and an economic analysis of Indian history, in addition to mastering the art of yoga in his cell. Without a doubt, a primary reason for not wanting to reform the penal code and its provisions for dealing with sedition was the fact that it was clearly a useful tool for the British in suppressing oppositional movements.

Take for example, Section 113 of the penal code, written by Macaulay in 1837. It was inexplicably not included in the adoption of the code of 1860 but was added ten years later in 1870. The logic behind the severe punishments and lack of restraint in cases of potential treason or subversion are fascinating:

> State crimes, especially the most heinous and formidable state crimes, have this peculiarity, that if they are successfully committed, the criminal is almost always secure from punishment. The murderer is

> in greater danger after his victim is dispatched than before. But the rebel is out of danger as soon as he has subverted the Government. As the penal law is impotent against a successful rebel, it is consequently necessary that it should be made strong and sharp against the first beginnings of rebellion, against treasonable designs which have been carried no further than plots and preparations.[15]

The usual causality between guilt and punishment is bizarrely inverted here; punishment must precede the crime, because the treasonous act could eliminate the means of punishment. It is clear why such a provision might prove invaluable for consolidating the sovereignty of the new national government in a country besieged by partition, suspicion of different groups, regional tensions, and a dazzling plurality of languages, practices, and beliefs. Rather than use the rule of law as a tool for developing the capacities of the citizenry, the British largely envisioned law as a tool for creating stability in the current regime. This trend continues with the anti-terrorist regulations that condone preventative detention today. The same laws that were used to try and prevent the birth of an independent India are the very ones that are used to prevent the country's "murder" today.[16]

Furthermore, the division between armed police and those who are empowered to investigate crimes persists. Remarkably, as fear of crime and disorder accelerate, armed police are offered as the solution. But the number of police who can investigate crimes remains comparatively small. Since independence, "all governments have seen fit to continue expanding the armed police battalions. This importance to specialized armed units has been at the cost of indifference to the investigative wings of the police."[17]

Colonialism and Policing

> To subdue the wild Mahrattas, to conquer the stalwart Sikhs and enroll then under our banner, that they might fight in our armies along with the haughty Rajpoot, the proud Mahometan of the north, and the trans-frontier Yusufzai, was a more imposing achievement than is suggested by the term "Police."
>
> —Sir Edmund Cox

While the machine gun has been touted as the source of English dominance around the world, more credit needs to be given to their system of policing. Before British administration of India, a variety of local systems of policing were in place, varying according to the region. There were village systems, whereby members of a lower caste were made responsible for all crimes committed, and in return for their efforts they were given a living by the rest of the village. These positions were often hereditary.[18] Another tradition was that of the *kavalkars*, who were responsible for a larger territory and appointed from above rather than selected from below, more closely resembling the feudal system of policing. Kavalkars asked for payment in return for safety; in British eyes, they resembled formal thuggery rather than policing. Lord Cornwallis made some attempt to extirpate these practices with the development of *daroghahs*, appointed commissioners responsible for twenty square miles with a small coterie of assistants also given formal titles. There were three ranks of officers (*daroghah, muharrir*, and *jamadar*) who were to turn all apprehended suspects over to the local British magistrate for judgment and punishment.[19] Crime increased drastically with the demise of the indigenous systems and the failure of the *daroghah* system. In 1817, Thomas Munro, who was to be appointed governor of Madras in 1820, argued that the village system was more useful to the British aim of colonial order.

> Our situation, as foreigners, renders a regular village establishment more important to us than native government; our inexperience, and our ignorance of the circumstances of people, make it more necessary for us to seek the aid of regular establishments to direct the internal affairs of the country, and our security requires that we should have a body of headmen of villages interested in supporting our dominion.[20]

Munro's argument is insightful. What happens when you empower a segment of society that does not have loyalty to either the population they are regulating or the parties in whose name they regulate?

Policing became the method by which colonial administrators were able to "order" a population and terrain that was simply bewildering to recent comers. Sir Edmund Cox's description is intended to inspire a romantic vision of the effort to build a police force that reported to the British administration. But it is also a reminder of how immense the task appeared, and how tenuous the ability to muster the illusion of control actually was.[21] As Stephen remarked in regard to the development of law in India,

> For my own part, I know just enough of the country to feel bound to say that no one who has not been in India can have the faintest conception of the enormous magnitude of the task which we have taken upon ourselves, or of the unspeakable difficulties by which it is encumbered. The wonder is, not that holes can be picked in the institutions and laws by which we have governed India, but that we have governed India at all.[22]

In 1855, a two-volume report, the *Report of the Commissioners for the Investigation of Alleged Cases of Torture in the Madras Presidency*, was published and circulated with graphic accounts of routinized police violence. As part of their charge to conduct investigations and take confessions—a necessity because of the frequent linguistic gaps between the accused and the magistrate—police officers were using physical coercion. These confessions would then be produced as evidence that in turn was used to convict the accused. However these policing efforts went beyond "rounding up the usual suspects" and involved creating evidence, torture to extract confessions, sodomy, and killing suspects.

The magistrates in India were quick to place blame upon the brutal tendencies of the system before their arrival. Alexander Campbell explained, "Under the native governments which preceded us at Madras, the universal object of every police officer was to obtain a confession from the prisoner with a view to his conviction of any offense; and not withstanding every endeavor of our European tribunals to put an end to this system, frequent instances have come before all our criminal tribunals of its use."[23]

Though the Madras Report was deeply embarrassing to the British in that it displayed the systemic violence that was inherent in the colonial regime in India, it also provided a rationale and convenient escape for the magistrates. The violence could be blamed upon the police, who were Indians. This further proved the inability of the Indians to govern themselves and the inherent superiority of British justice. Such practices were blamed upon the residue of native practices that had yet to be eradicated by the British, though they claimed they were certainly trying. The Madras Report observes, "The whole cry of the people, which has come before us, is to save them from the cruelties of their fellow natives, not from the effects of unkindness or indifference on the part of the European officers of Government."[24]

Yet it also appears that police brutality can be linked to the East India Company's need for more revenue. At the start of the nineteenth century, trade was decreasing, and the administrative needs of the Company were increasing. "British rule was distinguished from its predecessors by its more ambitious appetite. British revenue expectations were upwards of fifty percent of the gross produce of the land as compared to approximately thirty percent in the case of previous regimes."[25] Prices of crops kept falling, and eventually peasants were driven to moneylenders to pay their taxes. Revenue needed to be raised from the peasant population, the equivalent of drawing blood from a stone. Physical coercion was the surest way of accomplishing this. Douglas Peers's research from the first half of the nineteenth century in Madras concluded, "Torture appears to have been used primarily in revenue collection."[26] This may help account for the fact that "between 1806 and 1855, the superior criminal court in Madras, the *Faujdari Adalat*, issued no less than ten circulars designed to check the use of torture and other questionable practices within the police force."[27] The only lining in this storm cloud is that the methods of torture for revenue extraction were more mild than those used in extracting confessions. After all, the future working and tax-paying capacity of the peasant needed to be secured, not jeopardized.

In the House of Lords on April 14, 1856, there was a lively debate about the appropriate response to the revelations of torture in Madras. The Earl of Albemarle expressed outrage, listing in graphic detail the different kinds of torture that were described in the report as a method of forcing his peers into action. His conclusion was that the rents demanded by the British and extracted by the police in Madras were simply too high, "When rent could only be obtained by means of torture, it might safely be assumed that the land was rented too high."[28] The Duke of Argyll then urged swift and decisive action in order to protect the honor of the British government among "other countries of Europe" who would take the report as evidence of their inhumanity. He then contrasts the natural abhorrence that Europeans would feel for such practices with the placid acceptance of torture in India by uninformed minds.

The Marquess of Clanricarde makes a devastating observation, asking what the report reveals about the status of British sovereignty and the East India Company: Is either entity actually in control of things in India? "He could believe it possible that the Governors who were sent out to India were ignorant of these practices, but it was difficult to say whether it were a greater shame to be ignorant, or to be cognizant, of their existence."[29] The fact that the East India Company denied knowledge of the practice demonstrated ineptitude it if were true, and corruption if it was not.

In a fascinating subversion of responsibility, the debate then turned to the impossibility of regulating against such abuses on the part of authorities. After all, laws are relatively useless if a population is not willing to enforce or invoke them.

> Abuses like these were not to be extirpated by Act of Parliament or by philanthropic declamation. It was most difficult to get rid of oppression when you had to do with a people who would not complain. In the northern districts and in Scinde, where an independent spirit prevailed, it was possible to protect the people, but in Madras and Bengal districts, where the spirit of the people was cowed, and where they looked upon acts of oppression as a natural consequence of rule, it was difficult to repress evils of this kind.[30]

This formulation of the issue of police impunity perfectly encapsulates many of the tensions of the rule of law in the colonial context. There is doubt as to the suitability of the indigenous population to participate in the rule of law. Yet to acknowledge that the rule of law is not actually a system of laws but rather a set of behaviors undermines the British project of importing said laws in order to improve the indigenous population. The comment is also potentially dangerous to the assumption of the British capacity to rule in a colonial context. If such rule is dependent upon the informed consent and participation of colonized subjects, then these same subjects could presumably be self-legislating. What then, is the purpose, mission, or capacity of British colonial government?

These are all insoluble conundrums at the heart of the British colonial project. The different elements of British rule come to coexist in permanent tension. Institutions are built around conflicting assumptions, and the stated values of one institution of government are ignored with impunity by members of other institutions. But the Marquess of Clanricarde's statements about the East India Company expose the most pressing issue in regards to the rule of law. Is the East India Company more damned by its ignorance of torture or its complicity in it? The first option displays impotence, the second hypocrisy. If *both* conditions are at least partially true, then the rule of law is exposed as a meaningless invocation. There is no unified power capable of enforcing the rule of law, nor is the law effective in curbing state authorities. This fact is particularly devastating in combination with the rule of law's persistence as an evolving technique of governance and a mode of legitimating the British presence. The rule of law became regarded as an empty signifier, and institutionalized as an empty signifier by the division between the police who were to create order and the British who were to uphold the law.

The debate over the torture report concluded with some imprecise guessing at the current status of "the Native mind." The Lords proposed that perhaps in the past Indians would have accepted the prevalence of torture as inevitable. Lord Congleton believed that time was now past. "The Native mind had grown too large in the last twenty years for such a system to be perpetuated."[31] This schizophrenic vision of "the Native mind" debated in the House of Lords became institutionalized through colonial laws in the next fifteen years. Lord Congleton presciently asserted that a new form of rule of law would need to be developed. This is precisely what happened in the 1860s with the generation of new practices of policing and legal administration.

The Police Act of 1861 was a response to the Insurrection of 1857, and reformed the existing system and unified it across the entire territory. It was based upon the Irish model, dividing policing into two different forces, one of which was armed and staffed by Europeans in close cooperation with the regional state. David Arnold describes the two main goals of this system: to separate the military from internal population control and to create a system of police for internal control that would be staffed by indigenous populations who would be subordinate to Europeans. David Arnold characterizes the division of labor and authority as follows,

"Within this binary system, the European element represented domination and superintendence, the Indian element subordination and the passive execution of superiors' orders."[32] After the Insurrection, British officials determined that relying exclusively upon the military to keep order throughout the country was unreliable and costly. The overall effect of this innovation was to bring in more British subjects into the policing framework through the "superior division." These new men were recruited from the Indian Army and reportedly entirely lacking in initiative described as "the amiable detrimental, the younger son, or sporting public school boy, too lazy or too stupid for the Army, but prepared to go anywhere or do anything which did not involve prolonged drudgery."[33] Therefore, they did not bring a new spirit to the activities of policing in the country but instead seemed to add another layer of bureaucratic entitlement. Such a group was not inclined to question the methods or motivations of their subordinates if it meant that they could point to a larger number of resolved cases and reduced crime statistics.

The "subordinate" level of police continued along the same trajectory, as reports of torture, fear, and local animosity attest. The violence of the police had far-reaching implications for the experiences of the population. First of all, those who had crimes to report or evidence to submit only rarely came forward. In 1875, one district magistrate explained that a villager would rather keep the facts to himself "rather than be subjected to the inconvenience of being taken to the police station, where he will certainly be questioned and cross-examined, probably be tortured to give evidence in a certain way to suit the police view of the case, and possibly be himself suspected in the crime."[34] For this reason, crime statistics from this period are completely unreliable. Furthermore, villagers also learned that they could use the police to exact revenge upon neighbors and enemies. False reports of crime were common, and since police rarely held themselves to standards of fact or proof, filing a report could potentially lead to direct reprisals for the accused.

But the violence of policing can also be viewed as a condemnation of the ethnic, cultural, and linguistic divide between policing and law that was put into place in the nineteenth century. While some have argued that police brutality was a direct result of colonialism, it seems to me that a more plausible argument is that the logic of colonialism provided the dangerous divide between the application and mechanisms of criminal justice. When law and police follow two different structures, what happens is that the law provides for an authorization of a police force without a check upon its exercise. It is difficult to see what the alternatives in this particular situation could have been. As Rao argues,

> Magistrates with a poor command of native languages were often unfamiliar with the customary and/or religious codes that regulated persons and communities. They found themselves relying on confessions taken by the police rather than conducting their own inquiries. This suggests that the police often acted in a *de facto* judicial capacity, taking confessions, deciding guilt, and punishing wrongdoers.[35]

The rhetoric of British law in India met its comeuppance with the realities of the Indian police force. According to one scholar, "much evidence suggests that torture often resulted out of a sense of exasperation with the foreign procedures of the British-administered court system, since these courts often demanded types of evidence that a weak and poorly paid force could not provide."[36] The violence of policing is then engendered by the particularities of the legal system that administered the rule of law, not despite it.

However, the ingredients for police impunity can also be found in the criminal codes. The Rowlatt Act and Section 197 of the Criminal Procedure Code also give room for constables to exercise discretion in use of force while on "official duty." One legacy of colonial rule was a police force that was largely unlimited by stated and apparently irrelevant legalities but nonetheless responsible for maintaining justice and order in the void created by the realities of colonial administration. Another was a vastly underfunded system of legal administration, developed in order to maximize the obedience of the population at minimal costs. Both of these dynamics remain in force today. Naturally, the solution for both of these problems was to strengthen "the rule of law" in India through more staffing and oversight, and reformed codes.

Contemporary Policing in India

> Indian police is basically a colonial police, both in its organization and operations: it is basically a repressive force. But if the police retains its

> repressive colonial profile, it is due to the fact that the governing elites wish it so.
>
> —Upendra Baxi

The issue of policing in India reveals the particular abuses and difficulties that appear when a system of law is put into place and undermined by its own agents. The colonial regime could thrive given this divide, because the abuses of the police, when publicized, served as further evidence that the British needed to be there to govern. The racial difference between the British administrators who guarded the legal system and the Indian constables who were tasked with enforcing order was exacerbated by an institutional chasm between them. The colonial state could thereby "explain" the divergence between state value and state action. What about today?

A 2009 Human Rights Watch report, "Broken System: Dysfunction, Abuse and Impunity in the Indian Police," vividly illustrates the continuities between colonial and current police structures. Eighty-five percent of the police force are constables or head constables (local police station supervisors). None of these officers are given training in investigation or weapons management. During the colonial period, the police were considered a potentially revolutionary force, especially after the Insurrection of 1857. Therefore, the British wanted them to be segregated from the population at large, and to be given as few skills and weapons as possible in order to minimize their risk of destabilizing British dominance.

Each police station is staffed by constables; however, constables are not given training or the authority to write up official reports of crimes (FIRs). In response to the Madras Report of 1855, the British decided to have a European supervisor at every station. Constables were given little official discretion or any responsibility in order to try and curb the potential for abuse by those notoriously undisciplined "native minds." The hierarchical division of police work and segregation of duties continues today, even as the ethnic distinction between head constable and constables has disappeared.

Today, constables live in barracks and are considered on-call twenty-four hours a day. One constable remarked, "It's just like I'm a prisoner … There's no medical facilities, no toilet."[37] Many report having little sleep and no contact with their families. There are also very few police in India. The global average is 1 police per 333 people in a country; in India, the ratio is 1 per 1,037.[38] The police stations are crumbling and lack funds. Some police who were interviewed stated that they did not always have the forms available to file reports because police stations are given such meager funds and supplies. Others explained that they have to fill out procurements in order to attain fuel to go to the scene of an incident. Such requests can take days to be approved; therefore investigations are unlikely to happen. Some families looking for police help to investigate a crime offer to drive police to the scene of the crime in order to maximize the opportunity of an investigation. Police stations lack staffing and modern equipment, making tracking data, persons, and police activities impossible. "Case diaries and police registers are usually recorded in notebooks or loose leaf paper which are then tied with string and stored in corners of the station or atop tall cabinets."[39]

On the other hand, constables are also given imperatives to show a reduction in crime and to produce evidence in quick measure. While some constables who were interviewed said they sometimes lacked the paper forms to file an FIR; others remarked they were punished by their superiors if they filed too many. Why collect the evidence of the police station's failures? For this reason, the crime rates in India are startlingly low. In 2007 there were nineteen crimes per every 100,000 residents in India, as compared to one thousand reported crimes per every 100,000 resident in the United States.[40] One study concluded that in Lucknow, fewer than 5% of reported crimes were registered with an FIR.

Others have pointed out that one of the major continuities between colonial and postcolonial policing is the use of police largely as supports for the political, not the legal, system. Beatrice Jauregui has studied the dynamics of police delegitimization in contemporary India. One of the factors that she points out is the additional loss of scarce police resources to VIP bodyguard duty. Politicians in India do have reason to be frightened of assassination, but the demand of candidates and those in office for police attendants moves beyond personal security. Office holders are accompanied by a guard of anywhere from three to forty-five policemen; the number of policemen in your detail is a way of signaling to people the extent of political power at the VIP's fingertips. "In India, other power holders like elected officials, judges, political party functionaries, and some wealthy elites use police as props in performing their power to the world as a person who must be protected in order to continue the fight against the 'breakdown of law and order' that allegedly plagues Indian society."[41] Ironically, this practice of advertising for law and order significantly reduces already meager police resources. Jauregui was told by one commissioner in Uttar Pradesh that two hundred policemen were stationed at a single minister's house. This does have a significant impact on police capacity. For instance, in 2008, one-quarter of all policemen in Delhi were used to guard VIPs. When the police are used as props in a game of power signaling, their prestige is also diminished since they appear as lackeys for hire as opposed to independent agents. "Instead of people perceiving police as enforcing the law, they see police reduced to yes-men, robotic soldiers serving kingly and queenly leaders who are the 'true' sources of authority."[42]

While this means that others are culpable in the delegitimization of the police, their own actions also contribute to this process. A related matter is the continual involvement of police in public disturbances, protests, and interethnic and religious violence. A startling number of public protests happen in India every day. Even more remarkable, is the fact that violence occurs during 30% of protests.[43] The police are not a neutral force used to maintain order. Instead, they are known to take sides and even participate in the violence that occurs during such communal uprisings. K. S. Subramanian lists the most significant dates of police involvement in large-scale massacres: the 1969 Ahmedabad Riots, the massacre of the Sikhs in 1984, the 1987 massacre of Muslims in Maliana and Hashimura, and the Gujarat killings of 2002.[44] Since independence there has been a steady stream of incidents in which the police have been implicated in large-scale violence. After the assassination of Indira Gandhi in 1984 by her two Sikh bodyguards, the country was roiled by four days of mob violence against the Sikh population. The role of the Delhi police in helping organize the violence against Sikhs was the focus of a government inquiry, as apparently mobs were given voting lists that detailed the residences of Sikh families, making it possible for them to systematically pursue the population. The Marwah Commission was formed after the retaliatory killing of Sikhs to focus specifically on the role of the Delhi police in the violence. In 1985, the Marwah Commission was ordered to stop its inquiry, and only part of its findings were transferred to the Misra Commission. The Misra Commission was the first official report about the persecution of Sikhs and has been widely dismissed as a "whitewash" lacking any basis in truth. Tellingly, in two areas, Farsh Bazar and Karol Bagh, where police did immediately act to quell organizing mobs, there were no deaths reported in the four days after the assassination. Clearly, police action can influence the effects of public turmoil.

During the past fifteen years, the cycle of violence between Hindu and Muslim groups has periodically flared around Bombay. In all cases, investigations into police complicity were conducted. In 1992, a Hindu militant group destroyed a mosque, setting off riots in Bombay during which hundreds of people died. In the aftermath, Supreme Court Justice B. N. Srikrishna headed a commission that, once again, focused on the role of the Bombay police in refusing to try and control mob violence.

> The response of police to appeals from desperate victims, particularly Muslims, was cynical and utterly indifferent. On occasions, the response was that they were unable to leave the appointed post; on others, the attitude was that one Muslim killed was one Muslim less ... Police officers and men, particularly at the junior level, appeared to have an in-built bias against the Muslims which was evident in their treatment of the suspected Muslims and Muslim victims of riots. The treatment given was harsh and brutal and, on occasions, bordering on the inhuman ... The bias of policemen was seen in the active connivance of police constables with the rioting Hindu mobs, on occasions, with their adopting the role of passive on-lookers on occasions, and, finally, their lack of enthusiasm in registering offenses against Hindus even when the accused was clearly identified.[45]

The report recommended improvements in policing to avoid further loss of life in the event of future violence.

In 2002, there was retaliatory violence in Gujarat after Muslims burned a train which held Hindu activists (the group Vishwa Hindu Parishad) en route to construct a Hindu temple on the site of a mosque that had been destroyed in 1992. Similar mobs retaliated, systematically raping and attacking Muslims, and leading to between one and two thousand deaths.

A representative of Human Rights Watch observed, "The atrocities in Gujarat are a replay of events in Bombay in 1992 and 1993, had the recommendations of the Srikishna Commission been implemented, we might have been able to avoid the carnage of the last two weeks."[46]

Similar cases of police participation in systemic brutality and murder of specific groups has arisen in regards to the Dalits or Untouchables. In 2004, Dalits were barred from participating in a Hindu festival held in Tamil Nadu. A riot broke out in response to their attempts to integrate the event, and the police beat the Dalits. One human rights monitor reported that police told the Dalit protestors, "We will not rest until you are killed."[47]

There is another area in which there is a great deal of resonance between colonial and current practices. Reports of the use of torture in police investigation are still pervasive, eerily echoing the 1855 Madras Report on police torture. After the Hyderabad bombings in 2007, the police gathered suspects and detained them for questioning. The evidence of torture was so overwhelming that on November 13, the Andhra Pradesh government admitted to the torture of twenty-one people and paid compensation to the victims equivalent to six hundred US dollars per person. The subsequent investigation showed that the police failed to follow criminal procedure, including provisions that detainees appear in court within twenty-four hours and be interrogated at police stations, and that the police are required to notify one person outside of confinement of the detainee's custody.

What is interesting about this case is that the relationship of mutual incomprehension yet enablement between the police and government is evident. Even after the state admitted that detainees had been tortured and paid compensation, the police continued to deny it. When asked about the torture and report, the Andhra Pradesh minister for minority welfare, Mohammad Shabbir Ali, said he does not blame the police for the torture because "they do their work based on information, and sometimes information can be wrong."[48] The police force felt no need to concur with the government's story, and the government avoided charges of complicity by paying damages to victims of police torture, even as it explained and excused police brutality as a result of misinformation. This leads one to wonder if the police would have been justified if the suspects had been the perpetrators. Was the problem that they were torturing the wrong people?

Extrajudicial killings are also common in India. A suspicious number of detainees die in jail, an average of four per day. The Indian government has demanded an accounting of these custodial deaths from the National Human Rights Commission, which is charged with working as a watchdog agency for the police. But these figures do not necessarily account for what happens in a jail or prison cell. Death from natural causes is something that can only rarely be confirmed. There are also reports of "encounters" whereby police find a criminal, a struggle ensues during apprehension, and the criminal is killed. These incidents happen frequently enough to warrant suspicion, but there are never witnesses that step forward to testify against the police, particularly given the fact that the police will retaliate against formal complaints by arresting the person who accused them of misconduct.

Jinee Lokaneeta has challenged the common move to blame the violence of the Indian criminal justice system on "low-level police" and instead traces how the Supreme Court seems to tacitly, or even explicitly, accept the presence of torture in custody. Even though the court vociferously protests police violence in all cases, it also regards victims' demands for compensation with suspicion. For instance, one ruling refusing compensation stated:

> Where there is no independent evidence of custodial torture and where there is neither medical evidence about any injury or disability, resulting from custodial torture, nor any mark/scar, it may not be prudent to accept claims of human rights violation, by persons having a criminal records in a routine manner for awarding compensation.[49]

These guidelines virtually rule out any possible legal response to custodial torture. Only those who have been fully exonerated of their criminal accusation, who were able to achieve documentation by a medical official or the police while in custody or very soon thereafter, and who have permanent scars that can be traced to the documented incident are able to win compensation.

Lokaneeta examines the recent turn to narcoanalysis (a chemical injection followed by inquisition) and brain scanning during interrogations in police investigations in recent years. The court has approved these controversial techniques, in part, to avert the need for physical torture that seems an invariable element on the legal landscape. The court refers to physical coercion as "third-degree methods" and embraces these technological improvements as an alternative.

In *State of Andhra Pradesh v. Smt. Inapuri Padma and Ors.* (2008), the ruling affirming the use of these interrogation drugs and techniques stated:

> In the accusations made in India, the Police are attributed with applying third degree methods in eliciting information and there are instances of the culprits or suspects dying in lockups during the course of interrogation on account of application of third degree methods, therefore, *there is a blame* that the Indian police are flagrantly violating the human rights and fundamental rights guaranteed under Article 21 of the Constitution of India. Therefore there is every need to apply scientific tests to elicit the information from the culprits.[50]

The ruling takes for granted that coercive techniques of investigation will be utilized by the police. The self-appointed mission of the court is to make the methods used more gentle, so more prisoners will survive them. As Lokaneeta argues, it would seem that the Courts in India are not necessarily divided from the police in their views of what it takes to achieve justice. Like the British administration of Madras in 1855, the courts claim some level of ignorance along with an incapacity to govern practices done in the name of law and order.

The accounts of police violence, torture, and criminal neglect; the repeated yet seemingly fruitless government investigations; and the allegations of human rights violations are too numerous to be included here. While stories can be found of police brutality in virtually every country in the world, the division between practices of the police and the state's view of criminal justice is particularly stark in the case of India. Enter the reform commission.

Criminal Law Reforms: The Malimath Commission

The abuses of police power, the miserable conditions of prisons, and the vast numbers of prisoners who await trials or even charges have been recognized as factors in a national crisis by the Indian government. One of the first responses to the crisis was to start keeping official statistics on recorded instances or reports of police abuse. Figure 5.1 shows a report from 2014 compiled by the National Crime Records Bureau.

S.No.	Incidence of	No. of cases registered		No. of Cases found to be False		No. of Police Personal			
						Charge-sheeted		Convicted	
		State Plice	Central Paramilitary Force	State Police	Central Paramilitary Force	State Police	Central Paramilitary Force	State Police	Central Paramilitary Force
(1)	(2)	(3)	(4)	(5)	(6)	(7)	(8)	(9)	(10)
STATE:									
1	Disappearance of Persons	35	0	34	0	1	0	0	0
2	Illegal detention or arrests	0	0	0	0	0	0	0	0
	2.1 illegal detention or arrests of SCs	0	0	0	0	0	0	0	0
	2.2 illegal detention or arrests of STs	0	0	0	0	0	0	0	0
4	Fake encounter killings Humar Rights violation	0	0	0	0	0	0	0	0
5	Against Terrorists or Extremists	0	0	0	0	0	0	0	0
6	Extortion	3	0	0	0	4	0	0	0
7	Hurt/Injury	16	4	4	0	7	0	1	0
8	Failure in taking action Assault on women with	0	0	0	0	0	0	0	0
9	Intent to outrage her Modesty	14	3	3	0	11	1	2	0
10	Insult to the Modesty of Women	0	0	0	0	0	0	0	0
11	Atrocities on SCs	20	0	13	0	5	0	0	0
12	Atrocities on STs	1	0	7	0	2	0	0	0
13	Torture	1	0	1	0	0	0	0	0
	13.1 Torture of SCs	1	0	1	0	0	0	0	0
	13.2 Torture of STs	0	0	0	0		0	0	0
	13.3 Torture of Others	0	0	0	0	0	0	0	0
14	**Failure in Registering FIR Section 4 of ther SC/ ST (POA)**	0	0	0	0	0	0	0	0
15	**ACT, 1989 Sec. 23(4) of the Protection of Children from Sexual Offence Act, 2012**	1	0	0	0	0	0	0	0
16	Others Human Rights	1	0	0	0	0	0	0	0
17	Violations	6	3	0	0	0	2	0	0
Total Humar Rights Violation by Police		98	10	62	0	30	3	3	0

FIGURE 5.1 Incidence of Human Rights Violation by Police and Their Disposal During 2014.

What is notable about these figures is that they are clearly wrong. Even though assassination by a policeman is a frequent enough occurrence that it has its own term—"encountered"—in the thirty-five instances that police were suspected of being involved in the disappearance of a person, thirty-four were dismissed as false. There was not a single illegal detention or arrest in the entire country. Arguably, producing such a clearly falsified report is more damaging to the credibility of the rule of law than refusing to produce any information about policing in the country. It does not inspire confidence that the same government will be able to produce a solution to the issue.

In 2000, the Ministry of Home Affairs put together a Committee on Reforms of the Criminal Justice System that later became known as the Malimath Committee, named after its designated head. It had a large task at hand, including the following directives:

> To examine the fundamental principles of criminal jurisprudence, including the constitutional provisions relating to criminal jurisprudence and see if any modifications or amendments are required thereto;
>
> To examine in the light of findings on fundamental principles and aspects of criminal jurisprudence as to whether there is a need to re-write the Code of Criminal Procedure, the Indian Penal Code and the Indian Evidence Act to bring them in tune with the demand of the times and in harmony with the aspirations of the people of India;
>
> To make specific recommendations on simplifying judicial procedures and practices and making the delivery of justice to the common man closer, faster, uncomplicated and inexpensive;
>
> To suggest ways and means of developing such synergy among the judiciary, the Prosecution and the Police as restores the confidence of the common man in the Criminal Justice System by protecting the innocent and the victim and by punishing unsparingly the guilty and the criminal.[51]

It would seem that the state is perfectly attuned to the potential crisis of legitimacy for both law and the police in the eyes of "the common man."[52] The backlog of cases in the Indian court system has also reached epic proportions. At the end of 2013, then-Prime Minister Singh pointed out that there were only 15.5 judges per million residents in India, while the United States has 100 judges for every million residents. What this means is that there is a backlog in courts while people, many of them sitting in jail, wait for their trial. Tom Lasseter gave the following estimate of what it would take to clear the backlog: "At the end of 2013, there were 31,367,915 open cases working their way through the system, from the lowest chambers to the Supreme Court. If the nation's judges attacked their backlog nonstop—with no breaks for eating or sleeping—and closed 100 cases every hour, it would take more than 35 years to catch up."[53] The underfunding of the justice system is a time-honored tradition that has persisted to the present day.

The Malimath Report establishes from the outset that the penal code itself is of foreign origin, and that this legacy may be problematic. By repeatedly appealing to the sensibilities of this so-called common man, it would appear that the government is thinking not just about the ability to legitimate their criminal justice practices to an international community but about how the population perceives these practices. Hence, the committee positions its goal as the recalibration between the government, criminal justice, and the population. Given the long-standing perception that the government only *appears* to enforce laws and routinely breaks them, this would seem a laudable goal. There is an interesting echo in the commission's ventriloquism of "the common man" and "the native mind" that concerned the House of Lords in 1856.

The report, issued in 2003, has generated much debate but no specific reforms, which places it in the company of virtually all of the other reports and commissions I have mentioned in this chapter. It is six hundred pages in length, and begins on a very curious note. It introduces itself with a quote by Andre Gide: "Everything has been said already, but as no one listens, we must begin again." They admit that what they have compiled is common knowledge, as opposed to the unique insight of expertise; the problem is in responding to the information. Since the Indian government proliferates reports and commissions but seems to take no action in response to them, this biting introduction indicates a sense of estrangement from governance even within the government itself.

The committee proposes a large paradigm shift in criminal justice, pointing out that the country currently follows the adversarial system "inherited from British Colonial Rulers." The system is troubling in that it places too much emphasis upon the rights of the accused, and "is insensitive to the victims' plight and rights." The ability of criminals to be set free because of the procedural issues with presenting and finding evidence and the neutral role played by the judge has "seriously eroded the confidence of the people in the efficacy of the system." In short, the system inherited from the British provides too many protections for the accused and creates great inefficiencies.

The proposed solution is to move to an inquisitorial system that empowers police officers to investigate cases, prepare evidence, and pursue investigations under direction of the prosecutor. The primary reason for this shift, the committee argues, is that such a system would better capture Indian values. "The Indian ethos accords the highest importance to truth. The motto Satyameva Jayate (Truth alone succeeds) is inscribed in our National Emblem ... Our epics extol the virtue of truth. Gandhiji gave us truth—as the righteous means to achieve independence by launching the movement of Satyagraha."[54] The adversarial tradition directly undermines the independence movement. The issue of criminal procedural reforms is consistently reframed as a matter of tradition, and national honor. "The Adversarial System is the opposite of our ancient ethos. In the panchayat justice, they were seeking the truth, while in the adversarial procedure, the Judge does not seek the truth, but only decides if the charge has been proved by the prosecution."[55]

In the previous chapter, I examined the Indian Evidence Act as it was written by James Fitzjames Stephen. His attempt to regularize and create an empirical basis for what constitutes evidence was considered at the time the modernization of the legal process. It was intended to circumvent abuses and the falsification of evidence, particularly since the conviction rate in India courts was so low, it was clear that evidence was "produced" that was often completely unrelated to the crime. Today, this same system creates some paradoxical outcomes, such as the fact that torture must be proven by marks upon the body of the person who claims to have been tortured. In the case of chemical truth serums, there is no mark upon the body; hence there is no "proof" of torture. Others have argued that this system gives clear imperatives for the police to produce "proof," often subverting truth. In some sense then, the concern that "proof" and "truth" are not necessarily synonymous squares with many of the critiques of this system of legality. The report asserts that moving to an inquisitorial system will honor Indian values and bring criminal procedure in line with the perceptions of the "comman man"; it will reunite truth and justice.

The report argues the inquisitorial system will have advantages of speed and thrift as well. Citing the large percentage of imprisoned people who have not been charged, the report attributes this to the cumbersome legal investigation required to bring charges, not the lack of police staffing. By having police confessions and reports serve as the basis for the prosecution of criminals, the system will become much more efficient. The commission identified two major issues in the criminal justice system in India: court backlog and "the very low rate of conviction in cases involving serious crimes."[56]

By framing the issue of criminal justice in India in this way, the committee has decided to focus upon the issue of efficiency rather than on outcomes and procedures. Predictably, the report identifies ways of creating quicker rather than more substantive justice. Other observers have noted that the committee takes efficiency, not accuracy, as the measurement of success throughout their proposals.[57] Amnesty International issued a critique of the report, pointing out that the committee seems to value winning more convictions above other measurements of justice.[58] One can imagine the Bureau of Criminal Records that would like to show a conviction for every reported crime in order to assert the link between crime and punishment is infallible in India.

Right now, because of case backlog and the low rate of convictions, crime has become rampant. "Violent and organized crimes have become the order of the day. As chances of convictions are remote, crime has become a profitable business."[59] This observation contradicts the official statistics of India which show a very low crime rate, but I shall put that fact aside for the moment. The report insinuates that "the common man" in India is still truth seeking, and that it is on his behalf that the reforms must be undertaken. "For the common man truth and justice are synonymous. So when truth fails, justice fails."[60] The common man has lost faith in the criminal justice system, and lack of faith in the criminal justice system presumably erodes democracy, reducing it to "a rope of sand."

The report argues that the adversarial system "does not trust the police" in that it curtails the use of police confessions as evidence for prosecution, and that this hinders both the police's and the criminal justice system's abilities to function. Currently, only the accused, not the prosecution, are able to admit confessions given to police as evidence. The Malimath Committee wants to amend this. Acknowledging that there is a potential for coerced confession, they argue that increased documentation of confessions is necessary. They suggest placing video cameras in police stations so that police officers can document interrogations by other officers.[61] Given that police stations often lack paper, it is difficult to imagine how they would maintain and distribute video equipment.

The commission also finds that the rules that enforce the accused's right to silence and right to not self-incriminate are cumbersome to the judicial process. Though they admit that the accused may not be forced to speak, they suggest "amending the Code to provide for drawing appropriate inferences from the silence of the accused."[62] The commission also questions "the presumption of innocence" clause and suggests that it may hinder the prosecutor's ability to obtain convictions. They suggest some options such as a standard of proof lower than "proof beyond reasonable doubt." They also question the assumption that it is better to release those who are guilty than to punish those who are innocent, claiming that "it is as much a miscarriage of justice to acquit a guilty person as it is to convict an innocent."[63] In one last step for obtaining more convictions, the court also suggests that the accused be required to share their defense with the prosecution before the trial. Currently, "the accused is not required to disclose what his defence is going to be. He may spring a surprise at any stage. This is not fair and hampers dispensation of justice."[64]

Taken in conjunction with the systemic problems with police torture and violence in India, it is curious that the primary reform of criminal law on the table is the greater empowerment of the police and prosecutors within the justice system. By basing criminal prosecutions on policing, it seeks to overcome the institutional divide between the law and the police itself. Just as David Arnold observed that in Madras in the nineteenth century, the police had de facto ability to generate judicial evidence, the Malimath Commission seeks to make the production of such evidence de jure. In some sense, then, there will be agreement between what is official and what is practiced, and presumably the "common man" will perceive that his sense of justice is now being achieved. The emphasis upon justice as truth that is readily perceptible—a sense of easy justice—suggests that what may be emerging is a different interpretation of what the rule of law means. Do not seek to order the world by principles of justice; instead, order your system of justice so it reflects what is in the world.

After all, the truth is that Sikhs did assassinate Indira Gandhi, Muslims have detonated bombs, and Untouchables are still frequently considered different than the rest of the Hindu population. Should criminal law reflect these truths? While the recommendations themselves portend a revolution, what they in fact do is make the unfortunately common practice of policing and vigilantism into the code of law. These proposals can be seen as the ultimate postcolonial response to the colonial legacy, a shift toward eradicating the false adherence to standards of neutrality. On the other hand, they can also be seen as a continuation of that same legacy, exhibiting a disregard for the common man's existence in the name of his edification.

Since the Malimath Commission, there was a high profile Supreme Court decision, *Prakash Singh and Others v. Union of India and Others* (2006), that directed state and national governments to conduct police reforms. The issue with the ruling is that most of the violence and abuse happens at the local level, and these police are controlled by state regulations. All twenty-eight states would need to institute police reforms. But like other unfunded mandates, it is difficult to see how issuing new guidelines would substantially change the behavior and incentives for the police. They are understaffed, work under inhumane conditions, enjoy little or no respect from the population they are trying to work with, and have no resources.

The urgency with which reforms are suggested reflects the 1902–1903 Indian Police Commission which stated, "The police force throughout the country is in a most unsatisfactory condition, that abuses are common everywhere, that this involves great injury to the people and discredit to the government, and that radical reforms are urgently required."[65] The first post-independence examination of the Police Code was the 1979–1981 National Police Commission. The bulk of this commission's suggestions were about implementing a detailed system for investigating complaints of abuses by the police. These suggestions were never followed up. A series of eight different reports were issued, including consideration of case backlog in the system, rules for submitting and collecting evidence, the necessity of hiring more women police officers, public distrust of the police, the frequency of abuse by the police. The commission observed, "Police do in fact harass even those who try to help them."[66] Police training and recruitment were also considered. It is an extensive and complete list of all the potential reforms that would control and monitor police behavior.

There have been two more police commissions since then. The Ribeiro Committee (1998) made suggestions for police reforms, including updating the 1861 Police Act, and then the Padmanabhaiah Committee Report on Police Reforms (2000) also suggested that the Indian Evidence Act was not a sufficient guide for police work today. They suggested increasing specialization and providing now-absent opportunities for promotion and career planning for police so that they would not retire in the same position as they entered the force. Obviously, offering the possibility for advancement is one way to reward good behavior and provide an incentive for avoiding abuse. Currently since there is no possibility of advancement through the ranks of the police force, why would anyone try to achieve the difficult task of reform?

The commissions say over and over what should be done: reform the Police Code of 1861, reform the Indian Evidence Act, reform the criminal code. There have been five different commissions that point this out, but such resolutions—as the exasperated author of the Malimath Commission report points out—change nothing. This is remarkably similar to the frustrations and endless talk of reforming the criminal code of Great Britain, a discussion that has lasted for centuries at this point and to very little avail. Remember that J. F. Stephen was unable to codify English law and had to settle for codifying the laws of the Empire instead. Perhaps what this means is that India is indeed achieving maturity as a country where entrenched elites protect their own interests, and the ossification of law has occurred.

It would certainly seem that it is easier for an outsider to envision reform, just as Bentham believed. The temptation of the British colonialist was to see law in its simplicity and assume the omnipotence to drop it into a given context. Yet this book should display how complex this process turned out to be, along with the host of unintended consequences that it engendered. Colonialism provided a highly unusual historical circumstance, where one or a small handful of people were entrusted with assuring the law. The Aristotelian distinction between the rule of law and the rule of men collapsed; colonialism offered the possibility of having one, or just a few men, write the rule of law. It was an alluring, if impossible *aufhebung.*

Still another problem emerges when the outsider has the power to insist upon systemic change through the coercive use of power, as the legal crusaders in the British Empire employed. The paradox of disseminating the rule of law through force was bound to create resentment, and to vacate any meaning that the term might have possibly held. Today the debates of the Malimath Commission demonstrate that the inevitable failures of any system of law can all too easily be placed upon the outsiders that imported it. Just as the British blamed the "natives" for any violence that occurred, today there is a consistent deferral of responsibility. It would seem that the ability of the law to curb force is permanently crippled when force is so prominently used in its deployment.

Conclusion

The Rule of Law Today

The contemporary zeal for the rule of law says more about us than them.

—Tom Ginsburg

PROMOTING THE RULE OF LAW became a cause célèbre among policymakers and global NGOs in the first decade of the twenty-first century. The fascination with one solution that can presumably fix any turbulent society's problems resembles the fanfare around the promotion of civil society that was in vogue during the 1990s. In *Foreign Affairs* in 1998, Thomas Carothers called rule of law development "an elixir of transitions" because it promised a stable environment for economic development and the ground rules for political stability.[1] There is a cluster of specialists and programs deployed around the globe that has been labeled the Rule of Law Network.[2]

There has been a flurry of academic consideration and reconsideration about what the "best practices" for promoting the rule of law are. Should you focus upon building capacity among local institutions or building the motivation within a population to demand greater accountability? Will high-profile trials of perpetrators in a recent conflict serve to demonstrate the end of impunity? Or should courts focus more upon comprehensive prosecution of all criminal activity in a recent conflict?[3]

The growing industry that promotes the rule of law has attracted a number of critics, including Tom Ginsburg, who has noted,

> The rule of law is not only a philosopher's concept but a million-dollar industry and the dominant ideal of our time. As a concept, its success is in part a result of its vagueness, as it is broad enough to incorporate an overlapping consensus among free marketers, human rights activists, and promoters of the regulatory state. Countries as diverse as China, Chad and the Czech Republic agree on its virtue. At the same time, the idea of the rule of law has captured the policy-making imagination of the West and has become our modern *mission civilisatrice.*[4]

The similarities between the rhetoric attached to the rule of law and the discourses around civil society can provide some helpful insights. After all, civil society was also supposed to eradicate conflict, curb elite power, provide popular accountability, stabilize political shifts, and—oh yes—provide a better environment for economic development and foreign direct investment. Isn't it interesting that the rule of law is supposed to achieve the same goals?

One crucial difference between the rule of law and civil society fads is that the rule of law framework is more compatible with technocratic elite solutions that avoid the messy business of political involvement. Civil society development was meant to increase political stability and democratic accountability through empowering citizens. Rule of law adherents have the opposite relationships to political activism, as Richard Flathman noted: "Versions of institutionalism that strongly promote the rule of law typically accord high if not principle value to imperatival control and mandatory obedience. It is less than obvious that this stance is favorable to individuality, plurality, and freedom."[5]

Contemporary invocations of the rule of law are also more compatible with military intervention and the politics of empire more generally. Disturbingly, Niall Ferguson has called the rule of law an important enough venture that the United States and Europe need to take up the mantle of imperialism in order to enforce it—"if necessary … by military force"—anywhere on the face of the earth.[6] Lack of the rule of law is considered a justification for military intervention. Furthermore, policymakers are trying to figure out better ways for the rule of law to grow out of the barrel of a gun in volumes such as *Can Might Make Rights? Building the Rule of Law after Military Interventions*. This is why the time is ripe for a closer examination of how colonialism tried to promote the rule of law two centuries ago, and to what effect.

Disturbingly, even skeptics such as Tom Ginsburg point out the limited utility of rule of law programs, but then hypothesize that more substantive interventions might achieve better results. Noting the often counterproductive results of piecemeal intrusions into other regimes, Ginsburg notes, "I have come to conclude that only intervention on a far more intrusive scale, of a type no longer politically acceptable, has the potential to truly transform the societies and to enable them to achieve anything approaching 'the rule of law.' … We are insufficiently imperialistic to carry out social transformation from abroad."[7] Yet this book has demonstrated that colonialism is no way to deliver justice.

In some ways, focusing upon the rule of law sounds like resetting a country's internal clock so it can march along a predictable tick. It does not sound as ambitious as state building, but a close examination of the concept reveals that it amounts to the same thing. The rule of law is supposed to provide a boundary for normative politics by establishing frameworks of behavior for all citizens, and those who govern them. I am not the first to point out that there is a receding problem of enforcement. If laws are supposed to govern officials, who makes sure these laws are enforced? And who oversees those people? There is also a tautological problem in understanding the relationship of the rule of law and politics. Law is supposed to control people, but in the end, only politics can guarantee law, most specifically, the political involvement of the people who are to demand enforcement of norms and hold one another accountable to them.

One influential model in political science by Barry Weingast articulates the relationship between law and politics as a coordination problem. A stable regime that upholds the rule of law occurs only if all the relevant parties within a state are able to have a coordinated response against a regime that transgresses its boundaries that were established by law.[8] Weingast points out that countries with fractured constituencies are often unable to develop a coordinated response, particularly since one group is frequently favored by a sovereign power at the expense of others. He points out that optimally, citizen coordination insists upon universal applications of the law.

In suboptimal conditions, "the sovereign and one group of citizens form a coalition against the remaining citizens, transgressing the latter's rights."[9] This is a schematic way of describing the way that the rule of law operated under colonialism. Groups that were more closely affiliated with the British were given advantages, and the presence of British settlers within colonies also provoked the difficult task of sorting through which inhabitants of the colonies would be subject to which codes and in what area, as I described in Chapters Three and Four in the examples of Sierra Leone and India. Some groups enjoyed greater protection of the law, and others were devastatingly subjected to its vicissitudes.

Weingast's theory focuses upon what is required to have effective political mobilization to maintain the rule of law, but other social scientists have recently started to investigate the process of transferring codes of law from one location to another. Daniel Berkowitz, Katharina Pistor, and Jean-Francois Richard investigated whether the source of a country's laws had an impact on whether the rule of law was respected today. They found that the mode of transference had a great impact upon whether the rule of law was salient in a country. The authors of this study argued that whether the country was receptive to the legal importation matters more than the content of the codes. Further, they were interested in the relationship between rule of law and economic development and found that countries that had a greater respect for the rule of law enjoyed stronger economic development.[10] The conclusion of the study was that countries that recognize the need for a law and are receptive to being given it by another power will enjoy greater economic growth.

Clearly, this research is also pertinent for the colonial case, although once again, the model lacks historical specificity, and indeed the authors date the transference of law from the British Empire to locations in Asia and Africa from 1890–1914, which this book has demonstrated is incorrect. The authors posit that if the population does not perceive a use for the law, it is unlikely to be adopted, used, and enforced in any robust fashion. But here they assume "unfamiliarity" is the key predictor of a law's success. However, this demonstrates a lack of understanding of the ideological elements of colonialism, and an inability to recognize the power disparities that were involved. The authors take it as self-evident that laws will protect the rights of a population, but often laws protect the interests of elites. The assumption that the relationship between a country receiving law from a more powerful country can be encapsulated by a binary receptive/unreceptive score is problematic.

But contemporary social science is only reflecting a much longer tradition in political theory that looks to outsiders to solve problems that have arisen within a polity and have no apparent solution. The allure of delivering the rule of law through colonial power is reminiscent of the noble lies introduced in Plato's *Republic*, that is, stories from a stranger that will help order a population.[11] Like Plato's stories, laws can arrive from an outsider to launch a polity anew, as in Bentham's legislator of the world and Rousseau's lawgiver. In this way, the Western philosophical tradition provided encouragement to the project of delivering the rule of law through colonial order.

This book has provided examples of historical figures who tried to play these roles: James Stephen, and his attempt to serve as Rousseau's lawgiver for Britain's colonies, and his son, James Fitzjames Stephen, who attempted to play Bentham in India. Contemporary figures and organizations hoping to fulfill the same role should consider the lessons of Britain's colonial legal regime.

One of these lessons is the difficulty of balancing legal morality and enforcement from outside a society with the need to govern a society from within. The potentially disastrous implications of dividing the legal apparatus from the policing ones were described in detail in Chapter Five. In social science terminology, this same issue has recently been addressed as the dynamic between external and internal enforcement. The historical examples in the book have shown the slippery slope of legislating upon another population's behalf. If "they" cannot rule themselves, how can "they" be conceived as agents with responsibility? James Fitzjames Stephen wrestled with this conundrum and created a system of normativity with less and less agency.

The problem of how to relate foreign and domestic efforts for creating law is also a pattern from the colonial era that continues to haunt contemporary rule of law projects. Today there is a general notion that external international enforcement will be complementary with internal, local efforts. However, Ginsburg makes the case that external enforcement efforts can actually crowd out local ones. "Knowing that external actors will monitor the behavior of government, local actors will pay less attention to that behavior."[12] Even more, aid that is attached to the rule of law project creates a disincentive to effectively take over the internal enforcement of legality. "Stand on your own, and your country may be better off in some sense but risks a cutoff in aid as funds get shifted to other hot spots in worse condition. In any case, even if a country would be better off without support, the ruling coalition will almost certainly not be."[13] Taken on the level of personnel, Ginsburg points out that international agencies come to a country, find talent familiar with both national and international laws, hire them at a premium salary, and then take resources away from the local side of the equation. From the point of view of the rule of law aid worker, advertising failures is no way to keep contracts rolling and new projects funded. Small incremental steps and a continued level of mutual economic dependence characterize the attempt to build the rule of law from the outside. It is a partnership between international and local elites.

Counter to every idealistic invocation of the concept, in practice rule of law projects promote elite interests, whether these elites are indigenous or foreign. First, it is a way of championing the values of the greater powers and proclaiming national superiority. Ginsburg makes the point that though the rule of law interventions are couched in the name of altruism, promotion of human rights, and general stability, those engineering the interventions always have an investment in the outcome.

> The international criminal law project from the beginning has been as much about the intervenors as about the target societies. Nuremberg and Tokyo were self-conscious attempts to demonstrate that allied justice was of a higher quality than that of the Axis powers. This demonstration was as much for the home audience as for the target society. *We* are different from them; *we* follow procedures, whereas *they* pursue summary justice.[14]

The fact that the rule of law cottage industry burgeoned in the United States during the era of state-sanctioned torture and the legal chasm of Guantanamo Bay (not to mention other black zones of legality) should give us pause. If the United States is so invested in promoting the rule of law, why does the country abstain from participating in the International Criminal Court?

Second, the rule of law project protects elite interests in both political and economic ways. As I explored in Chapter Three, the growth of extraterritorial law through British colonial administration made the world ripe for economic exploration and appropriation. Rule of law projects have similar goals today. Richard Miller noted, "As the luster of structural adjustment has faded, the allure of the rule of law project has grown."[15] Populations have grown to distrust the so-called market imperatives of structural adjustment and austerity programs. Very few people would have the wherewithal to argue against the rule of law, because it currently stands as a largely uncontested self-evident good. Which it is, in theory. It is the application that presents difficulties.

Third, rule of law programs are intended to solve the problem of politics—violence, criminality, corruption, exploitation—but they do so by creating a stable system of power, not necessarily justice. In Chapter One, I discussed Judith Shklar's characterization of Montesquieu's understanding of the rule of law. While more recent invocations emphasize the universal application of rules and the benefits of limiting government power, Montesquieu saw the rule of law as an agreement between elites to guard their advantages against encroachment by other elites, an overt power-sharing arrangement. Given the global political and economic landscape where states struggle to regulate and even tax the accumulation of wealth by an increasingly transnational elite, Montesquieu's description is a more apt one for our time. After all, he developed his theory at a time when the power of sovereign states was as uncertain as it is today.

Does the rule of law have to be used in this way? I do not think so, but the first step toward having the rule of law serve as a protection for the more vulnerable citizens of a society is to critically evaluate whether it is something anyone has achieved at home, abroad, or anywhere. James Stephen became a model for me in this regard, because he saw it as an always incomplete project that required humility above all. As soon as we think we know the secret recipe or ingredients of the rule of law, we have lost the battle to achieve justice. We also need to recognize that it is not a neutral instrument that governs disparate power relations; it is an element that has been tightly bound within the development of our radically unequal economic and political global systems.

NOTES

Introduction

1. Alexis de Tocqueville, *Democracy in America*, trans. George Lawrence (New York: Harper and Row, 1966), 264.
2. United Nations Website, "The Responsibility to Protect," http://www.un.org/en/preventgenocide/adviser/responsibility.shtml.
3. Qtd. in Antony Fenton, "The Responsibility to Protect. The International Commission on Intervention and State Sovereignty," http://www.un.org/en/preventgenocide/adviser/responsibility.shtml.
4. Walter Benjamin, "Theses on the Philosophy of History," in *Illuminations: Essays and Reflections*, ed. Hannah Arendt (New York: Schocken Books, 1988), 261.
5. Duncan Bell encapsulates the moment in "Victorian Visions of Global Order: An Introduction," in *Victorian Visions of Global Order: Empire and International Relations in Nineteenth Century Political Thought*, ed. Duncan Bell (Cambridge: Cambridge University Press, 2007).
6. See C. A. Bayly, *Imperial Meridian: The British Empire and the World 1780–1830* (New York: Longman, 1989), for a complete account of the shifts in "the Second British Empire."
7. J. Holland Rose, A. P. Newton, and E. A. Benians, *The Cambridge History of the British Empire* (Cambridge: Cambridge University Press, 1940), vol. II, vi.
8. Thomas Carothers, "Rule of Law Revival," *Foreign Affairs*, March 1998, 99.

Chapter 1

1. See, for instance, the work of Uday Mehta, *Liberalism and Empire*; Carole Pateman, "The Settler Contract"; and David Armitage, "Locke and the Constitution of the Carolinas."
2. H. F. Morris, "How Nigeria Got Its Criminal Code," *Journal of African Law* 14, no. 3 (1970): 137.
3. J. S. Read, "Criminal Law in the Africa of Today and Tomorrow," *Journal of African Law* 7, no. 1 (1963): 5.
4. Peter Fitzpatrick, "Terminal Legality: Imperialism and the (De)composition of Law," in *Law, History, and Colonialism: The Reach of Empire*, ed. Diane Kirkby and Catharine Coleborne (Manchester: University of Manchester Press, 2011), 19.
5. Nasser Hussain, *The Jurisprudence of Emergency: Colonialism and the Rule of Law* (Ann Arbor: University of Michigan Press, 2003).
6. Ged Martin, "Was There a British Empire?," *The Historical Journal* 15, no. 3 (1972): 562.
7. Jeanne Morefield, *Empires without Imperialism: Anglo-American Decline and the Politics of Deflection* (Oxford: Oxford University Press, 2014).
8. C. A. Bayly, *Imperial Meridian: The British Empire and the World 1780–1830* (London: Longman, 1989), 75–77.
9. Hannah Arendt, "On Violence," in *The Crisis of the Republic* (New York: Harcourt, Brace, Javonovich, 1972), 178.
10. Bayly, *Imperial Meridian*, 100.
11. Jennifer Pitts, *A Turn to Empire: The Rise of Imperial Liberalism in Britain and France* (Princeton, NJ: Princeton University Press, 2005), 6.
12. Karuna Mantena, *Alibis of Empire: Henry Maine and the Ends of Liberal Imperialism* (Princeton, NJ: Princeton University Press, 2010), 149.
13. Ibid., 149.
14. The first attempt at revising Company/Crown relations was the Regulation Bill of 1773 which decentralized the Company's power greatly. Hastings complained that it was impossible to govern under these conditions. The 1784 Act learned from many of the difficulties of this initial reform and proved to be more effective.
15. James Mill to Brougham, 27, viii. 34, quoted in Alexander Bain, *James Mill: A Biography* (London, 1882), 375.
16. The Maine Papers in the India Office Archives reveal this pattern.
17. Henry Maine Papers, India Office Archives, April 22, 1867, MSS EUR C179 (underline in original).
18. Allan C. Hutchinson and Patrick Monahan, "Introduction," in *The Rule of Law: Idea or Ideology?*, ed. Hutchinson and Monahan (Toronto: Carswell, 1987), xiv.
19. Judith Shklar, "Political Theory and the Rule of Law," in *The Rule of Law: Idea or Ideology?*, ed. Hutchinson and Monahan (Toronto: Carswell, 1987), 1.

20. Ibid., 3.
21. Ibid., 2.
22. Ibid., 4.
23. Ibid., 4.
24. Thomas Metcalf, *Ideologies of the Raj* (Cambridge: Cambridge University Press, 1994), 18.
25. In W. W. Hunter, *Life of Mayo*, vol. 2, 168–169.
26. Shklar, "Political Theory," 5–6.
27. Ernest Marshall Howse, *Saints in Politics: The Clapham Sect and the Growth of Freedom* (London: George Allen and Unwin, 1960), 22. Quoted from George Stephen, *Antislavery Recollections.*
28. See Richard Cosgrove, *The Rule of Law: Albert Venn Dicey, Victorian Jurist* (Chapel Hill, University of North Carolina Press, 1980), for an excellent intellectual history of Dicey's thought. Anthony Brundage and Richard Cosgrove's *The Great Tradition: Constitutional History and National Identity in Britain and the United States, 1870–1960* (Stanford, CA: Sanford University Press, 2007), places Dicey in a larger and transcontinental legal context.
29. Carl Schmitt, *Political Theology: Four Chapters on the Concept of Sovereignty*, trans. George Schwab (Chicago: University of Chicago Press, 2005), 14.
30. Bernard Cohn, *Colonialism and Its Forms of Knowledge: The British in India* (Princeton, NJ: Princeton University Press, 1996), 65.
31. Committee of Circuit to Council at Fort Williams, August 15, 1772, in J. E. Colebrooke, *Supplement to a Digest of the Regulations and Laws*, 1, 1807, p. 8. Also referenced, Governor and Council at Bengal to the Court of Directors (COD), November 3, 1772, Seventh Report from the Committee of Secrecy on the state of the East India Company, May 6, 1773, *Reports from Committees of the House of Commons*, vol. iv, 1772–1773, p. 346. Quotation and citation in Radhika Singha, *A Despotism of Law* (Delhi: Oxford University Press, 1998), 2.
32. Cohn, *Colonialism*, 69.
33. Ibid., 69.
34. See Andrew Dilts, "To Kill a Thief," *Political Theory*, and Keally McBride, *Punishment and Political Order*, ch. 4.
35. Lindsay Farmer, "Reconstructing the English Codification Debate: The Criminal Law Commissioners, 1833–45," *Law and History Review* 18, no. 2 (2016): 399–400.
36. Metcalf, *Ideologies of the Raj*, 37.
37. Hall, *Macaulay and Son.*

Chapter 2

1. See M. Foucault, *Society Must Be Defended* (London: Penguin, 2003), 1–19, for Foucault's discussion of genealogy as method.
2. Leslie Stephen, *The Life of Sir James Fitzjames Stephen* (London: Smith, Waterfield, 1895), 1.

3. Ibid., 2.
4. There were four generations of lawyers in the family who were named James Stephen. The first who was imprisoned for debt was born "about 1733" according to Leslie Stephen and does not feature in the annals of history. The second (1758–1832) was an abolitionist politician who is described here; the third (1789–1859) is the primary subject of this and the next chapter; the last was James Fitzjames Stephen (1829–1894), famed for his exegesis of criminal law, who plays a central role in Chapter Four.
5. Leslie Stephen, *The Life of Sir James Fitzjames Stephen*, 16. Italics in the original. See also James Stephen, *The Slavery of the British West India Colonies Delineated, As It Exists Both in Law and Practice and Compared with the Slavery of Other Countries, Ancient and Modern* (London: J. Butterworth and Son, 1823), preface, vol. 1, for a description of the trial.
6. James Stephen wrote the original character sketch of the group in his book, *Essays in Ecclesiastical Biography* (London: Longmans, Green, 1891). It is not an impartial portrait.
7. See Catherine Hall, *Macaulay and Son: Architects of Imperial Britain* (New Haven, CT: Yale University Press, 2012), esp. chapters 1 and 2.
8. Paul Knaplund, "Colonial Problems and Colonial Policy, 1815–1837," in *The Cambridge History of the British Empire. Vol. II: The New Empire 1783–1870*, ed. Ross, Newton, and Benians (Cambridge: Cambridge University Press, 1940), 276.
9. Ernest Marshall Howse, *Saints in Politics: The "Clapham Sect" and the Growth of Freedom* (Toronto: University of Toronto Press, 1952), 115. For a more balanced history of the Claphamites, see *The Clapham Sect: How Wilberforce's Circle Transformed Britain* (London: Lion Hudson Press, 2010).
10. Quoted in Hall, *Macaulay and Son*, 61.
11. Ibid., 108.
12. James Stephen, *Essays in Ecclesiastical*, 584.
13. T. P. Thompson, cited in Hall, *Macaulay and Son*, 69.
14. Henry Adams, *History of the United States of America: The Second Administration of Thomas Jefferson, 1805-1809*. New York: Charles Scribner, 1890. 50.
15. James Stephen gained the firm friendship of Pitt when he figured out how supplies were being run to the French through blockades with ships sailing fake flags. His tract "War in Disguise" enabled the British to resurrect some maritime regulations that helped to squelch the practice, giving them an advantage in the war. Hence his service to the British war cause is what gave him entry into Parliament where he cantankerously advocated for abolitionism in all its guises. He knew that simply making slavery illegal would not eradicate it. Hence he spent years figuring out loopholes that slavers exploited and trying to close them.
16. Leslie Stephen, *The Life of Sir James Fitzjames Stephen*, 22.
17. James Stephen, *The Slavery of the British West India Colonies Delineated*..

18. *The Autobiography of Sir Henry Taylor*, quoted in Leslie Stephen, *The Life of Sir James Fitzjames Stephen*, 44–45.
19. Russell Smandych, "'To Soften the Extreme Rigor of Their Bondage': James Stephen's Attempts to Reform the Criminal Slave Laws of the West Indies, 1813–1833," *Law and History Review* 23, no. 3 (Fall 2005): 555.
20. Letter to Sir Alfred Stephen. Included in Sir James Stephen, *Letters*, with biographical notes by Caroline Stephen (Cambridge: W. Heffer and Sons, 1906), 16.
21. Quoted in D. B Swinfen, *Imperial Control of Colonial Legislation 1813–1865: A Study of British Policy towards Colonial Legislative Powers* (Oxford: Clarendon Press, 1970), 22.
22. C. H. Currey, *British Colonial Policy 1783–1915* (London: Oxford University Press, 1916), 27–28.
23. Letter to the Duke of Newcastle, August 29, 1853, Stephen Papers.
24. James Stephen, *Essays in Ecclesiastical*, 546.
25. February 23, 1846, Stephen Papers.
26. June 27, 1858, Stephen Papers.
27. Richard Ely, "From Sect to Church: Sir James Stephen's Theology of Empire," *Journal of Religious History* 19 (1995): 74–91.
28. August 7, 1830, Stephen Papers.
29. Leslie Stephen, *The Life of Sir James Fitzjames Stephen*, 116.
30. James Stephen, *Lectures on the History of France* (New York: Harper and Brothers, 1875), 225–226.
31. See Ged Martin, "Was There a British Empire?," *The Historical Journal* 15, no. 3 (1972): 562–569, for a smart encapsulation of the black holes of British imperial administration.
32. Brian Tamanaha, *On the Rule of Law: History, Politics, Theory* (Cambridge: Cambridge University Press, 2004), 4.
33. "Reinventing the Rules" by USAID Rule of Law and Democracy Projects. See http://reinventingtherules.com/2014/01/06/interview-with-usaids-wade-channell-on-rule-of-law-reform/.
34. Philippe Nonet, "The Rule of Law: Is that the Rule that Was?," in *The Rule of Law: Ideal or Ideology?*, ed. Hutchinson and Monahan (London: Carswell Publishing, 1987), 128.
35. Bonnie Honig has also explored the role of the outsider in providing foundations upon which polities are built, or solving problems for different regimes. See *Democracy and the Foreigner* (Princeton, NJ: Princeton University Press, 2003). Jennifer Pitts provides an excellent exploration of Bentham's relationship to British colonialism in "Legislator of the World? A Rereading of Bentham on Colonies," *Political Theory* 31, no. 2 (2003): 200–234.
36. Nonet, "The Rule of Law," 130.
37. Ibid., 133. Nonet's thinking about judgment was considerably refined in "Judgment," *48 Vanderbilt Law Review* 987 (1995). Here he also questions

whether the application of reason might block our understanding of the law. His description of law as a more spiritual practice would have found resonance with Stephen's personal experience.

38. D. M. Young, *The Colonial Office in the Early Nineteenth Century* (London: Longman, Green, 1961), 12.
39. Ibid.
40. R. B. Pugh, "The Colonial Office," In *The Cambridge History of the British Empire,* vol. III (Cambridge: Cambridge University Press, 1967), 712.
41. For more information about the mechanisms of the Colonial Office during this era, see H. T. Manning, "Who Ran the British Empire 1830–1850?," *Journal of British Studies* 5, no. 1 (1965); H. L. Hall, *The Colonial Office: A History* (London: Longmans, Green, 1937); and John Ward, "The Retirement of a Titan: James Stephen 1847–1850," *Journal of Modern History* 31, no. 3 (1959): 189–205.
42. Young, *The Colonial Office,* 5.
43. Leslie Stephen, *The Life of Sir James Fitzjames Stephen*, 45.
44. CO 323/40.
45. Pugh, "The Colonial Office," 723.
46. Leslie Stephen, *The Life of Sir James Fitzjames Stephen*, 50.
47. Ibid., 61.
48. Ibid., 51.
49. Virginia Woolf, "A Sketch of the Past," in *Moments of Being*, ed. Jeanne Schulkind (London: Hogarth Press, 1985), 68.
50. Leslie Stephen, *The Life of Sir James Fitzjames Stephen*, 63.
51. CO 323/40, September 18, 1815, n. 92.
52. CO 323/40, July 18, 1816.
53. Undated letter to Sir. T. F. Buxton in *Letters of Sir James Stephen*, 45–46.
54. CO 267/77, October 31, 1826, to Hay.
55. CO 323/40, December 10, 1816.
56. CO 343/40, July 11, 1817.
57. James Stephen, *Essays in Ecclesiastical Biography* (London: Longmans, Green, 1891). 636.
58. *Letters of Sir James Stephen*, 213.
59. See David Lieberman, "Bentham on Codification," and Philip Schofield, "Jeremy Bentham, the Principle of Utility, and Legal Positivism," both in Jeremy Bentham, *Selected Writings*, ed. Stephen Engelmann (New Haven, CT: Yale University Press, 2011).
60. See Jennifer Pitts, *A Turn to Empire, and "Great and Distant Crimes": Empire in Bentham's Thought*, in Jeremy Bentham, *Selected Writings*, 487–499.
61. William Empson, "Jeremy Bentham," *Edinburgh Review* LXXXVIII (1843): 56. Quoted in David Lieberman, "From Bentham to Benthamism," *The Historical Journal* 28, no. 1 (1985): 202.

62. The Bentham Project website states, "In 1968 when the first two volumes of the new Collected Works appeared, Maurice Cranston wrote in *The Guardian*: 'Of all the great theorists of the Age of Reason, Jeremy Bentham has hitherto been the most neglected.' This neglect was attributable in part to the unsatisfactory nature of the only collection of his works which then existed, brought out by his disciple Sir John Bowring in 1843, eleven years after Bentham's death. This edition was unattractive in format and so closely printed as to be barely legible. Moreover, it omitted a number of works that had been published in Bentham's lifetime (notably those concerning religion), as well as many substantial works which had not been published but which survived in manuscript. The memoir of Bentham contained in the last two volumes, which was described by Sir Leslie Stephen as one of the worst biographies in the English language, included only a fraction of his correspondence. Much of the editing was of very poor quality, and several of the works included by Bowring were translations into English of French versions of Bentham's writings which had been edited and published in the early nineteenth century by his Genevan follower, Etienne Dumont." http://www.ucl.ac.uk/Bentham-Project/about.
63. David Lieberman, *The Province of Legislation Determined: Legal Theory in Eighteenth-Century Britain* (Cambridge: Cambridge University Press, 2002), 245.
64. Ibid.
65. See Michael Lobban, *The Common Law and English Jurisprudence 1760–1850* (New York: Oxford University Press, 1991).
66. Jeremy Bentham, "Place and Time," in *Jeremy Bentham, Selected Works*, ed. S. Engelmann (New Haven, CT: Yale University Press, 2011), 179.
67. See Philip Schofield, *Bentham: A Guide for the Perplexed* (London: Continuum, 2009), chapter 1.
68. See his letter reprinted in *"Legislator of the World": Writings on Codification, Law and Education*, ed. Philip Schofield and Jonathan Harris (New York: Oxford University Press, 1998).
69. Jeremy Bentham, "Place and Time," 195.
70. Ibid., 179.
71. See Lieberman, "Bentham and Codification," 463.
72. Jeremy Bentham, "Place and Time," 208.
73. Jeremy Bentham, "Codification Proposal to All Nations Professing Liberal Opinions..." (London: J. M'Creery, 1822), 17.
74. Jennifer Pitts, "'Great and Distant Crimes': Empire in Bentham's Thought," in *Selected Writings*, ed. S. Engelmann (New Haven, CT: Yale University Press, 2011), 490.
75. Ibid., 481.
76. Jeremy Bentham, *A Fragment on Government* (Oxford: Clarendon Press, 1891), 98.
77. Jeremy Bentham, *Fragment*, 99.

78. James Fitzjames Stephen, *Lectures on the History of France* (New York: Harper and Brothers, 1875), vii., dedicatory letter, critiquing current system of education.
79. See Colin Dayan, *The Law Is a White Dog: How Legal Rituals Make and Unmake Persons* (Princeton, NJ: Princeton University Press, 2011), 13–15, for a fascinating description of Bentham's lifelong fear of ghosts and how it shaped his legal philosophy.
80. Michael Paul Rogin, *Fathers and Children: Andrew Jackson and the Subjugation of the American Indian* (New York: Vintage Books, 1975), 14.
81. James Stephen, Diary, Stephen Family Papers, University Archives, Cambridge Library, July 24, 1857. MSS 7511.
82. Nonet, "The Rule of Law," 136.
83. James Stephen to Thomas Carlyle, October 15, 1853, Stephen Family Papers, Cambridge University.

Chapter 3

1. James Stephen, July 11, 1817, CO 323/40.
2. The Sierra Leone Correspondence is held at the National Archives, Kew, CO 267.
3. See Tcho Mbaimba Caulker, *The African-British Long Eighteenth Century: An Analysis of African-British Treaties, Colonial Economics, and Anthropological Discourse* (Lanham, MD: Lexington Books, 2009), especially ch. 2 for a close study of the treaties in the first three decades of the colony.
4. Radhika Singha, *A Despotism of Law: Crime and Justice in Early Colonial India* (Delhi: Oxford University Press, 1998), and Elizabeth Kolsky, *Colonial Justice in British India* (Cambridge: Cambridge University Press, 2010).
5. See C. R. Pennell, "The Origins of the Foreign Jurisdiction Act and the Extension of British Sovereignty," *Historical Research* 83, no. 221 (August 2010): 466–485.
6. Carl Schmitt, *Political Theology: Four Chapters on the Concept of Sovereignty*, trans. George Schwab (Chicago: University of Chicago Press, 2005), 11.
7. Carl Schmitt, *The Nomos of the Earth in the International Law of the Jus Publicum Europaeum*, trans. G. L. Ulmen (Candor: Telos Press, 2003), 91.
8. Schmitt, *Political Theology*, 82.
9. Schmitt, *Nomos*, 148.
10. Ibid., 188.
11. Ibid., 132.
12. Ibid., 238–239.
13. Ibid., 235.
14. Thomas Ludlam and William Dawes, "Report of the Commissioners of African Inquiry; Use of the Navy, 1811," *Parliamentary Papers* x (101) (1812): 1–2.
15. Catherine Hall, "Making Colonial Subjects: Education in the Age of Empire," *History of Education* 37, no. 6 (2008): 777.
16. Zachary Macaulay, Diary Sierra Leone Governor, October 1, 1793, Huntington Library MY 418 (1–5), Box 19.

17. James Stephen, *Essays in Ecclesiastical Biography*, 5th Ed. (London: Longmans, Green and Co. 1891), 538.
18. Hall, "Making Colonial Subjects," 2008.
19. See Bruce L. Mouser, "African Academy-Clapham 1799–1806." *History of Education* 33, no. 1 (January 2004): 87–103, for an account of the school, its students, and its philosophies.
20. William A. Green, "The West Indies and British West African Policy in the Nineteenth Century—A Corrective Comment," *Journal of African History* 15, no. 2 (1974): 247–259. Green argues that British policies in Africa were driven in large part by the needs of their Caribbean territories. While he is certainly correct to point out an interdependence between different areas of the British Empire, I think he underestimates the British strategy to outmaneuver the French in West Africa.
21. See Stephen J. Braidwood, *Black Poor and White Philanthropists: London's Black and the Foundation of the Sierra Leone Settlement 1786–1791* (Liverpool: Liverpool University Press, 1994).
22. See Christopher Fyfe, *A History of Sierra Leone*, and Kenneth Morgan, "Sierra Leone: Origins, 1787–1808," in *Encyclopedia of African History. Vol. III*, ed. Kevin Shillington (New York: Fitzroy Dearborn, 2005), 1352–1353.
23. Macaulay remains deeply suspect of the character and motives of even those settlers who claim to convert. In his journal he remarks about a discussion with one of his school teachers: "I asked the Schoolmaster who was one of Moses' preachers respecting the three converts, and he told me they were the very worst children in the school. He had tried he said to persuade their parents as Moses of the folly and impunity of allowing Girls like them to let themselves up as subjects of Conversion, and to talk about Grace Sense of his forgiveness, when their whole conduct was so incorrigibly petulant and rude as to lay him under the necessity of frequently punishing them with stripes. And while they were so ignorant as not to be able to tell him who was the Savior of Sinners. I was pleased with this frank avowal." Nov. 28th 1796, Huntington Library MY 418 (1–5) Box 19. For more about Macaulay in Sierra Leone, see Catherine Hall, *Macaulay and Son: Architects of Imperial Britain* (New Haven, CT: Yale University Press, 2012), and "Making Colonial Subjects: Education in the Age of Empire," *History of Education* 37, no. 6 (2008): 773–787.
24. Fyfe, *A History of Sierra Leone*, 116.
25. "Civilization of Africa-Sierra Leone-Liberated Africans," James M'Queen, Glasgow, to R. W. Hay, Esq., undersecretary of state, *Blackwood's Edinburgh Magazine*, December 1826, 20: 120, 882.
26. James Stephen, Minute, December 8, 1840, CO 325/37.
27. Stephen quoted in Fyfe, *A History of Sierra Leone*, 217.
28. A. Anghie, "Finding the Peripheries: Sovereignty and Colonialism in Nineteenth Century International Law," *Harvard International Law Review* 40, no. 1 (1999): 1–80, 6.

29. James Stephen, Minute, June 20, 1842, CO 87/28.
30. Ibid. Also described by Fyfe, *A History of Sierra Leone*, 220.
31. Fyfe reports that in April 1841, 612 émigrés went to Jamaica, Trinidad, and British Guiana (219).
32. Letter from Governor MacDonald, January 26, 1842, CO 267/175.
33. Sierra Leone, Law 1, 1841. Included in CO 267/175, January 26, 1842.
34. Ibid.
35. April 24, 1842.
36. CO 96/2.
37. CO 96/2, May 27, 1843.
38. Fyfe, *A History of Sierra Leone*, 223–224.
39. James Stephen, memo to Hope, December 23, 1842, CO 96/2.
40. Ibid.
41. FO 97/497.
42. FO 97/497, May 16, 1845.
43. FO 97/497, March 5, 1845.
44. Ibid., 7.
45. Ibid., 11–12.
46. Ibid., 8.
47. Ibid.
48. Quoted in R. Derek Wood, "The Treaty of Nanking: Form and the Foreign Office 1842–1843," *Journal of Imperial and Commonwealth History* 24, no. 2 (1996): 192.
49. Pennell, "Origins," 484.
50. Ibid.
51. Quoted in ibid., 465.
52. Schooner Exchange v. M'Faddon, 11 U.S. 116 (1812). Quoted in Teemu Ruskola, *Legal Orientalism: China, The United States, and Modern Law* (Cambridge, MA: Harvard University Press, 2013), 114.
53. Ruskola, *Legal Orientalism*, 130.
54. Ibid., 130. Emphasis in the original.
55. Ruskola lists the nineteen countries in the order in which they received the extraterritorial privilege: Great Britain, the United States, France, Sweden, Norway, Russia, Germany, Denmark, the Netherlands, Spain, Belgium, Italy, Austria-Hungary, Peru, Brazil, Portugal, Japan, Mexico, and Switzerland (287).
56. See Gerrit Gong, *The Standard of "Civilisation" in International Society* (Oxford: Clarendon Press, 1984).
57. Quoted in John Spagnolo, "Portents of Empire in Britain's Ottoman Extraterritorial Jurisdiction," *Middle Eastern Studies* 27, no. 2 (1991): 272.
58. Ruskola, *Legal Orientalism*, 156.
59. Quoted in Wood, *The Treaty of Nanking*, 193.

60. W. R. Johnston, *Sovereignty and Protection: A Study of British Jurisdictional Imperialism in the Late Nineteenth Century* (Durham, NC: Duke University Press, 1973).
61. Spagnolo, "Portents of Empire," 272.

Chapter 4

1. It is also known as the First War of Indian Independence, the Great Rebellion, the Indian Mutiny, the Sepoy Rebellion, and the Great Mutiny. Any event with this many names is surely world historical.
2. Sir James Stephen wrote the bill abolishing slavery in the British Empire in 1833, but it was enacted in Jamaica in 1834.
3. Bernard Semmel, *Jamaican Blood and Victorian Conscience: The Governor Eyre Controversy* (Cambridge: Houghton Mifflin, 1963), 33.
4. See Gad Heuman, *"The Killing Time": The Morant Bay Rebellion in Jamaica* (Knoxville: University of Tennessee Press, 1995).
5. For instance, in a review of a law in Tabago that replaced confinement with working on chain gangs as preferable and more humane option, Undersecretary Stephen noted: "It is difficult to understand why the same rules of Natural Justice should be inapplicable to the case of slaves in our last Indian Colonies. To say that daily labour in the public chain is a condition to be preferred to detention in the Gaol at Tabogo, is in other words to give a description of prisons in that Colony the truth of which is difficult to believe. A place of confinement must be wretched indeed if more irksome that the suffering and disgrace that the Law has condemned the worst class of criminals; and even if it could be supposed that such a representation of the Goal of Tobago was well founded, it would be improper not to object to an Act recognizing the existence and virtually supporting the continuance of such establishment." September 18, 1815, N. 92 (CO 323/40).
6. Semmel, *Jamaican Blood and Victorian Conscience*, 40.
7. See both Heuman, *"The Killing Time"*, and R. W. Kostal, *A Jurisprudence of Power: Victorian Empire and the Rule of Law* (Oxford: Oxford University Press, 2005), for more elaborate descriptions of the event.
8. There is considerable disagreement amongst historians as to whether the Morant Bay Rebellion was elaborately planned in advance and in fact an insurgency, or whether it was a tempest in a teapot, a small outbreak of discontent to which the British overreacted. Heuman sees the Rebellion as an organized revolutionary movement. Semmel favors the later opinion. Recognizing the political implications of both interpretations, as well as the possibility that both views may be correct and in fact compatible, I have drawn from both accounts here. Semmel focuses more upon British colonial office politics; Heuman's archival research of events in Jamaica is rich in detail.
9. Semmel, *Jamaican Blood and Victorian Conscience*, 52.
10. Ibid., 13–14.

11. Kostal, *A Jurisprudence of Power*, 37.
12. Cited in Kostal, *A Jurisprudence of Power*, 155.
13. See Semmel, *Jamaican Blood and Victorian Conscience*, and K. J. M. Smith, *James Fitzjames Stephen: Portrait of a Victorian Rationalist* (Cambridge: Cambridge University Press, 1988), for more on how the controversy impacted Stephen's thought.
14. Quoted in Leslie Stephen, *The Life of Sir James Fitzjames Stephen* (London: Smith, Elder, 1895), 228.
15. J. F. Stephen, *A History of the Criminal Law of England*, vol. 2 (London: Macmillan, 1883), 345.
16. In addition to his brother Leslie's biography, *The Life of Sir James Fitzjames Stephen*, there have been two others: James A. Colaiaco, *James Fitzjames Stephen and the Crisis of Victorian Thought* (New York: Palgrave Macmillan, 1983), and K. J. M. Smith, *James Fitzjames Stephen: Portrait of a Victorian Rationalist* (Cambridge: Cambridge University Press, 1988). On Stephen and the criminal laws, see Leon Radzinowicz, *Sir James Fitzjames Stephen, 1829–1894, and His Contribution to the Development of Criminal Law* (London: Bernard Quarich, 1957); Richard Posner, "The Romance of Force: James Fitzjames Stephen on Criminal Law," *Ohio State Journal of Criminal Law 10*, (2012) 263–275; and Stephen Morse, "Thoroughly Modern: Sir James Fitzjames Stephen on Criminal Responsibility," *Ohio State Journal of Criminal Law 5*. (2008) 505–522. For an interesting essay on J. F. Stephen as academic, thinker, and codifier, see John Heydon, "Reflections on James Fitzjames Stephen," *University of Queensland Law Journal 29*, no. 1 (2010). 43–65.
17. Radika Singha, *A Despotism of Law: Crime and Justice in Early Colonial India* (Oxford: Oxford University Press, 1998).
18. See Bernard Cohn, *Colonialism and Its Form of Knowledge: The British in India* (Princeton, NJ: Princeton University Press, 1996), for a description of this fiasco.
19. See H. H. Dodwell, "The Development of Sovereignty in British India," in *The Cambridge History of the British Empire*, vol. 4 (Cambridge: Cambridge University Press, 1929), 589–590.
20. Ibid., 590.
21. Smith, "Macaulay's Indian Penal Code," 146.
22. J. F. Stephen, "Legislation Under Lord Mayo," in *Life of the Earl of Mayo*, 2nd ed, ed. William Hunder, 143–226 (London: Smith, Elder, 1876), 185.
23. J. F. Stephen, "The Law of Evidence," speech to Supreme Council of India, March 31, 1871. Printed in Henry Raymond Fink, *The Indian Evidence Act* (Calcutta: Wyman), Appendix, 4.
24. See Sanford Kadish, "Codifiers of the Criminal Law: Wechsler's Predecessors," *Columbia Law Review* 78, no. 5 (1978), and Richard Posner, "The Romance of Force: James Fitzjames Stephen on Criminal Law," *Ohio State Journal of Criminal Law* 10, no. 263.

25. Stephen, James Fitzjames, "English Jurisprudence," *The Edinburgh Review CXIV*, 67.
26. Smith, *James Fitzjames Stephen*, 55.
27. J. F. Stephen, *A History of the Criminal Law of England*, vol. 2 (London: Macmillan, 1883), 96.
28. Ibid., 81–82.
29. Leslie Stephen, *The Life of Sir James Fitzjames Stephen* (London: Smith, Waterfield, 1895), 235.
30. J. F. Stephen, *Liberty*, 71.
31. J. F. Stephen, "Codification in Indian and England," *Fortnightly Review* 18 (1872): 649.
32. J. F. Stephen, *Liberty, Equality, Fraternity* (Cambridge: R. J. White, 1967 [1873]), 70.
33. J. F. Stephen, "Legislation under Lord Mayo," in *Life of the Earl of Mayo*, 2nd ed, ed. William Hunter, 143–226 (London: Smith, Elder, 167).
34. Leslie Stephen, *The Life of Sir James Fitzjames Stephen*, 243.
35. J. F. Stephen, "Legislation under Lord Mayo," 169.
36. J. F. Stephen, *Liberty*, 90.
37. J.F. Stephen, "Legislation under Lord Mayo" 158–159.
38. J. F. Stephen, "Codification," 661.
39. Ibid., 672.
40. Ibid.
41. J. F. Stephen, "Codification," 668.
42. Quoted in Calaiaco, 1983, 103.
43. Elizabeth Kolsky, *Colonial Justice in British India* (Cambridge: Cambridge University Press, 2010), 11.
44. Elizabeth Kolsky, "Colonial Order, British Law: Codification and the Rule of Colonial Difference," *Law and History Review* 23, no. 631 (2005): 666.
45. Quoted in Kolsky, *Colonial Justice*, 4.
46. Ibid., 96.
47. Kolsky, "Colonial Order," 677.
48. Ibid., 667.
49. Ranabir Samaddar, "Crimes, Passion and Detachment: Colonial Foundations of Rule of Law," in *Challenging the Rule(s) of Law: Colonialism, Criminology and Human Rights in India*, ed. Kalpana Kannabiran and Ranbir Singh (New Delhi: SAGE, 2008), 355.
50. Ibid., 361.
51. Gerrit Gong, *The Standard of 'Civilisation' in International Society* (Oxford: Clarendon Press, 1984), 25.
52. Carl Schmitt, *The Nomos of the Earth in the International Law of the Jus Publicum Europaeum*, trans. G. L. Ulmen (New York: Telos Press)

53. David Armitage, *The Ideological Origins of the British Empire* (Cambridge: Cambridge University Press, 2000), 8.
54. Quoted in Armitage, *Ideological Origins of the British Empire*, 11. For more on this line of thinking, see Miles Taylor, "IMPERIUM OR LIBERTAS? Rethinking the Radical Critique of Imperialism during the Nineteenth Century," *Journal of Imperial and Commonwealth History* 19 (1991).
55. K. J. M. Smith, "Macaulay's Indian Penal Code: An Illustration of the Accidental Functions of Time, Place, and Personalities in Law Making," in *Legal History in the Making*, ed. W. M. Gordon and T. D. Fergus (London: Humbledon Press, 1991), 146.
56. Lindsay Farmer, "Reconstructing the English Codification Debate: The Criminal Law Commissions 1933–45," *Law and History Review* 18, no. 2 (2000): 399–400.
57. Karuna Mantena, *Alibis of Empire: Henry Maine and the Ends of Liberal Imperialism* (Princeton, NJ: Princeton University Press, 2010), 91.
58. Stephen, "Codification in Indian and England," 654.
59. E. P. Thompson, *Whigs and Hunters: The Origin of the Black Act* (New York: Pantheon Books, 1975), 266.
60. John Roach, "James Fitzjames Stephen 1829–94," *Journal of the Asiatic Society of Great Britain and Ireland* (April 1956): 1–16, makes a similar observation.
61. A. Rao and S. Pierce, "Discipline and the Other Body: Correction, Corporeality, and Colonial Rule," *Interventions* 3, no. 2 (2001): 160.
62. J. F. Stephen, *Liberty, Equality, Fraternity*, 231. See also Russell Kirk, "The Foreboding Conservatism of Stephen," *Western Political Quarterly* 5, no. 4 (1952): 563–577, for an excellent discussion of Stephen's views about executive force and law.
63. Radika Singha, "Punished by Surveillance: Policing 'Dangerousness' in Colonial India 1872–1918," *Modern Asian Studies* 49, no. 2 (2015): 241–269.
64. Ranabir Samaddar, "Crimes, Passion and Detachment: Colonial Foundations of Rule of Law," in *Challenging the Rule(s) of Law: Colonialism, Criminology and Human Rights in India*, ed. Kalpana Kannabiran and Ranbir Singh (New Delhi: SAGE, 2008), 379.

Chapter 5

1. There was a group of seven Hindu nationalists who traveled to Delhi with the intent of killing Gandhi. When the first attempt failed, the police apprehended a member of the cohort, Madanlal Phawa, who explained the entire operation to the police and led them to the hotel room where they were staying. The police decided not to pursue the group at that time, and Nathuran Godse, another member of the group, killed Gandhi a week later. The matter was a subject of debate in the Constituent Assembly of India and the J. L. Kapur Commission of Inquiry into the Conspiracy to Murder Mahatma Gandhi.

2. According to *Snapshots: Prison Statistics India* in 2013, 66.7% of prisoners were awaiting charges.
3. David Arnold, *Police Power and Colonial Rule: Madras 1859–1947* (Delhi: Oxford University Press, 1986), 3.
4. Dilip Das and Arvind Verma, "The Armed Police in the British Colonial Tradition," *Policing: An International Journal of Police Strategies and Management* 21, no. 2 (1998): 355.
5. Nasser Hussain's *The Jurisprudence of the Emergency: Colonialism and the Rule of Law* (Ann Arbor: University of Michigan Press, 2003) is an excellent discussion of many of these issues, and my thoughts are indebted to his analysis.
6. Thomas Munro, "On the Ultimate Aim of British Rule in India," 1824. Reprinted in Anil Chandra Banerjee, ed., *Indian Constitutional Documents 1757–1947*, vol. 1, 3rd ed. (Calcutta: A. Mukherjee and Co., 1961), 206–207.
7. V. D. Kulshreshtha, *Landmarks in Indian Legal and Constitutional History*, 3rd ed. (Lucknow, India: Eastern Book Company, 1968), 278. See 263–283 for a concise description of the developments of Indian criminal law before the penal code.
8. George Campbell, *Modern India; A Sketch of the System of Civil Government. To which is Prefixed, Some Account of the Natives and Native Institutions* (London: J. Murray, 1852), 465. Quoted in Kulshreshtha, *Landmarks*, 278.
9. Fitzjames Stephen, "Codification in India and England," *Fortnightly Review* 12 (1872): 644.
10. As I have observed, the position was initially offered to James Stephen, then colonial undersecretary. One can only assume that he suggested his close friend as an alternative.
11. V. B. Mishra, *Evolution of the Constitutional History of India 1773–1947* (Delhi: Mittal Publications, 1987), 110–111.
12. Thomas Paine, *Rights of Man, Common Sense, and Other Political Writings*, ed. M. Philp (New York: Oxford University Press, 1995)
13. See K. McBride, "Severing the Sanguinary Empire," in *Punishment and Political Order* (Ann Arbor: University of Michigan Press, 2007), ch. 4; Thomas Dumm, *Democracy and Punishment* (Madison: University of Wisconsin Press, 1987); and Gustave de Beaumont and Alexis de Tocqueville, *On the Penitentiary System in the United States and Its Application in France.* Trans. Frances Lieber. (Philadelphia: Carey, Lea and Blanchard. 1833).
14. Rudrangshu Mukherjee, ed., *The Penguin Gandhi Reader* (New York: Penguin, 1993), 18.
15. Quoted in Ujjwal Kumar Singh, "Penal Strategies and Political Resistance in Colonial and Independent India," in *Challenging the Rule(s) of Law: Colonialism, Criminology and Human Rights in India*, ed. Kalpana Kannabiran and Ranbir Singh (Dehli: SAGE, 2008), 227.
16. See Singh, "Penal Strategies and Political Resistance," for a complete discussion.
17. Das and Verma, "The Armed Police in the British Colonial Tradition," 363.

18. In Southern India these were called *taliari*; in the North, *chaukidars*.
19. William Morley describes the criminal justice system in India in a volume that was published the year after the Insurrection. *The Administration of Criminal Justice in British India* (Delhi: Delux Offset Printers, 1976). First edition published 1858.
20. Quoted in David Arnold, *Police Power and Colonial Rule Madras 1859–1947* (Delhi: Oxford University Press, 1986), 10.
21. See Ranajit Guha, *Dominance without Hegemony: History and Power in Colonial India* (Cambridge, MA: Harvard University Press, 1997), for a fascinating discussion of discipline, persuasion, and obedience in Colonial India.
22. Stephen, "Codification," 647.
23. *Select Committee Report*, 114, quoted in Anupama Rao, "Problems of Violence, States of Terror: Torture in Colonial India," *Interventions* 3, no. 2 (2001): 191
24. Madras Report, 35, quoted in Anuj Bhuwania, "'Very Wicked Children': 'Indian Torture' and the Madras Torture Commission Report of 1855," *International Journal on Human Rights* 6, no. 10 (2009): 13.
25. Douglas M. Peers, "Torture, the Police, and the Colonial State in the Madras Presidency 1816–55," *Criminal Justice History 12* (1991) 40..
26. Ibid.
27. Ibid., 34.
28. "Torture in Madras," *Hansard Parliamentary Debates*, HL Deb 14, April 1856, vol. 141, cc964–99.
29. Ibid.
30. Ibid.
31. Ibid.
32. Arnold, *Police Power and Colonial Rule*, 69.
33. J. C. Curry, *The Indian Police*, 54, quoted in Edward Thompson, *The Rise and Fulfillment of British Rule in India* (London: MacMillan, 1934), 480.
34. Arnold, *Police Power and Colonial Rule*, 132.
35. Rao, "Problems of Violence, States of Terror," 191.
36. Peers, "Torture, the Police, and the Colonial State," 44.
37. Human Rights Watch, *Broken System: Dysfunction, Abuse, and Impunity in the Indian Police* (Washington, DC: Human Rights Watch, 2009), 7.
38. Ibid., 26.
39. Ibid., 24.
40. Ibid., 46.
41. Beatrice Jauregui, "Beatings, Beacons, and Big Men: Police Disempowerment and Delegitimation in India," *Law and Social Inquiry* 38, no. 3 (Summer 2013): 659.
42. Ibid., 659.
43. T. K. Vinod Kumar, "Public Order in India: An Empirical Study," *Journal of Contemporary Criminal Justice* 25, no. 2 (2009): 159.

44. K. S. Subramanian, *Political Violence and the Police in India* (New Delhi: SAGE, 2007.
45. Report of the Justice B. N. Srikrishna Commission on the Mumbai riots of 1992–1993.
46. Human Rights Watch, "Prevent Further Communal Violence in India," March 12, 2002, http://hrw.org.
47. Human Rights Watch, "India: Probe Police Attacks on 'Untouchables,'" July 9, 2004.
48. Human Rights Watch, "India: Hold Torturers Accountable," November 17, 2008.
49. Quoted in Jinee Lokaneeta, *Transnational Torture: Law, Violence, and State Power in the United States and India* (New York: New York University Press, 2011), 162.
50. *State of Andhra Pradesh v. Smt. Inapuri Padma and Ors* (2008), quoted in Jinee Lokaneeta, "Creating a Flawed Art of Government: Legal Discourses on Lie Detectors, Brain Scanning, and Narcoanalysis in India," *Journal of Law, Culture and the Humanities*, November 2014.
51. Ministry of Home Affairs (India), "Committee on Reforms of Criminal Justice System" (Malimath Report), March 2003, 7, available at http://www.mha.nic.in/hindi/sites/upload_files/mhahindi/files/pdf/criminal_justice_system.pdf.
52. It is interesting to me that the report does not refer to "the average citizen" as someone used to the US vernacular would expect.
53. Tom Lasseter, "India's Stagnant Courts Resist Reform," *Bloomberg Businessweek*, January 8, 2015.
54. Malimath Report, 28.
55. Ibid.
56. Ibid., 4.
57. "Criminal Justice Reforms," *India Together*, November 2003.
58. Amnesty International, "India: Report of the Malimath Committee on Reforms of the Criminal Justice System: Some Observations," September 18, 2003.
59. Malimath Report, 4–5.
60. Ibid.
61. Having police be in charge of guarding against police corruption through the wonders of technology is a simply preposterous notion, but videotaping confessions is sure to help provide a sense of their infallibility.
62. Malimath Report, 52.
63. Ibid., 68.
64. Ibid., 56.
65. *History of Police Organization in India and Indian Village Police, being Select Chapters of the Report of the Indian Police Commission 1902-1903*. University of Calcutta: 1913. 44.
66. Ibid., 47.

Conclusion

1. Thomas Carothers, "Rule of Law Revival," *Foreign Affairs*, March 1998, 99.
2. See Richard Miller, "Might Still Distorts Right: Perils of the Rule of Law Project," in *Getting to the Rule of Law*, ed. James Fleming (New York: New York University Press, 2011), 265–292.
3. There are a number of excellent volumes that provide a survey of rule of law programs, offer suggestions for improvement, and critique both the premise and execution of such rule of law programs. See James Fleming, ed., *Getting to the Rule of Law*; James J. Heckman, Robert Nelson, and Lee Cabatingan, eds., *Global Perspectives on the Rule of Law* (New York: Routledge, 2009); Thomas Carothers, ed., *Promoting the Rule of Law Abroad: In Search of Knowledge* (Washington, DC: Carnegie Endowment for Peace, 2006); and Jane Stromseth, David Wippman, and Rosa Brooks, eds., *Can Might Make Rights? Building the Rule of Law After Military Interventions* (Cambridge: Cambridge University Press, 2006).
4. Tom Ginsburg, "In Defense of Imperialism/The Rule of Law and the State-Building Project," in *Getting to the Rule of* Law, 224–240.
5. Richard Flathman, "Liberalism and Political Institutionalization," in *The Rule of Law*, ed. Ian Shapiro (New York: New York University Press, 1995).
6. Miller, "Might Still Distorts Right," 279.
7. Ginsburg, "In Defense of Imperialism," 225.
8. Barry Weingast, "The Political Foundations of Democracy and the Rule of Law," *American Political Science Review* 91, no. 2 (1997): 245–263.
9. Ibid., 251.
10. Daniel Berkowitz, Katharina Pistor, and Jean-Francois Richard, "Economic Development, Legality, and the Transplant Effect," *European Economic Review* 47 (2003): 165–195.
11. See Bonnie Honig, *Democracy and the Foreigner* (Princeton, NJ: Princeton University Press, 2003), for a nuanced discussion of this dynamic.
12. Ginsburg, "In Defense of Imperialism," 228.
13. Ibid., 229.
14. Ibid., 237.
15. Miller, "Might Still Distorts Right," 286.

BIBLIOGRAPHY

Manuscript and Archival Collections

Argyll Papers, India Office Records
Colonial Office Records (CO), National Archives, Kew
Foreign Office Records (FO), National Archives, Kew
Kenneth Macaulay Diaries, Huntington Library
Maine Papers, India Office Records
Stephen Papers, Cambridge University Library

List of Works Cited

Adams, Henry. *History of the United States of America: The Second Administration of Thomas Jefferson, 1805–1809*. New York: Charles Scribner, 1890, 50.

Amnesty International India. *Report of the Malimath Committee on Reforms of the Criminal Justice System: Some Observations.* September 18, 2003.

Anghie, A. "Finding the Peripheries: Sovereignty and Colonialism in Nineteenth Century International Law." *Harvard International Law Review* 40, no. 1 (1999): 1–80.

———. *Imperialism, Sovereignty, and the Making of International Law.* Cambridge: Cambridge University Press, 2005.

Arendt, H. "On Violence." In *The Crisis of the Republic.* New York: Harcourt, Brace, Javonovich, 1972.

Armitage, D. *The Ideological Origins of the British Empire.* Cambridge: Cambridge University Press, 2000.

———. "John Locke, Carolina, and the *Two Treatises of Government.*" *Political Theory* 32, no. 5 (2004): 602–627.

Arnold, D. *Police Power and Colonial Rule: Madras 1859–1947*. Delhi: Oxford University Press, 1986.

Bain, Alexander. *James Mill: A Biography*. London: Longmans, Green, 1882.

Bayly, C. A. *Imperial Meridian: The British Empire and the World 1780–1830*. London: Longman, 1989.

Beaumont, Gustave de and Alexis de Tocqueville, *On the Penitentiary System in the United States and Its Application in France*. Trans. Frances Lieber. Philadelphia: Carey, Lea and Blanchard. 1833.

Bell, D. "Victorian Visions of Global Order: An Introduction." In *Victorian Visions of Global Order: Empire and International Relations in Nineteenth Century Political Thought*. Edited by Duncan Bell. Cambridge: Cambridge University Press, 2007.

Benjamin, W. "Theses on the Philosophy of History." In *Illuminations: Essays and Reflections*. Edited by Hannah Arendt. New York: Schocken Books, 1955.

Bentham, J. "Codification Proposal to All Nations Professing liberal Opinions..." London: J. M'Creery, 1822.

Berkowitz, Daniel, Katharina Pistor, and Jean-Francois Richard. "Economic Development, Legality, and the Transplant Effect." *European Economic Review* 47 (2003): 165–195.

Bhuwania, A. "'Very Wicked Children': 'Indian Torture' and the Madras Torture Commission Report of 1855." *International Journal on Human Rights* 6, no. 10 (2009): 7–28.

Braidwood, S. J. *Black Poor and White Philanthropists: London's Black and the Foundation of the Sierra Leone Settlement 1786–1791*. Liverpool: Liverpool University Press, 1994.

Brundage, A., and R. Cosgrove. *The Great Tradition: Constitutional History and National Identity in Britain and the United States, 1870–1960*. Stanford, CA: Stanford University Press, 2007.

Campbell, G. *Modern India; A Sketch of the System of Civil Government. To Which Is Prefixed, Some Account of the Natives and Native Institutions*. London: J. Murray, 1852.

Carothers, Thomas. "Rule of Law Revival." *Foreign Affairs*. March 1998, 95–106.

Carothers, Thomas, ed. *Promoting the Rule of Law Abroad: In Search of Knowledge*. Washington, DC: Carnegie Endowment for Peace, 2006.

Caulker, T. M. *The African-British Long Eighteenth Century: An Analysis of African-British Treaties, Colonial Economics, and Anthropological Discourse*. Lanham, MD: Lexington Books, 2009.

Cohn, B. *Colonialism and Its Forms of Knowledge: The British in India*. Princeton, NJ: Princeton University Press, 1996.

Colaiaco, J. A. *James Fitzjames Stephen and the Crisis of Victorian Thought*. London: Macmillan, 1983.

Colebrooke, J. E. *Supplement to A Digest of the Regulations and Laws*. 1807.

Cosgrove, R. *The Rule of Law: Albert Venn Dicey, Victorian Jurist.* Chapel Hill: University of North Carolina Press, 1980.

Christina, A. "Interview with USAID's Wade Channell on Rule of Law Reform." *Reinventing the Rules: A Blog.* 2014. reinventingtherules.com.

Currey, C. H. *British Colonial Policy 1783–1915.* London: Oxford University Press, 1916.

del Valle, J. Letter printed in *"Legislator of the World": Writings on Codification, Law and Education.* Edited by P. Schofield and J. Harris. New York: Oxford University Press, 1998.

Das, D., and A. Verma. "The Armed Police in the British Colonial Tradition." *Policing: An International Journal of Police Strategies and Management* 21, no. 2 (1998): 354–367.

Dayan, C. *The Law Is a White Dog: How Legal Rituals Make and Unmake Persons.* Princeton, NJ: Princeton University Press, 2011.

Dilts, A. "To Kill a Thief: Punishment, Proportionality, and Criminal Subjectivity in Locke's *Second Treatise.*" *Political Theory* 40, no. 1 (2012): 58–83.

Dodwell, E. "Alphabetical List of the Honourable East India Company's Bengal Civil Servants, From the Year 1780 to the Year 1838." London: B. Bensley, 1839.

Dodwell, H. H. "The Development of Sovereignty in British India." In *The Cambridge History of the British Empire*, vol. 4, 589–608. Cambridge: Cambridge University Press, 1929.

Dumm, T. *Democracy and Punishment.* Madison: University of Wisconsin Press, 1987.

Ely, R. "From Sect to Church: Sir James Stephen's Theology of Empire." *Journal of Religious History* 19 (1995): 74–91.

Empson, W. "Jeremy Bentham." *Edinburgh Review* 78 (1843) 460–516.

Farmer, L. "Reconstructing the English Codification Debate: The Criminal Law Commissioners, 1833–45." *Law and history Review* 18, no. 2 (2000): 397–425.

Fenton, Anthony. "The Responsibility to Protect. The International Commission on Intervention and State Sovereignty." 2009. http://www.un.org/en/prevent-genocide/adviser/responsibility.shtml.

Flathman, Richard. "Liberalism and Political Institutionalization." In *The Rule of Law.* Edited by Ian Shapiro. New York: New York University Press, 1995.

Foucault, M. *Society Must Be Defended.* London: Penguin, 2003.

Fitzpatrick, P. "Terminal Legality: Imperialism and the (De)composition of Law." In *Law, History, and Colonialism: The Reach of Empire.* Edited by Diane Kirkby and Catharine Coleborne. Manchester: University of Manchester Press, 2011.

Fyfe, C. *A History of Sierra Leone.* Oxford: Oxford University Press. 2000.

Gandhi, Mohatma. "Chapter One: Critique of Modern Civilization." In *The Penguin Gandhi Reader.* Edited by R. Mukherjee. New York: The Penguin Group, 1993.

Ginsburg, Tom. "In Defense of Imperialism/ The Rule of Law and the State-Building Project." In *Getting to the Rule of Law.* Edited by James Fleming, 224–240. New York: New York University Press, 2011.

Gong, G. *The Standard of "Civilisation" in International Society*. Oxford: Clarendon Press, 1984.

Green, William A. "The West Indies and British West African Policy in the Nineteenth Century—A Corrective Comment." *Journal of African History* 15, no. 2 (1974): 247–259.

Guha, R. *Dominance without Hegemony: History and Power in Colonial India*. Cambridge, MA: Harvard University Press, 1997.

Hall, C. "Making Colonial Subjects: Education in the Age of Empire." *History of Education* 37, no. 6 (2008): 773–787.

———. *Macaulay and Son: Architects of Imperial Britain*. London: Yale University Press, 2012.

Hall, H. L. *The Colonial Office: A History*. London: Longmans, Green, 1937.

Heckman, James J., Robert Nelson, and Lee Cabatingan, eds. *Global Perspectives on the Rule of Law*. New York: Routledge, 2009.

Heuman, Gad. *"The Killing Time": The Morant Bay Rebellion in Jamaica*. Knoxville: University of Tennessee Press, 1995.

Heydon, John. "Reflections on James Fitzjames Stephen." *University of Queensland Law Journal 29. No. 1* 2010. 43–65.

Honig, B. *Democracy and the Foreigner*. Princeton, NJ: Princeton University Press, 2003.

Howse, E. M. *Saints in Politics: The Clapham Sect and the Growth of Freedom*. London: George Allen and Unwin, 1960.

Human Rights Watch. *Broken System: Dysfunction, Abuse, and Impunity in the Indian Police*. Washington, DC: Human Rights Watch, 2009.

Human Rights Watch India. "India: Hold Torturers Accountable." 2008. https://www.hrw.org/news/2008/11/17/india-hold-torturers-accountable

Hunter, W. W. *The Life of the Earl of Mayo*. London: Smith, Elder, 1876.

Hussain, N. *The Jurisprudence of Emergency: Colonialism and the Rule of Law*. Ann Arbor: University of Michigan Press, 2003.

Hutchinson, A. C., and P. Monahan. "Introduction." In *The Rule of Law: Idea or Ideology?* Edited by. Hutchinson and Monahan. Toronto: Carswell Publishing, 1987.

India Together. "Criminal Justice Reforms." November 2003. http://indiatogether.org/malimath-human-rights.

Jauregui, B. "Beatings, Beacons, and Big Men: Police Disempowerment and Delegitimation in India." *Law and Social Inquiry* 38, no. 3 (2013): 643–669.

Johnston, W. R. *Sovereignty and Protection: A Study of British Jurisdictional Imperialism in the Late Nineteenth Century*. Durham, NC: Duke University Press, 1973.

Kadish, S. H. "Codifiers of the Criminal Law: Wechsler's Predecessors." *Berkeley Law Scholarship Repository* 78 (1978): colum. L, rev. 1098.

Kirk, Russell. "The Foreboding Conservatism of Stephen." *The Western Political Quarterly* 5, no. 4 (1952): 563–577.

Knaplund, P. "Colonial Problems and Colonial Policy, 1815–1837." In *The Cambridge History of the British Empire. Vol. II: The New Empire 1783–1870*. Edited by. Ross, Newton, and Benians. Cambridge: Cambridge University Press, 1940.

Kolsky, E. "Codification and the Rule of Colonial Difference: Criminal Procedure in British India." *Law and History Review* 23, no. 3 (2005): 631–683.

———. *Colonial Justice in British India*. Cambridge: Cambridge University Press, 2010.

Kostal, R. W. *A Jurisprudence of Power: Victorian Empire and the Rule of Law*. New York: Oxford University Press, 2005.

Kulshreshtha, V. D. *Landmarks in Indian Legal and Constitutional History*. 3rd ed. Lucknow: Eastern Book Company, 1968.

Lasseter, T. "India's Stagnant Courts Resist Reform." *Bloomberg Businessweek*, January 8, 2015.

Lieberman, D. "From Bentham to Benthamism." *The Historical Journal* 28, no. 1 (1985): 199–224.

———. *The Province of Legislation Determined: Legal Theory in Eighteenth-Century Britain*. Cambridge: Cambridge University Press, 2002.

Lobban, M. (1991). *The Common Law and English Jurisprudence 1760–1850*. New York: Oxford University Press, 1991.

Lokaneeta, J. *Transnational Torture: Law, Violence, and State Power in the United States and India*. New York: New York University Press, 2011.

———. "Creating a Flawed Art of Government: Legal Discourses on Lie Detectors, Brain Scanning, and Narcoanalysis in India." *The Journal of Law, Culture and the Humanities*. Published online by SAGE.

Ludlam, T., and W. Dawes. "Report of the Commissioners of African Inquiry; Use of the Navy, 1811." *Parliamentary Papers* x (101), 1–2.

Macaulay, Zachary. Diary Sierra Leone Governor. MY 418 (1–5), Box 19. Huntington Library. Maine Papers, India Office Archives. April 22, 1867. MSS EUR C179.

Manning, H. T. "Who Ran the British Empire 1830–1850?" *Journal of British Studies* 5, no. 1 (1965). 88–121.

Mantena, K. *Alibis of Empire: Henry Maine and the Ends of Liberal Imperialism*. Princeton, NJ: Princeton University Press, 2010.

Martin, G. "Was There a British Empire?" *The Historical Journal* 15, no. 3 (1972): 562–569.

McBride, K. *Punishment and Political Order*. Ann Arbor: University of Michigan Press, 2007.

Metcalf, T. *Ideologies of the Raj*. Cambridge: Cambridge University Press, 1994.

Mehta, U. *Liberalism and Empire: A Study in Nineteenth Century Political Thought*. Chicago: University of Chicago Press, 1999.

Miller, Richard. 2011. "Might Still Distorts Right: Perils of the Rule of Law Project." In *Getting to the Rule of Law*. Edited by James Fleming, 265–292. New York: New York University Press, 2011.

Ministry of Home Affairs (India). "Committee on Reforms of Criminal Justice System" (Malimath Report). March 2003. http://www.mha.nic.in/hindi/sites/upload_files/mhahindi/files/pdf/criminal_justice_system.pdf.

Mishra, V. B. *Evolution of the Constitutional History of India 1773–1947*. Delhi: Mittal Publications, 1987.

Morefield, J. *Empires without Imperialism: Anglo-American Decline and the Politics of Deflection*. Oxford: Oxford University Press, 2014.

Morse, Stephen. "Thoroughly Modern: Sir James Fitzjames Stephen on Criminal Responsibility." *Ohio State Journal of Criminal Law* 5 (2008): 505–522.

Morgan, K. "Sierra Leone: Origins, 1787–1808." In *Encyclopedia of African History*. 3rd ed. Edited by Kevin Shillington, 1352–1353. New York: Fitzroy Dearborn, 2005.

Morley, W. *The Administration of Criminal Justice in British India*. Delhi: Delux Offset Printers, 1976. First edition published 1858.

Morris, H. F. "How Nigeria Got Its Criminal Code." *Journal of African Law* 14, no. 3 (1970): 137–154.

Mouser, B. L. "African Academy-Clapham 1799–1806." *History of Education* 33, no. 1 (2004): 87–103.

M'Queen, James. "Civilization of Africa-Sierra Leone-Liberated Africans" A Letter to R. W. Hay, Esq. Undersecretary of State. Glasgow. *Blackwood's Edinburgh Magazine* 20, no. 120 (1826): 872–892.

Munro, T. "On the Ultimate Aim of British Rule in India." *Indian Constitutional Documents 1757–1947*. 3rd ed. Edited by A. C. Banerjee. Calcutta: A. Mukherjee, 1961. First edition published 1824.

National Crimes Records Bureau (India). "Snapshots." Prison Statistics 2013. Ncrb.nic.in/PSI-2013/Snapshots-2013.pdf.

Nonet, P. "The Rule of Law: Is that the Rule that Was?" *The Rule of Law: Ideal or Ideology?* Edited by A. D. Hutchinson and P. Monahan. London: Carswell Publishing, 1987.

Paine, T. *Rights of Man, Common Sense, and Other Political Writings*. Edited by M. Philp. New York: Oxford University Press, 1995.

Pateman, C. "The Settler Contract." In *Contract and Domination*. Carole Pateman and Charles Wade Mills. Cambridge: Polity, 2007.

Peers, D. "Torture, the Police, and the Colonial State in the Madras Presidency, 1816–55." In *Criminal Justice History 12 (1991)* 29–56.

Pennell, C. R. "The Origins of the Foreign Jurisdiction Act and the Extension of British Sovereignty." *Historical Research* 83, no. 221 (2010): 466–485.

Pitts, J. "Legislator of the World? A Rereading of Bentham on Colonies." *Political Theory* 31, no. 20 (2003): 200–234.

———. *A Turn to Empire: The Rise of Imperial Liberalism in Britain and France*. Princeton, NJ: Princeton University Press, 2005.

———. "Great and Distant Crimes: Empire in Bentham's Thought." In *Jeremy Bentham, Selected Writings*. Edited by S. Engelmann. New Haven, CT: Yale University Press, 2011.

Posner, Richard A. "The Romance of Force: James Fitzjames Stephen on Criminal Law." *Ohio State Journal of Criminal Law* 10, no. 1 (2012) 263–275.

Pugh, R. B. "The Colonial Office." In *The Cambridge History of the British Empire*. Vol. III. Cambridge: Cambridge University Press, 1967.

Radzinowicz, L. *Sir James Fitzjames Stephen, 1829–1894, and His Contribution to the Development of Criminal Law*. London: Bernard Quarich, 1957.

Rao, A. "Problems of Violence, States of Terror: Torture in Colonial India." *Interventions* 3, no. 2 (2001): 186–205.

Rao. A., and S. Pierce. "Discipline and the Other Body: Correction, Corporeality, and Colonial Rule." *Interventions* 3, no. 2 (2001): 159–168.

Read, J. S. "Criminal Law in the Africa of Today and Tomorrow." *Journal of African Law* 14, no. 3 (1963): 137–154.

Roach, John. "James Fitzjames Stephen 1829–94." *Journal of the Asiatic Society of Great Britain and Ireland*. April 1–16, 1956.

Rogin, M. P. *Fathers and Children: Andrew Jackson and the Subjugation of the American Indian*. New York: Vintage Books, 1975.

Rose, J. H., A. P. Newton, and E. A. Benians, eds. *The Cambridge History of the British Empire*. Cambridge: Cambridge University Press, 1940, Volume 4.

Ruskola, T. *Legal Orientalism: China, the United States, and Modern Law*. Cambridge, MA: Harvard University Press, 2013.

Samaddar, R. "Crimes, Passion and Detachment: Colonial Foundations of Rule of Law." In *Challenging the Rule(s) of Law: Colonialism, Criminology and Human Rights in India*. Edited by K. Kannabiran and R. Singh, 355–381. New Delhi: SAGE, 2008.

Schmitt, C. *The Nomos of the Earth in the International Law of the Jus Publicum Europaeum*. Translated by G. L. Ulmen. Candor: Telos Press, 2003.

———. *Political Theology: Four Chapters on the Concept of Sovereignty*. Translated by George Schwab. Chicago: University of Chicago Press, 2005.

Schofield, P. *Bentham: A Guide for the Perplexed*. London: Continuum Publishing, 2009.

———. "Place and Time." In *Jeremy Bentham, Selected Writings*. Edited by S. Engelmann. New Haven, CT: Yale University Press, 2011.

Semmel, B. *Jamaican Blood and Victorian Conscience: The Governor Eyre Controversy*. New York: Houghton Mifflin, 1963.

Shklar, J. "Political Theory and the Rule of Law." In *The Rule of Law: Idea or Ideology?* Edited by. Hutchinson and Monahan. Toronto: Carswell Publishing, 1987.

Singh, U. K. "Penal Strategies and Political Resistance in Colonial and Independent India." In *Challenging the Rule(s) of Law: Colonialism, Criminology and Human Rights in India*. Edited by K. Kannabiran and R. Singh, 227–256. Dehli: SAGE, 2008.

Singha, R. *A Despotism of Law: Crime and Justice in Early Colonial India*. Delhi: Oxford University Press, 1996.

———. "Punished by Surveillance: Policing 'Dangerousness' in Colonial India 1872–1918." *Modern Asian Studies* 49, no. 2 (2015): 241–269.

Smandych, R. "'To Soften the Extreme Rigor of Their Bondage': James Stephen's Attempts to Reform the Criminal Slave Laws of the West Indies, 1813–1833." *Law and History Review* 23, no. 3 (2003): 537–588.

Smith, K. J. M. *James Fitzjames Stephen, Portrait of a Victorian Rationalist.* Cambridge, Cambridge University Press, 1988.

———. "Chapter 10: Macaulay's 'Utilitarian Indian Penal Code': An Illustration of the Accidental Function of Time, Place, and Personalities in Law Making." In *Legal History in the Making: Proceeding of the Ninth British Legal History Conference, Glasgow, 1989.* Edited by W. M. Gordon and T. D. Fergus. London: Hambledon Press, 1991.

Spagnolo, J. "Portents of Empire in Britain's Ottoman Extraterritorial Jurisdiction." *Middle Eastern Studies* 17 (1991): 256–282.

Stephen, G. *Anti-Slavery Recollection: In a Series of Letters to Mrs. Beecher Stowe.* Piccadilly, London: Thomas Hatchard, 1854.

Stephen, James. *Sir James Stephen Letters.* With Biographical Notes by Caroline Stephen. Cambridge: W.Heffer and Sons, 1906.

Stephen, James. 1823. *The Slavery of the British West India Colonies Delineated, As It Exists Both in Law and Practice and Compared with the Slavery of Other Countries, Ancient and Modern.* London: J. Butterworth and Son, 1823.

Stephen, James. *Essays in Ecclesiastical Biography*, 5th ed. London: Longmans, Green and Co, 1891.

Stephen, James Fitzjames. "Codification of India and England." *The Fortnightly Review.* July–December 1872,

———. *Liberty, Equality, Fraternity.* London: Smith, Elder, 1873.

———. *Lectures on the History of France.* New York: Harper and Brothers, 1875.

———. "Legislation Under Lord Mayo." In *Life of the Earl of Mayo*, 2nd ed. Edited by William Hunder. London: Smith, Elder, 1876.

———. *A History of the Criminal Law of England.* London: Macmillan, 1883.

———. *Essays in Ecclesiastical Biography.* London: Longmans, Green, 1891.

Stephen, L. *The Life of Sir James Fitzjames Stephen.* London: Smith, Waterfield and Co, 1895.

Stromseth, Jane, David Wippman, and Rosa Brooks. *Can Might Make Rights? Building the Rule of Law After Military Interventions.* Cambridge: Cambridge University Press, 2006.

Subramanian, K. S. *Political Violence and the Police in India.* New Delhi: SAGE, 2007.

Swinfen, D. B. *Imperial Control of Colonial Legislation 1813–1865: A Study of British Policy towards Colonial Legislative Powers.* Oxford: Clarendon Press, 1970.

Tamahana, B. *On the Rule of Law: History, Politics, Theory.* Cambridge: Cambridge University Press, 2004.

Taylor, M. "IMPERIUM OR LIBERTAS? Rethinking the Radical Critique of Imperialism During the Nineteenth Century." *Journal of Imperial and Commonwealth History* 19 (1991): 1–23.

Thompson, E. *The Rise and Fulfillment of British Rule in India*. London: MacMillan, 1934.

Thompson, E. P. *Whigs and Hunters: The Origin of the Black Act*. New York: Pantheon Books, 1975.

Tocqueville, Alexis de. *Democracy in America*. Translated by George Lawrence. New York: Harper and Row, 1966.

Tocqueville, Alexis de, and de Beaumont, G. *On the Penitentiary System in the United States and its Application in France*. Carbondale and Edwardsville: Southern Illinois University Press, 1964.

Tomkins, S. *The Clapham Sect: How Wilberforce's Circle Transformed Britain*. London: Lion Hudson Press, 2010.

"Torture in Madras." *Hansard Parliamentary Debates*. HL Deb 14, April 1856, Vol. 141 cc964–999.

United Nations. "The Responsibility to Protect." http://www.un.org/en/prevent-genocide/adviser/responsibility.shtml. Accessed January 12, 2016.

Vinod, Kumar, T. K. "Public Order in India: An Empirical Study." *Journal of Contemporary Criminal Justice* 25, no. 2 (2009): 148–169.

Ward, J. "The Retirement of a Titan: James Stephen 1847–1850." *Journal of Modern History* 31, no. 3 (1959): 189–205.

Weingast, Barry. "The Political Foundations of Democracy and the Rule of Law." *The American Political Science Review* 91, no. 2 (1997): 245–263.

Wood, R. D. "The Treaty of Nanking: Form and the Foreign Office 1842–1843." *Journal of Imperial and Commonwealth History* 24, no. 2 (1996): 181–196.

Woolf, V. "A Sketch of the Past." In *Moments of Being*. Edited by Jeanne Schulkind. London: Hogarth Press, 1985.

Young, D. M. *The Colonial Office in the Early Nineteenth Century*. London: Longman, Green, 1961.

INDEX